# How We Got Over

*Growing up in the Segregated South:*
*A Collection of Narratives*

DR. HELEN BENJAMIN, EDITOR

JEAN NASH JOHNSON, COEDITOR

ISBN: 979-8-9853177-0-1 (Paperback)
ISBN: 979-8-9853177-1-8 (Hardcover)

Book cover design by Melanie Belanger
Book interior design by Najdan Mancic

First printing edition 2021.

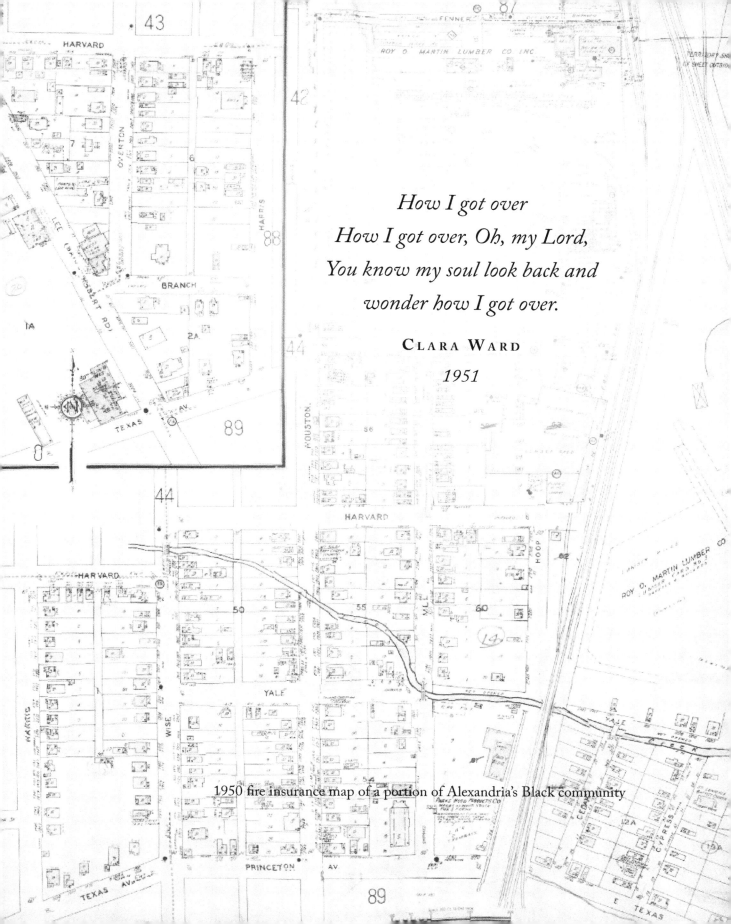

*How I got over*
*How I got over, Oh, my Lord,*
*You know my soul look back and*
*wonder how I got over.*

CLARA WARD

*1951*

1950 fire insurance map of a portion of Alexandria's Black community

# TABLE OF CONTENTS

PART THREE: **Peabody: Our Community's High School**

## PART FOUR: Our Community's Fight for Civil Rights

# ACKNOWLEDGMENTS

CREATING A WORK such as this requires the efforts of many hands from idea to reality. The genesis for this book came to me in October 2020. I was engaged in a professional development activity via Zoom with a focus on diversity, equity, and inclusion. The facilitator, Natalie Gillard, creator of the Factuality Game, was discussing structural inequality in America, using redlining as an example. She used maps from various cities and historical information to explain redlining in detail and its impact on African Americans. I knew about redlining but had never thought about it deeply. I had a visceral reaction that day. I was immediately transported to the 1950s to my old neighborhood in Alexandria, Louisiana, because we lived in an area similar to the one she described. It limited our economic and intellectual growth as well as our ability to live healthy lives.

The moment was both emotional and epiphanous for me. I thought of the major railway systems with tracks literally at the back doors of some homes. I remembered the ever-present noise and air pollution, resulting from the numerous railway systems that ran through our communities and plants releasing toxic chemicals. In that moment, I thought about the extent to which we had been taken advantage of as a people in a different way. It was a gut-wrenching, painful moment. The facilitator called on me to comment, and I could not speak because I was emotionally wrought. When I spoke, I had a tremor in my voice. I asked her to come back to me. I thought about my life and the lives of my high school classmates and decided in that moment that we had stories to tell, stories that had to be preserved and shared. We had survived redlining and the numerous indignities placed on us. We got over by the grace of God! Clara Ward's "How I Got Over" in the powerful voices of Mahalia Jackson and Aretha Franklin came to me instantly. We survived unfiltered racism in the segregated South as so many have done.

It was not only important that our stories be told but also that the historical context for our narratives be recognized and included in this volume. I am not a historian, but I am interested in history. So began my deep dive into the past. I remember being in the required Louisiana history course in eighth grade, but I was not taught any of the known facts I have discovered in my research for this volume. So much has been kept from us, but it is there to be found. My hope is that this book will educate and inspire readers to think deeply about their personal histories and commit to learning more and sharing what they learn.

Yes, many hands contributed to the completion of this project. I enumerate and offer thanks to them here.

- The greatest debt of gratitude is owed to my 24 Peabody High School classmates whose narratives comprise this volume and make it possible. For some of them, writing was the last activity in which they wanted to participate, but they had in common the desire to tell their stories. I thank them all for first, feeling the sense of urgency to write, and then writing.

- Family and friends were indeed an asset to the project. My dear baby brother, Michael, found things (historical books on Rapides Parish, the 1950 fire insurance map for Alexandria detailing every street and edifice in town) and assisted with all technical interpretations. My daughter, Traci, provided all manner of technical assistance from retrieving files I lost in the process, advising me on publishing, to reviewing copy and in needed moments, eagerly being my listening ear. My son, Michael Patrick, served as advisor and reviewer, challenging and questioning and giving meaningful feedback throughout the project. My brother, Justus, Jr., I thank for technical advice and last-minute photography in Alexandria. Barbara McClain, Tess Caldwell, and

Dr. Debbie DiThomas reviewed essays and worked with individual writers. Linda Lamar and Dawn Benjamin typed handwritten essays submitted by contributors. Cheryl Jones, my friend since first grade, sent me information on the first Black schools in Rapides Parish and connected me with resources in the Rapides Parish School Board office. Sadly, we lost her a few months before publication. She was a champion of this project. Graduate school friend and colleague, Dr. Phyllis Elmore, contributed her keen critical analytical skills and brought only the clarity that she can bring to all things Black. Dear friend, Dr. Elsie Burnett conducted the final review of all except the narratives before we sent the book off to the designer. Throughout the project, Dr. Cindy Miles, business colleague, provided sage advice, and college roommate, Rebecca Harrison, kept me sane.

- Mr. Earnest Bowman, who taught many of us calculus and trigonometry, did not hesitate when asked to write about his teaching experience at Peabody under the leadership of Professor Iles. Thanks for an accurate and honest portrait of our principal.

- Two Peabody alums, Charles F. Smith (Class of 1959) and William Douglas (W.D.) Johnson (Class of 1946) helped us tremendously. Mr. Smith shared documents and stories about Professor J.B. Lafargue that would have otherwise been unknown to us. Mr. Johnson, aside from being our cheerleader for the project, shared photographs from the 1940s and filled in historical gaps important to the project. Many thanks to both of you!

- Librarians in the Rapides Parish Library system in Alexandria and LeCompte were most helpful in providing invaluable assistance in the research effort: Sophia Pierre Louis, Kyle Franklin, and Sonia Span. Sonya Jeter, manager at the main branch, was available to me any time I called and ran down numerous rabbit trails with me in validating facts. She was a joy to work with. Thanks is extended as well to Patricia Boone of the Alexandria Historical and Genealogical Library and Museum in acquiring photos and information from pre-Civil War local newspapers.

- The *Town Talk* was a major source of information otherwise unavailable for historical aspects of this work.

- Melanie Belanger and her team created the front, back, and inside covers.

- Rev. Ameal Jones, longtime friend and preacher extraordinaire, engaged in numerous conversations with me about our town and surrounding communities. He has an incredible memory and made sure the facts were straight, especially the ones about churches and plantations.

- Michael Johnson, another person I have known since first grade, has lived and breathed this project day and night since its inception because he is married to the coeditor. He has been witness to and sometimes a part of early morning and late night phone calls about the project, on the receiving end of finding photographs, as well as sending them, solving technology problems, including staying up half the night to find files that seemed to be forever lost. He is owed a ton of thanks. All he has asked me is, "When do I get my wife back?" I can now say we are done. Thanks so much, Michael, for your sacrifices as well as your support in every way.

- Rev. Larry Smith, classmate and longtime friend, has assisted from the beginning of the project. After hearing my pitch, he joined me in making initial contact with classmates and building the contributors to 24. He obtained and shared historical information, photos, and ideas and has been an advisor on every aspect of the project. He has been a great supporter, encourager, and partner. His written contributions and other input on the historical pieces make a positive difference in the content.

- I end with my coeditor who has been an invaluable asset throughout the project, laboring with me in every aspect from the beginning to completion/final product. She was the first person with whom I shared the idea. Her commitment to the efforts of the Peabody Class of 1968 did not begin with this project. She has been associated with us for many years as she is the wife of one of our classmates. Jean has had an extensive career of discovering, reporting, writing, and editing news and features stories focusing on African American history, culture, and lifestyle for *The Dallas Morning News*. She brought that expertise to this publication. Thank you, Jean Nash Johnson! You rock!

These individuals and others contributed to the development and completion of this work, allowing the contributors to share experiences in the context of the town and the times in which we lived and how we got over.

Helen Benjamin

Dallas, Texas

October 2021

# PREFACE

*"There is that great proverb — that 'until the
lions have their own historians, the history of
the hunt will always glorify the hunter'."*
— CHINUA ACHEBE,
1994 interview, *The Paris Review*

W HEN ASKED TO participate in the writing of this book, we each agreed without hesitation. What is the probability in the middle of the 2020 global pandemic, coming up on 53 years after our 1968 high school graduation, that two dozen of us — Baby Boomers, all classmates from the same central Louisiana all Black high school, most of us now living in other cities and states—would rise to write about growing up in midcentury Jim Crow America?

We received the "Call for Participation" in December 2020 from Helen, inviting us to tell our stories of early childhood, family, school, work, and spiritual life. In a year fraught with not only the deadly COVID-19 virus, but also the police killing of George Floyd and a contentious U.S. Presidential election, how could we not respond affirmatively? We were ready to tell our stories. If truths are not chronicled by those living to tell, history is rewritten or tragically goes away. Consensus and commitment were verbally solidified in our first meeting in January 2021.

Writing our stories was hard work. Between group Zoom meetings and one-on-one telephone edits, Helen and Jean turned us into documenters, carefully recalling and substantiating events, and, in some cases, researching historical background information for accuracy, crafting our best words, and producing drafts for them. *How We Got Over* is a collection of stories about our daily lives. We were children born black, gifted, and without access to what this country routinely afforded white Americans in the 1950s and 1960s. We share genuine feats and honest daring anecdotes of what it was like to live the first 18 years of our lives in the segregated Deep South under the strictest of this country's laws. Our stories are unfiltered, recounting the racial, social, and economic strife we faced before the Civil Rights Movement took hold in our hometown and the impact of those experiences on our lives as adults.

Our narratives reveal raw details of personal and family experiences, unfair employment tactics, discriminatory healthcare practices, and one-sided homebuyer strategies, as well as other discriminatory practices prevalent during segregation. We go deep and share accounts of distress and despair amid survival and success. We praise our supportive all Black community for providing the dependable security that kept us blanketed from some of the coldhearted barriers and challenges that dominated our way of life. We share the realities of living in a town in which we depended on the whims of the white people who presided over our community and who were committed to the segregationist system they created. We give you glimpses into the contradictions in our lives with the sense of security and vulnerability in having a teacher, grocer, preacher, and doctor who looked like us, alongside a police sector, city government, and state leaders who did not. Further, we reveal facts of our adult lives in the military, college, our homes, and the workplace.

We now consider ourselves memoirists and remain hopeful as we reflect on our lives in our early 70s. We view our accounts as universal and, as a package, a reflection of the human experience. We hope that amid the instances of troubling encounters of bigotry, you, our reader, discover endurance and appreciate—even connect with—everyday joy and courage in Black life. Amid humorous and heartwarming childhood experiences, our stories clearly illustrate how much all peoples and cultures have in common.

As members of the Peabody High School class of 1968 (PCOSE), we consider this act of writing the continuation of our commitment to paying it forward begun in 2016 with our establishment of an annual scholarship to graduating seniors at our alma mater. Our establishment and funding of this scholarship was a testament to our appreciation for what Peabody did for all of us and our pledge to paying it forward. Some of the proceeds from the sale of this book will fund our scholarship.

We hope you find our stories compelling, significant, inspiring, and worthy of being preserved and shared—that the names (past and present), images, places and treasured things within this volume narrate forward the story of our people, and that their names will not be, as John Keats lamented, "writ on water."

The Contributors

October 2021

# INTRODUCTION

IN MANY WAYS, the year 1968 was a watershed in American history. For example, the ongoing Vietnam war caused dissention and chaos in the streets of American cities, as young Americans protested the draft and the immorality of the war itself. Two American icons for social justice were assassinated — Robert F. Kennedy and Dr. Martin Luther King, Jr. Dr. King's assassination led to more urban racial violence that had come to characterize the struggle by African Americans for racial justice. Dr. King's assassination sent a clear message to African Americans that even a nonviolent movement, such as Dr. King's, would result in a violent reaction from those who opposed it. As conflicts raged in the streets of many of the country's cities and in its politics, the Republican Party under the leadership of Richard Nixon and others promoted a new "southern strategy." The "southern strategy" took advantage of white resistance to civil rights for African Americans to literally attract and convert the former Solid Democratic South to the GOP.

Historians have written extensively about the social and political changes in American society that seemed to characterize the United States in 1968. They have written about how America "unraveled" and how racial and identity politics emerged to dominate the nation's political landscape. They have also written about how the Black Power and Black Arts Movement provoked a new sense of racial pride among the younger generation of the period. They have also shown how, in spite of the new laws against racial discrimination and the Supreme Court cases that ended the legal foundation of racial segregation, white resistance to desegregation and racial justice continued unabated.[1]

With only a few exceptions, historians have not examined how the social and political changes that occurred in 1968 affected the daily lives of the African Americans who experienced and lived through them.[2] Thus, the current book fills a gap in the historical narrative about the period and provides first person stories about what happened to the class of 1968. Set in Alexandria, Louisiana, the personal stories of these 1968 graduates of Peabody High School go beyond the traditional, macro viewpoints of African American life that we assume was the typical African American experience in the American South. Instead, they provide us a micro lens into the daily lives of African Americans, who in spite of growing up in a segregated and hostile environment, lived lives of love and success.

While the recent explosion in studies about the African American experience has given us a wealth of materials on the history and culture of African Americans from the antebellum period to the present, we still lack the studies that give us a lens into the lives of the everyday, grassroots African American. This book excels in doing just that. From the Peabody High School graduates of 1968, we learn about their experiences with family, work, religion, love and marriage, education, attending historically black colleges, beginning their careers in various occupations, and indeed, "how they got over." Their personal stories of encountering and confronting a racist and hostile society that was just beginning to accept African Americans as equals are truly unique.

---

[1]       See Alan J. Matusow, *The Unraveling of America: A History of Liberalism in the 1960s* (New York: Harper & Row, 1984); Mark Kurlansky, *1968: The Year That Rocked the World* (New York: Ballantine Books, 2003); Larry Neal, "The Black Arts Movement," *Drama Review* (Summer 1968); and LeRoi Jones and Larry Neal, eds., *Black Fire: An Anthology of Afro-American Writing* (New York: Morrow, 1968).

[2]       See especially Ann Moody, *Coming of Age in Mississippi* (New York: Bantam Dell, 1968); and Stokely Carmichael and Charles V. Hamilton, *Black Power: The Politics of Liberation* (New York: Vintage Books, 1967). See also "The First," *The Atlantic*, September 29, 2020, a five-part series about the children who desegregated America's public schools.

As a 1968 high school graduate myself, I identified with many of the stories in this book, and I am excited that I have had the opportunity to read it.

W. Marvin Dulaney

Associate Professor of History Emeritus

University of Texas, Arlington

# PART ONE

# OUR COMMUNITY: ENSLAVEMENT, THE CIVIL WAR, AND RECONSTRUCTION

*"We are not makers of history. We are made of history."*
—DR. MARTIN LUTHER KING JR.

THE CONTRIBUTORS TO THIS book were born in the middle of the 20th century, their lives shaped by the people, places, events, and laws associated with Alexandria, Louisiana, before and after their birth. To fully understand the experiences shared in their stories, the early history must be illuminated with a view of the city's racial past. From the arrival in the central Louisiana region of the first slaves in the 1790s to 2018, the marker for Alexandria's first elected African American mayor, 20-20 hindsight reveals that the journey from slavery to freedom under law has been jarring.

This early history provides the backdrop for Alexandria, the village and place of origin for the contributors to this volume. Experiences there from the time of their birth influenced them greatly and created the moral, intellectual, and social foundation from which they speak. This overview covers deliberations on the part of the enslaver and effects of legislation designed to ensure subjugation of African Americans. The narratives in this section show the impact of slavery and segregation on the lives of the writers into the 21st century, particularly the lives of women as heads of households, job discrimination, and how they managed to survive it and, at times, thrive.

## OUR COMMUNITY: ENSLAVEMENT, THE CIVIL WAR, AND RECONSTRUCTION

Historian Daniel Usner estimates that some 500 African slaves were brought into Louisiana near New Orleans in 1719 by the French during the transatlantic slave trade. For farmers, those slaves were a welcome change as replacements for undesirable European convicts and other less reliable workers. Slave laborers were expected to perform the manual and mechanical work required to settle a colony rich in economic potential. After the initial purchase of slaves, for the farmers, there was no better investment for business than unsalaried Black people living in a land foreign to them with little or no freedom of movement and no rights and privileges. Because of the

difficult journey across the Middle Passage to the Americas, many enslaved people
died enroute or after reaching their destination.

Alexandria is in the center of Louisiana on the south bank of the Red River in
Rapides Parish.[3] Small bayous meander throughout the city and surrounding areas.
White inhabitants, first the French, followed by the Spanish, had control of Alexandria
until the United States purchased 827,000 square miles of land west of the Mississippi
in 1803. Before the French descended on Rapides Parish, it was inhabited by indigenous
peoples, including Caddo, Choctaw, The Natchez, and The Natchitoches. Only traces
of the indigenous people can be seen today, as they were systematically extracted from
the environment by disease, effects of enslavement, and involuntary relocation. Black
inhabitants initially were brought to Louisiana as enslaved people from the Caribbean
and Africa to provide free labor in the agriculturally rich area in which cotton, sugarcane, and other staples grew in abundance. Ensuing actions in Alexandria's history
highlight its racist past and the lasting effects of marginalization on people of color.

*Red River*

---

[3]         Parishes are geographical units known as counties in the other 49 states.

*Bayou Robert*

## Enslavement in Alexandria

The acquisition of slaves in Rapides Parish began much later than it did in the southernmost parts of the state. Rapides Parish population information from the U.S. Census in the years indicated in the table below reveals the extent to which Blacks swiftly outnumbered whites in the parish, while all the financial and physical resources, as well as power and authority, were in the hands of the white minority. (That remains true today. Based on U.S. Census estimates, the current population of Alexandria is 45,412 with 55.29% being Black or African American and 39.62%, white)

## TABLE 1

|             | 1799 | 1810  | 1820  | 1830  | 1840   | 1850   | 1860   |
|-------------|------|-------|-------|-------|--------|--------|--------|
| Whites      | 530  | 996   | 2,491 | 3,113 | 3,243  | 5,037  | 9,711  |
| Black Slaves| 175  | 1,081 | 3,487 | 5,329 | 10,511 | 11,340 | 15,358 |
| Black Freemen | 2  | 123   | 85    | 113   | 378    | 184    | 291    |
| Total       | 706  | 2,200 | 6,063 | 8,555 | 14,132 | 16,561 | 25,360 |

The table below reflects the U.S. Census results for 1850 and 1860 with Alexandria's population statistics compared to the parish statistics for 1850 and 1860 only. The table shows that larger numbers of enslaved and free Blacks lived in the rural areas where the more plentiful and challenging work was done, where cotton and sugarcane were grown and harvested. Alexandria was the hub that provided consumer services for the outlying areas. Black slaves who lived in town worked in the "service" industry and as servants to the wealthy.

## TABLE 2[4]

|                     | ALEXANDRIA | | RAPIDES PARISH | |
|---------------------|------|------|--------|--------|
|                     | 1850 | 1860 | 1850   | 1860   |
| Whites              | 394  | 980  | 5,037  | 9,711  |
| Black Slaves        | 168  | 314  | 11,340 | 15,358 |
| Black Free men/women| 26   | 131  | 184    | 291    |
| Total               | 588  | 1425 | 16,561 | 25,360 |

---

[4]      The information in Tables 1 and 2 was gleaned from data presented in Carl Laurent's *From This Valley: A History of Alexandria, Pineville, and Rapides, Louisiana.*

In her 1944 thesis on slavery legislation in antebellum Louisiana, Ethel Kramer points out that because of its central location, Alexandria in 1826 was one of three depots established in the state for runaway slaves. Slaveholders and prominent citizens placed notices in the daily newspapers to recapture fleeing slaves, to sell a "fresh crop" of slaves, and to sell trustworthy, experienced slaves as shown in the samples below from two issues of the *Louisiana Democrat* in 1859.

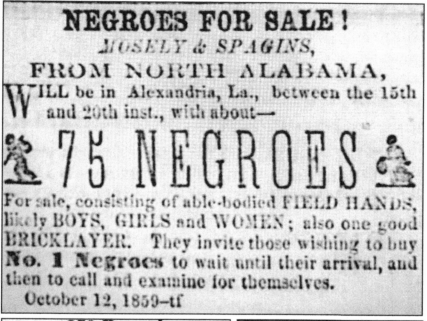

Slaves were a valued monetary commodity. According to Carl Laurent, one slave could be purchased in Alexandria in the 1850s for $1,800, enough to buy a sugar mill. The *Code Noire* (Black Code) was enacted in 1724. The codes were designed to maintain control of Blacks by limiting their education, movement, and ability to think freely and assemble in groups. A French invention, the Code became more critical to whites as the slave population grew, a challenge of their own making in their desire for economic gain through free labor.

Laurent gives a glimpse into the social lives of slaves in his description of "Negro balls" hosted by a white socialite in Alexandria in her attempt to provide an entertainment outlet for slaves. The balls, frequently attended by white men in search of Black women, often resulted in altercations reported in the local papers. The low regard in which slaves were held and the extent to which they were included in the community also were reflected in local newspapers. In the May 13, 1848, issue of the *Red River Republican*, the following racist statement appeared regarding Black attendance at an upcoming circus: "every man, woman, child and nigger (for it is fashionable for all) in and about town, will be delighted to learn that there will soon be a circus here."

Throughout slavery, similar references on the treatment of slaves who lived in Alexandria are found in newspapers. Regarding freedom of movement of Blacks, the Alexandria Board of Trustees released the following statement in the January 6, 1849, edition of the *Red River Republican:*

> "Be it ordained, that it shall be the duty of the town constable, after the ringing of the nine o'clock bell, to strike every slave found off of his or her master's premises without a pass or something to indicate that he or she is on his or her master's business, 25 lashes."

As population numbers for slaves grew and exceeded those of whites, Blacks became more of a threat to whites, especially after whites learned about revolts in other places. While no major rebellions are recorded in Alexandria, one did occur in nearby Cheneyville, as portrayed in the 2016 film *12 Years a Slave*, based on abolitionist Solomon Northrup's 19th century book/memoir.

There is substantial documentation of at least 25 plantations in and around Alexandria before the Civil War. Slaves played a significant role in the development and profitability of plantations. "The greatest incidence of slaveholding occurred among the attorneys, physicians, merchants, and lodging keepers. ...the census recorded a number of single or widowed women slaveholders," according to Terry Seip in his research on slaves and free Blacks. He notes further that the number of slaveholders nearly doubled between 1850 and 1860, showing slavery at its height in Alexandria prior to the Civil War. Neighborhoods and plantation sites bear the names today: Annandale, Hard Times, Inglewood, Kent House, Mooreland, and Willow Glen.

State Library of Louisiana (http://www.state.lib.la.us)

*Blacks picking cotton on the Inglewood Plantation on the outskirts of Alexandria, date unknown*

*"Fellow Citizens, we cannot escape history."*

— ABRAHAM LINCOLN

A month after the November 6, 1860, election of President Abraham Lincoln, South Carolina seceded. The following April, Confederates fired on federal troops at Fort Sumter, off the coast of Charleston, and started the Civil War. Lincoln's antislavery backing had worried Southerners. If slaveholding became illegal, slaveowners would lose economic advantage. With South Carolina first up, a bevy of southern states seceded from the Union. Louisiana seceded January 26, 1861. Most men went off to war in other states, leaving white women to fend for themselves with slaves as their aides. By 1863, Alexandria was occupied by the Union forces, and the Union forces set fire to the town May 13, 1864, burning most of its buildings. In 1868, three years after the war, Louisiana was restored to the Union under a rewritten state Constitution that abolished slavery and granted citizenship to former slaves. The 1870 census data show the impact of the Civil War on the population with the dramatic shift in the numbers of Blacks in Rapides Parish.

|                       | 1860   | 1870   |
|-----------------------|--------|--------|
| Whites                | 9,711  | 7,742  |
| Black Slaves          | 15,358 | 0      |
| Black Free men/women  | 291    | 10,267 |
| Total                 | 25,360 | 18,015 |

Although Black people in Rapides Parish moved from enslavement to freedom, little changed for them. They began their lives as "free" people with no advantages. If they chose to remain in the South, they likely would remain beholden to whites. Those in rural areas moved from chattel status to sharecropping, another form of oppression. Blacks in Alexandria benefitted very little from Reconstruction, 1865-1877, during which attempts were made to redress the inequities of slavery. However, at the state level and in some Louisiana towns and cities, Blacks were elected to public office in this period. Of note, is P.B.S. Pinchback, who served as lieutenant governor and governor of Louisiana briefly from 1872-73. According to the historical marker honoring Pinchback in downtown Alexandria, he lived for a brief period in Alexandria and influenced the inclusion of the creation of Southern University in the 1879 Louisiana state constitution. No evidence could be found that such progressive action as electing Blacks to public office was taken in Alexandria.

Freed slaves in Rapides Parish were likely hungry for postwar progress, though events occurring in the region during Reconstruction may have created fear and hesitancy. No doubt, Black Alexandrians had heard about the April 1873 Colfax Massacre, a horrific Easter Sunday attack, a few miles from Alexandria. Black militia men there had surrendered and were murdered, attempting to exercise their equal rights as included in the rewritten Louisiana State Constitution after the Civil War. Throughout the state during Reconstruction, Blacks were systematically discouraged from embracing mandated freedoms. Stripped of political, economic, and social autonomy, Black Alexandrians were powerless but managed to move forward.

# A STORY, A STORY. LET IT COME, AND LET IT GO

*"Where there is love, there is no darkness."*
BURUNDIAN PROVERB

## Rosa Ashby Metoyer

I AM ROSA MARIE Ashby Metoyer, daughter of Thomas Joseph Ashby Sr. and Rosa Taffaro Ashby. I feel that I am not a good historian, not because I'm a senior citizen, but because I've had problems recalling childhood events even as a young adult. However, I do have memories of my childhood that come in bits and pieces, like little skits often without dialogue. I have memories from different ages in my life but not every age. These glimpses, taken as a whole with my classmates, can provide a window into growing up in the segregated South.

*This place that fueled my passion for acting had been a source of degradation and despair for my parents.*

So, the narrative I have prepared depicts small vignettes in my life that my brain has opened. Some memories are easily recalled and put to paper, yet others were sparked by hearing stories, and some came after reaching out to childhood friends and doing a little research.

My story is a plain and simple one. My childhood was good. I had a mother and a father who loved me and took care of me, and I had family and friends in a community that nurtured me. I always had food and clothes, and life was carefree. As a teenager, I realized that few things were as simple as they seemed, and the carefree life I'd always lived was anything but carefree for my parents and our Black community. As children, we were often protected from the darkness of the real world.

## GROWING UP: FAMILY LIFE

In the 1950s and 1960s, segregation was the law, and Jim Crow was alive and well in Alexandria, LA. Segregation affected us all whether we knew it or not. Our perspective on events and the circumstances of our daily lives, however, is what makes our stories different.

I was born December 10, 1950, in Huey P. Long Charity Hospital in Pineville, LA., "Charity Hospital" as it was called by many people. My first residence was with my mom, dad, and sister on Solomon Street, off Lower Third Street. Alice Faye, 11 years my senior, took her role as big sister seriously, as she loved me as if I were her doll baby. With our age difference, she assumed she could discipline me. When I was 7 or 8 maybe, story has it, that she spanked me, and I let her know through words that she would never whip me again "or else," and according to our parents, that was her last time.

*My parents at Jones Street Junior High event in 1960s*

Because of this narrative, I did more research into my family history, and I learned that we lived on Lot 4 of William Ashby addition to the City of Alexandria. It was called Ashby Alley, then Ashby Street early in its existence, and years later, it was changed to Solomon Street as it exists today. Solomon Ashby was my grandfather.

My great grandfather, William Ashby, migrated to America from Barbados on a ship that docked in Baltimore, Maryland in 1867. He became a naturalized citizen in 1869. William moved to Rapides Parish near Lecompte where he met and married Josephine Washington. They later moved to Alexandria and acquired this land. Apparently, the land was divided among William and Josephine's seven children. We lived next door to my grandmother. The next two houses were her brothers' families. Across the street was Pilgrim Baptist Church where my grandmother attended. That church is still operating today. I owned property on Solomon Street until 1993. The majority of what was once Ashby land is now owned by the Pilgrim church community.

My uncle, William Ashby, and his family lived on Leonard St, one street north of Solomon. My cousin, "Buddy" Ashby, and his family lived two streets south of Solomon on John Thomas Street. My uncle, Solomon, or Toby, as we all called him, and his wife, Aunt Dot (Dorothy), lived on John Thomas as well. Our family and extended neighborhood felt safe, and we all looked out for one another.

In 1955, we moved a little farther down Third Street to Woodard Street. My brother, Thomas Jr. was born July 2, 1957. I was 6 years old, somewhat spoiled, and not willing to share my parents and sister with this little boy. Let's just say his early years were a little rocky with me. I loved my baby brother, but I would be mean to him sometimes. As we grew, so did our bond, and eventually I did stop being the mean sister. Sadly, my brother died on March 26,1983, from a gunshot wound. He was 26.

After we moved to Woodard Street, we were not side by side with family, but we were still within walking distance. For a while after we moved, I spent part of the week at my grandmother's house because I attended Augustana Lutheran School on Third Street, a short walk from the house. When I stayed with my grandmother and the nights would be cold, I remember she would heat an iron and wrap it in a towel then tuck it in at the foot of my bed to keep me warm. I never forgot that. I loved my grandmother dearly. Josephine Ashby Ellis died August 18, 1965. She was 85 years old.

Augustana Lutheran Church was established in 1915. It was pastored by Rev. E.R. Berger at its beginning. The church ran a successful lower elementary school from 1932 through the 1970s. Mrs. S.B. Berger was the lead teacher at the school in the early days. From approximately 1944 through 1971, hundreds of Black kids in the Lower Third area were educated at Augustana before moving to upper elementary school. Augustana became a licensed daycare center in 1972 and was in operation until at least 1976.

Augustana Lutheran Church was my first church. My daddy was baptized there when he was a baby. I was a member until the early 1980s when I converted to Catholicism to worship with my husband. My mother and sister were Baptist and my brother, and I were Lutheran. As kids, we visited each other's churches. Augustana school was my first school. I went there through second grade and then to Silver City Elementary.

At the beginning of Woodard Street was a large cotton gin that fronted Third Street and extended about two or three blocks down Woodard on the left side. I remember it being a loud bustling entity in the neighborhood. In the air there was a sweet smell of cottonseed. We lived on the last block of Woodard at 719. The end cross street was Ninth Street. Across Ninth was the canal.

Our house had a living room, dining room, kitchen, three bedrooms and one bath. My father and his brothers and other family built that house. Several Ashby men were carpenters. Uncle Solomon taught carpentry at the Alexandria Vocational Technical School. We had a big backyard that my parents took advantage of to raise chickens from time to time. I remember my mother wringing the necks of chickens, and she was an expert! She would grab a chicken and wring its neck, then whip it up into the air and snap it down toward the ground. The neck would still be in her hand, while the headless bird would be flopping all over the yard until it was dead.

I specifically remember two painful accidents that happened to me while living in our house. First, in the kitchen, we had a wringer washing machine. The washer had a round body that held gallons of water and on top were two rollers that closed together to wring the water from the clothes. Articles of clothing had to be fed between the rollers carefully to prevent one's fingers from being caught in the rollers. One day, I took what I remember to be doll clothes out of the washer and carefully placed them one at a time between the rollers. All was well until a piece of clothing got bunched up in the wringer. I decided to pull it out — bad idea. My hand got caught and was slowly pulled into the wringer. I was screaming and naturally trying to pull my hand out, but that only made the pain worse. My hand was pulled in as far as my wrist and the wrist bone kept it from moving farther inside, but the wringer kept turning, causing a second-degree burn across the top of my left hand. My mother released me from the washing machine disaster and took me to the doctor where I was treated. The burn healed but the scar, although faded, remains. I learned a powerful lesson that day about being careful around household machinery.

The second incident happened when I was in the fifth grade. I apparently forgot how dangerous household machinery could be, and one of the most dangerous of all was the gas space heater. One morning, I was fooling around taking too much time getting ready for school. I was wearing a long nightgown and a long robe. It was cold outside, and the heater was on in my room. We had space heaters that were freestanding on four legs with a ceramic top and grates where flames came from. My mother had told me to get ready several times, but I was cold and didn't want to go to school. I was warming myself with my back to the heater. It felt good, until the heat got more intense, and I looked back to realize that my gown and robe were on fire! Instead of stopping, dropping, and rolling, I did the opposite by panicking, screaming, and running. My mother caught me in the hall and snuffed the fire and took me straight to the doctor. I remember being in Dr Robinson's office and being treated again for second-degree burns. This time I did learn my lesson, a few lessons in fact. I learned not to stand too close to the heater, and in case your clothes catch fire, you stop, drop, and roll. At the time, I attended Silver City Elementary, and my mother would send me to school with a special pillow to sit on for a couple of days, as my burns continued to heal.

## My Hardworking Parents

I remember my parents were hard workers, but racism certainly took a toll on them. My parents worked for and around white people, but as a small child, I only got glimpses of that world. I remember going to their respective workplaces from time to time. My father, a grown man being the head of his own household, was different around these people than he was at home. I never saw him treated badly, but I never saw him treated like the white employees. There was definitely a color line. My daddy was a responsible, trusted employee but not a valued employee. He was expected to be happy, obedient, and available when he was needed and that's what he did to succeed. He was a drinker, as were most of our family and their friends, and his drinking increased over his lifespan, yet all the while he was able to keep the same job for 36 years.

My father worked at R.J. Jones and Sons Building Company. He was a smart man and very good in math. He could tell you exactly how much building material it took to build a house, down to the last nail regardless of size. I remember him having a stool and a tall desk on the loading dock. I also remember people asking him where to find things in the store and about how much material they needed for their projects.

My daddy also worked as the Jones' chauffeur, and he was a bartender at their social events. He worked for the Joneses for 36 years until the day that he had a stroke and fell off his stool on the loading dock. He was taken to Rapides General Hospital where he had surgery and never recovered. His doctor, Dr Chicola, said it looked like he had been kicked in the head by a horse. Dr Chicola was white, and he treated many Black people in Alexandria/Pineville. Thomas Joseph Ashby Sr. died February 1, 1985. He was 62 years old.

My mother worked in private homes. Before I was born, she cooked in a café and, at some point, she worked in a medical clinic. Throughout my life, especially when I expressed an interest in nursing, Madear would say she could have been a nurse if she had really applied herself. I believe she could have been a great nurse. I didn't spend much time with my mother on any of her jobs. I would go with my dad to pick her up sometimes. I remember some of the employers, but I never had a relationship with any of them. My mother worked hard, but she was not one to take a lot of crap. If she felt disrespected on the job, she would say what she felt on her way out. Remember this was the '60s, so she knew how far to go. "My mama didn't raise no fool," she would say as she recounted her experience. She would also say, "you can't let these white people treat you any type of way." As you can see, my mama had a bit of an attitude.

Daddy was drinking daily by the time I was a teen. Madear drank mostly on the weekends. They had friends who came over that drank as well. While there were good times with family and friends, my parents ran the gambit of little fusses to huge alcohol-fueled arguments. My bedroom and books were my retreat.


## THE NEIGHBORHOOD: IN BLACK AND WHITE

In the late 1950s, Lower Third was bustling, and there was a store or business on every block. In the vicinity around Solomon Street there were churches, a fish market and a cleaner. There also were bars, several mom-and-pop stores, and, of course, the three large, white-owned grocery stores. The grocery stores were where I would see white people regularly in the '50s and early '60s.

At the corner of Third and Solomon was a "Cree-Mee" hamburger place, which was the Dairy Queen of our time. They had the best soft serve ice cream cones. Needless to say, there were "white" and "colored" windows for service. According to my sister, during the time, people complained about the signs, and there was even some talk of a boycott. Eventually the signs were removed, and there was no violence associated.

We frequented the "Mom and Pop" stores, as well as the bigger ones. You could buy cigarettes out of the pack, two or three for a nickel. There were packs of tobacco with rolling papers, so you could roll your own cigarettes. Kids could buy cigarettes during those days. Our parents would send us to the store for odds and ends, and we could get some penny candy or a bottle of Coke. My sister loved to put peanuts in her Coke bottle. Anyone else ever tried that? I loved it too back in the day.

I don't remember there being a problem with race in the white-owned stores in the neighborhood. The Food Mart, F & F, and K & S groceries were all family businesses. Owners had their children running around behind the counters or in the store. I never played with these white children, but they grew up in the neighborhood during the day and interacted with neighborhood kids. Also, my parents were able to cash their checks at these stores, and for the most part, they had good relationships with the owners until they closed in my adult years.

I saw white people on Woodard Street regularly. The Union National life insurance man would come to our house weekly to collect, and the mercantile man, who sold a variety of household items, like Chenille bedspreads and curtains, also would come with his wares. Today, when I think about our interaction with white people in my youth, I would say it was limited. Our neighborhoods, our schools, our churches, our parks, our swimming pools, movie theaters, and so much more were all Black. We had two Black doctors in Alexandria, Dr. Hines, and Dr. Robinson. There was a pharmacy on Third and Bogan run by a white man, Mr. Redmond, who filled prescriptions and prepared medicine. There were six Black-owned funeral homes that I was aware of in Alexandria.

## My Education: In and out of School

After Silver City Elementary, I went on across the street to Jones Street Junior High. I loved music, so I joined the band. My daddy was a musician. He played tenor saxophone in a band, and he also wrote and arranged music. So, playing music came naturally for me. My parents bought me a B flat clarinet from a music store in town, I can't recall the name, and they paid it off over time. I still have that instrument today, and it is in fair condition. I have played that clarinet from time to time over the last 50 plus years. It has been years since the last time I picked it up, but I feel like I can still play a tune.

Later at Peabody, I was in the marching and the concert bands. Our band director, Mr. Andrews, encouraged us to learn more than one instrument. My major instrument was the clarinet, and I also played oboe and baritone horn. I thought about majoring in music in college. Because of Mr. Andrews' instruction and encouragement, just after graduating from Peabody, I was able to play with the Rapides Symphony Orchestra for a short time. The white orchestra members were not friendly, and I remember hearing a remark about my lips being too big to play oboe, so I showed them how a big-lipped Black girl could play. I practiced with them for three to four months before I left.

By this time in my life, as a teenager, I had been exposed to the real world. I had been "to town," so to speak. I knew that when we rode the city bus, we sat at the back, and when we went to the Paramount or the Don Theater, we had to sit in the balcony. I knew that we could order food at Kress's lunch counter, but we couldn't sit there to eat. Although I had lived in the real world, I had not experienced overt racism.

After two years at Jones Street, the home of the "Rattlers", we were one summer break away from entering Peabody High School, the third point in the triangle of schools on Jones Street. In that summer of 1964, there was a get-together every weekend at someone's house on my end of Woodard and Ninth Streets. I was not an introvert or shy, just more of a homebody. I had friends, animals, and books. I typically stayed home reading, and I was content. My mother and sister encouraged me to go to some of the get-togethers that summer. These were at friends' houses and their parents were home. There was food, dancing, and fun.

On one summer evening, I went to a get-together at Ennis Miles' house, and my whole life changed. I met Joseph Metoyer that night. He was a good-looking boy, with piercing eyes that stole my heart for all eternity. We were 14 years old when we met. We talked and danced, and he walked me home, which was just a few doors up the street. My sister says they couldn't wipe the smile off my face that night. I liked him a lot, and I could hardly wait until the next get-together. Alice still tells that story, and she exaggerates it more every time she tells it. What's not exaggerated is the fact that the Summer of 1964 was transformative for me. Joe came from a big family, four sisters and three brothers. They attended St. James Catholic Church and School. That summer I met his friends and family, and he met mine. And somehow, in spite of that, we kept seeing each other.

Our courtship was not perfect. He broke up with me in high school for nearly a year because of his family's concern that we were seeing too much of each other. He was also being advised by a priest who was close to his family that because I had planned to go away to college, and he had planned to join the U.S. Air Force that we should cut ties. So, he broke up with me. I was miserable. We lived one street apart, so we saw each other at games, downtown, or in passing in the neighborhood. Mutual friends told me that he was miserable too. When he decided in his heart and mind what he wanted, he came back. We built a relationship that expanded to 42 years and one month of marriage, four children, six grandchildren and one on the way in 2021. Our life together was not perfect, but it was beautiful. Our children were born in the 1970s and 1980s. The racial climate had improved for them, but there were still hills that they had to climb. We did our best as parents to keep them safe and secure and always aware of who they are and whose they are. My sweet precious husband died October 3, 2013. He was 62 years old. I miss him every day.

I loved high school! Joe went to St. James, the Catholic school for Blacks, and I went to Peabody. My years at Peabody were some of the happiest of my life. My friends and I were no longer "Rattlers" from Jones Street, we were "Warhorses", the Mighty Warhorses, if you will. Along with us were students from Lincoln Road Junior High, the home of the "Bulldogs". We had been fierce competitors for the past two years in all sports and school activities. I'm sure we brought some of that competitive spirit with us as we crossed the threshold and walked down the hallowed halls of Peabody. We got to know each other in classes and as we participated in sports and other activities together. The teachers lived in or near our neighborhoods and Mr. Iles, our principal, convinced all of us that he knew our families personally. Also, the teachers were available to help with any problems we felt comfortable sharing with them.

For me, the Peabody experience gave me a sense of community like the one I had growing up with family on Ashby Street. Our books and equipment were second-hand, mostly coming from Bolton, the seemingly rich public white high school across town. Our teachers, however, were dedicated to giving us the best education with the equipment at hand, and they pushed us to be more than we thought we could be. They were supportive but firm, and they taught us that we couldn't be as good as white students; we had to be better. They expected us to do well, and most of us did. That being said, we weren't all sitting around singing happy songs and watching the real world go by. I did not slide through high school. I don't think any of us did. Some days were tough, and there were times when I doubted my own ability, but my teachers walked me through difficult studies and situations.

We walked through the doors of Peabody as "Rattlers" and "Bulldogs". We bonded in high school, old friends and new, and four years later, we walked across the stage and received diplomas as a part of the strong, proud, unified Peabody Class of 1968, P-COSE. This book of narratives is a testament to our bond.

Throughout high school, I was asked to speak, narrate, or serve as mistress of ceremony for school and community events. I was in the band, drama club, Future Nurses of America, and other clubs at different times. My involvement in school activities afforded me the opportunity to be involved in Alexandria community events.

I was chosen along with a group of students to usher at the Rapides Parish Coliseum when Dr. Martin Luther King Jr. spoke at the opening of the Louisiana Education Association convention in 1966. I remember that being a very exciting night, and I was thrilled to be a part of it. Hearing Dr. King speak in person was easily one of the most important experiences in my life.

After graduation, I was determined to make my family and Peabody proud. I decided to stay home instead of going away for college, so I enrolled at LSU-A, majoring in nursing. I did not like LSU-A at all, but it was affordable. I could stay home and monitor things, and I could see Joe every day. It was like a huge high school with mostly white people. There were no Black instructors, and I sensed that the white ones were prejudiced as were most of the students. Before I got a car, I rode a bus to school. LSU-A had a bus stop in the mall parking lot where students were picked up and dropped off. I met Black students from different places and other schools. I met students who were willing to share rides, and when I got my car, I did the same.

In 1970, I was part of a group of Black students that organized the first Black student organization on campus. We applied to the committee on student organizations at LSU-A and were approved by the committee and the Dean. Uhuru na Umoja (Freedom and Unity) was born. I was the treasurer of the group. Our purpose was to strive to attain equality throughout the campus and the community, to merit a voice on campus affairs and to aid the Black communities through tutorship sessions, improvement plans, and by enlightening others of the true heritage of people of Afro-American descent. I found out while researching for this narrative that Uhuru na Umoja was only active that one year.

During my stay at LSU-A, I participated in school activities to make my presence known. I was in a couple of plays, I danced in student programs, and I participated in homecoming activities. Willie D. Weaver and I entered the Miss LSU-A pageant in 1970, to add a little color, and although we did not win, we had a good time in the process. I'm not sure, but I think we were the first Black students to enter that pageant. While I did not like LSU-A, the nursing program was known to be hard, and it was highly rated in the state. The percentage of graduates who passed the State

Board Exam on their first try was always near 100 percent. Through hard work and determination, I earned an Associate Degree in Nursing. I'm proud to say that I passed the State Board exam on my first attempt and became a registered nurse.

Years later, I returned to school and earned a Bachelor of Science degree in Health Arts from the College of St. Francis in Joliet, Illinois. I wanted to participate in the commencement ceremony. Joe and the kids, nor my mom was able to go, so my sister flew from Texas to Chicago to be with me. I was thrilled that she was there. We had a great time. Alice and I have had many special times together as adults. Our bond has never been stronger. She is 81years old, and she still thinks she's the boss of me.

## CURTAIN CALL IN SECOND ACT

I love nursing, and it has served me well for nearly 50 years. I've been a school nurse, I've worked ICU and general medicine, a plasma donor center, and nearly 30 years in psychiatric/mental health nursing. Mental health nursing felt like my calling. I remember that people who had mental health problems, people who were different or didn't fit in most places, were welcome in our home. Those were the people drawn to my mother, and they sought her counsel. Rosa Ashby Sr was a mental health nurse/counselor before I knew what that was. My mother taught me to treat others the way I wanted to be treated. She WAS the nurse she always said she could be. In my work, I approached each patient respectfully with the attitude that "this is somebody's child, but for the Grace of God, this could be me or one of mine." My staff and students know that respect for our patients is my Number 1 rule. Since retiring from state service in 2012, I have enjoyed teaching prospective clinical medical assistants at a local career college.

I am proud to say that I never strayed too far from my creative side.

I have established myself as a professional storyteller and an actress on stage and screen. I was active in theater at Peabody and LSU-A, and I never lost that love for the stage. After working for years and raising a family, I auditioned for a play with City Park Players, which is Alexandria's oldest community theater. The local theaters were and still are predominantly white with few Blacks involved in productions or audiences.

I did not get a part in the first play I auditioned for, but the next time there was a performance, I got a small part. After that I kept coming, I worked behind the scenes and on stage frequently. I pushed for more Black plays to get more Black actors involved, but there was always pushback. I was given the opportunity to direct plays, particularly the yearly Black play that they were comfortable putting on. I was fortunate enough to have starring roles in some of City Park Players' most successful productions. While theater is not as noble a calling as nursing, I give God the Glory for affording me this talent. If my performance helps one person who is burdened leave the theater feeling better, I've done a good job.

My mother would come to see me perform, and we would talk about the plays afterwards. One day she told me this story: When I was a little girl, my daddy's employer Robert Jones of R.J. Jones and Sons Building Company gave Daddy two tickets to see a play at City Park Players. This was probably late '50s, early '60s, the height of segregation in the Deep South. Who knows why Mr. Jones would give my dad those tickets, but I know why my dad would take them and go to a play at a segregated theater. He went because his boss expected him to go. My mother did not remember the

*Rosa as Sarah Delaney in Crowns*

play or much about their treatment inside the theater, but she had a clear memory of them coming out of the theater to a slashed tire. That's all I got because that's all she remembered. That story left me stunned. This place that fueled my passion for acting had been a source of degradation and despair for my parents. I thought about cutting ties with the theater, but I decided to stick around to try to make things better.

I was asked to sit on the Board of Directors of City Park Players in 2000. A few years later, I became the first Black president of that board. I sat on the design committee for the Coughlin-Saunders Performing Arts Center, and along with other board members, I had the honor of laying one of the first bricks as the building was being constructed. Later, I played the role of Sadie Delany in the play *Having Our Say: The Delany Sisters' First 100 Years.* Along with Sylvia Davis as Bessie Delany, we represented City Park Players in the American Association of Community Theaters festivals, and we had the good fortune of winning state and regional competitions for the production of the play. Our performance at nationals led to an invitation to the international festival in Strasburg, Germany. The theater held fundraisers, and we got lots of donations. Our goal was reached, and it was off to Germany. We were accompanied by five City Park Players supporters who worked as our crew. Joe was able to come with me, so it made for a perfect trip.

I had success and good times with City Park Players. I can't blame people in the present for sins of people in the past. Yet, every time I presided at a board meeting or performed with City Park Players, I recalled the story that my mother told me, and I thought, "This is for you, Mom and Dad. This is for the racism and the disrespect showered on you. Your baby girl has the keys to their building and Black folks are encouraged to come in."

I didn't change much at City Park Players. Times changed, and I received the respect my mother and father deserved when they went to a play there when I was a child. My mother died June 2, 2010.

This is my story. Plain and simple. My life has had ups and downs, but my perspective has always been that life is good. God has been good to us even in the bad times, and I am grateful. Madear always said, "Thank God for what it is." It is my hope that the simple accomplishments that I have made in my life have been a source of pride to my parents and to my school.

I am thankful for this opportunity to tell my story as a member of the Peabody Class of 1968.

# ONE MORE THING

*"He that dwelleth in the secret place of the most High shall abide under the shadow of the Almighty."*

PSALM 91:1

## Dr. Helen Benjamin

I AM NOT UNIQUE among the masses of African Americans whose ancestors were brought to America as enslaved people. I see myself as a survivor of the legacy of horror that symbolized that terrible time. As such, I have endeavored to honor the memories of those who lost their lives in the Middle Passage and those who survived and enabled my birth. I have not always considered myself a survivor. I grew into this awareness as I learned more about and reflected on my heritage. Doing so allowed me to call up the strength and determination instilled by my forebears so that I could participate fully in a society determined to denigrate and exclude me.

*Whether conscious of it or not, I think now that I was always living with a sense of urgency, always involved in something meaningful and engaged in multiple activities toward a greater purpose.*

## A BIT OF FAMILY HISTORY

We have a huge family. I have close to 70 first cousins. Family members on both sides have spent considerable time exploring our lineage, which has been traced to five and six generations because of records in family Bibles, stories passed down by family members, and genealogical research. There are many stories worthy of noting, but I shall mention only one. My mother's maternal ancestry goes back to Africa to Celestine Adams Baptiste (Scilisteen) who was born in either 1815 or 1823. The story has been passed down through six generations. When Scilisteen was around 6 years old, she and her mother, along with others, were lured onto a slave ship, presumably off the West African coast, to shop for bolts of colorful bright fabric. After taking some time to select the fabric for purchase, they discovered that the ship had deliberately sailed so far out to sea, it was impossible for them to get off and get back to their African village. They were forever tormented by thoughts of leaving their families behind and never knowing what happened to them. They belonged to their captors and became slaves, first in Texas, then in Louisiana. We have a photo of her.

My parents, Justus Benjamin and Dorothy Givens Benjamin, were born and reared in Natchitoches Parish, Louisiana. Specifically, both sides of my father's family settled in the Flora/Cypress area soon after the Civil War. Both sides of my mother's family settled in the Lena (Rapides Parish)/Marco/Chopin areas long before the Civil War. My father's parents, George Benjamin and Virena Talton Benjamin, began their lives together as sharecroppers in 1925 and became parents to 12 children. My father was their oldest child. My mother's parents, Willie Givens and Sarah Murphy Givens, were also sharecroppers who married in 1930, both for the second time. They had six children together and a total of 14 children including those from prior marriages. My grandparents settled in Marco, my grandmother having lived in Chopin prior to the marriage. My mother, Dorothy, was their oldest child together.

*My parents in early 1950s*

My father served in the U.S. Navy during World War II and returned to the Cloutierville/Derry area after the war ended. Church attendance brought our parents together. Our mother was in a quartet with three of her friends. They sang at a service Dad attended. In a video in which Dad reflects on his life, he says our mother was "the prettiest girl I had ever seen". My mother remembers seeing him for the first time walking toward her and a group of friends on their way from church. They married on February 26, 1949, on the front porch of her parents' house facing Cane River.

My mother and grandmother had made a special trip to Alexandria and bought her wedding dress at Schwartzberg's. My parents moved to Alexandria in 1953, after what Dad humorously described as his miserable failure at sharecropping. Alexandria, he determined, would offer more employment opportunities. With just me (I was the only child until 1954), they moved first to Woodside, then to the Sonia Quarters on Poplar Street where we lived until I was 12. My three siblings were added in 1954 (Justus Jr), 1955 (Patricia), and 1960 (Michael). Our parents were married for over 68 years, until Dad's passing in 2017.

## MY FIRST NEIGHBORHOOD

The house we lived in was on one of four tree-named (Poplar, Locust, Cypress, Cedar) streets, hemmed between two railroad tracks and the businesses that employed Black men and women in the surrounding community: an oak flooring plant, a sawmill, and a chicken processing plant. The latter emitted the worst stench imaginable *every single day*. I never got used to the smell and have never forgotten it. The placement of these homes was and remains typical of neighborhoods designed in cities and towns throughout the country for Black people. Interestingly, the homes on those streets were owned by Blacks. We rented our house from Mr. Henry who had converted one room of the house we lived in into a store. It was a small store typical of its time. Folks were in and out all day for cookies, "lunch" meat, candy, pickles, slices of cheese. Entrepreneurial and a tough businessman, Mr. Henry represents for me those in the Black community with a desire, and in some cases, a gift for business, but lacked the opportunity and resources to capitalize on those skills. Within those four streets were two churches; my siblings and I attended St. Lawrence. I loved that church. I was a regular at Sunday School and Vacation Bible School. The pastor, Rev. D.D. Smith, was a proponent of Christian education and recruited all the children in the neighborhood for participation in church activities. Just about everything I know about the Bible, I learned in the church's excellent programs. Ask me the major and minor prophets, I can tell you. I am ever grateful for that exposure to the Bible.

Ours was a lively, close-knit neighborhood with plenty of children, elders, and young couples. We were one of the few families with a television. I remember it well. It was a "floor model" with a blonde finish and doors that made it appear to be a cabinet when closed. Children would gather at our house to watch "TV". One of my friends called my mother recently and brought that memory back to her. Westerns were popular in the 1950s and 1960s and reflected in the one activity boys loved: riding stick horses. They would get long sticks, attach "reins" and commence to ride. I wish I'd had a video camera to capture the kids riding their horses up and down Poplar Street. The boys also used to roll tires. That was also a sight to see. Girls made all manner of things from mud and played with paper dolls made from pages of the Sears catalog in the absence of the "store bought" ones. What we could do with popsicle sticks showed the depth of our creativity. We used what we had to entertain ourselves.

## My Grandmother's House

Although we lived in Alexandria, my three siblings and I had much to look forward to, as we spent our summers on Cane River, primarily in Marco. My maternal grandparents lived close to the point where Cane River began. In those years, the Red River ran alongside Colfax and served as the dividing line between Grant and Natchitoches Parishes. The two rivers formed a "T", with Red River forming the top of the "T" and Cane River, the vertical line," rambling its way through Natchitoches Parish from that point. There were no plantations on the Marco end of Cane River, but white landowners constructed houses for themselves and the sharecroppers who worked the land hoeing and picking cotton in summer and fall, picking pecans during winter, and fishing in Cane River year-round. My grandparents merely crossed the road and walked down the hill to the banks of Cane River. It holds a distinct place in the lives of those who grew up in its presence. It was the source for many meals with its variety of fish, including buffalo, cat, gar, and gasper goo. Many of our family members on both sides, including our parents, my baby brother, and I, were baptized in it. Some family members and friends of the family lost their lives in it. With the houses facing the river, cottonfields on both sides and behind the houses for rows and rows, and scores of pecan trees behind the cottonfields, my grandparents and others who lived "on the river" were surrounded by their livelihood. They all lived off the land, some, of course, better than others. My paternal grandparents (Big Momma and Big Poppa) lived further up the river in Cloutierville/Derry until 1956 when they shed their sharecropping existence for the more lucrative highway construction work in other parts of Louisiana and Mississippi.

We were on Cane River every first and fourth Sunday of the month attending my mother's (St. Mary) and father's (Bright Morning Star) home churches, respectively, both established during the early 1900s. Muh, what we call our mother, and Daddy maintained their membership in those home churches for many years after leaving for town, as Alexandria was called by them. The church as well as the services were different from those in town. The services were still steeped in the traditions from slavery. There was no piano. Every song was a capella and beautifully accompanied by patting feet and clapping hands. People told their determinations, prayed strong, unforgettable prayers in the tradition of the ancestors, and shouted from being filled with the spirit. Rev. A.J Jenkins, a man with a calm demeanor and strong commitment to the Word, pastored both churches and was the grandfather of my classmate, Larry Jenkins. People adored Rev. Jenkins who was atypical for his time. More than 60 years later, I can still see and hear them all in my mind's eye. Mr. Jim (Cleveland), as we called him, prayed soul stirring prayers and sang from the depths of his soul. The equally powerful women, my grandmother and Miss Jo (Mr. Jim's wife) among them, enhanced the services with their prayers, songs, and testimonies. Church gave them power and hope in a world that offered little. It was a place all their own. They had power and control in church that they did not experience in their daily lives.

*My parents (1971) at Marco. St. Mary B. C. in the background*

My maternal grandfather died in 1953. Mama, my grandmother, never remarried. I know now that she was the strongest and bravest woman I have known personally. I saw her in action run that farm and support her family against the odds. Nobody messed with her. There are wonderful stories about her toughness. Until I was 13, I spent most summers at her house. I loved being in the "country" as we called it. Those experiences in the sharecropping environment are integral to the person I am today; I was immersed in the culture and traditions that I love. I did all kinds of things from feeding chickens to collecting the eggs they laid in

*Sarah Murphy Givens, Mama,*
*my maternal grandmother*

the chicken house which often had snakes that "collected" the eggs as well. However, I never learned to milk the cow whom we called Blossom. I tortured her. Getting the right tilt on the rope to get a full bucket of water from the cistern was a challenge as well. My aunts would tell me it was a good thing I was a good student because I would never make it on a farm. Nevertheless, I enjoyed my time there.

My grandmother's house, built in 1950 by the landowner, appeared to be on stilts. We used to play under that house. Peach trees lined one side, and a flower garden with a chinaberry tree was set in the corner of the yard. The opposite side had a cistern with water flowing into it from the gutters surrounding the edges of the tin roof of the house. A crib for storing the cotton once picked and a scale for weighing it were across from the cistern. A chicken coop and a large garden were in the back of the house. The house had front and back porches that all of us enjoyed. Neither the house nor the crib was painted. Row upon row of cotton on both sides of the house and behind it were hoed and picked by the Givens family for many years. Of course, there was an outdoor toilet. A gate led to the front porch, and a very wide gate on the other side allowed vehicles or wagons to enter the yard for access to the crib and the fields. The house and setting were emblematic of the agricultural life lived by Black people in Louisiana at that time. Even as there were reminders of poverty and separation, being there was a source of comfort and pleasure because family and community were there. My mother shares stories of the entire family listening to Joe Louis fights and Los Angeles Dodgers games on the radio with Jackie Robinson as a member of that team. They cheered for Jackie Robinson as though he was a member of the family. Every family member, especially my grandmother, loved the Dodgers because they hired Jackie Robinson. One of their own had become the first to make the big leagues and made them proud. *Jet* and *Ebony* magazines were a staple in the household. They provided connections to an aspirational Black world.

In 1958 when I was in third grade, I had the opportunity to live with my grandmother for a few months and attend Springhill, the school in Chopin. Although their school, like my South Alexandria Elementary, was segregated, there were glaring differences in the investment made in these schools and what were considered grossly underfunded schools in town. We seemed to fare better by far. (Everything is relative!) Children attending these schools were from Black sharecropping families and seemed to have fewer resources. Their physical environment had moved directly from slavery to "freedom". In 1958, they were in the same setting in which their ancestors had been enslaved with little change, a generation removed from slavery but still suffering its indignities to what appeared to be at a greater degree than Black schoolchildren in Alexandria! They rode several miles on a bus to get to school. Several grades were taught in one classroom. They often missed school because of the need to help the family bring in the crop. Despite the inequities, the teachers were committed to the community and the students, and they were able to provide excellent instruction and extracurricular activities for the children to the extent possible under the circumstances. I had a memorable experience. On reflection, those times in the country made me appreciate the character-building qualities of work, family, worship, and community that as an adult allowed for a more confident transition for me into the outside world.

My paternal grandmother, Virena Talton Benjamin (Big Mama), passed away in 1960 when I was 10. Two weeks before she passed, I had spent part of my summer with her in Amite, LA. Her passing broke my heart. She gave birth to 12 children and was ahead of her time in so many ways. Her legacy lives on in her numerous grandchildren.

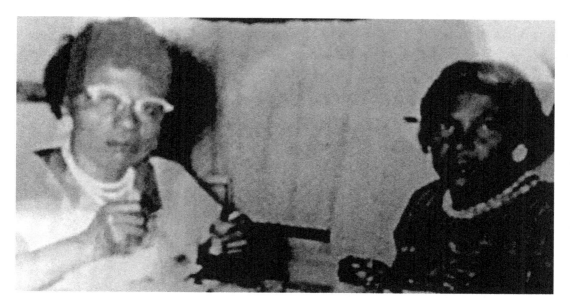

*Big Mama (right) with her sister, Essaphine, in 1954 in Los Angeles.*

## THE BENJAMIN HOUSEHOLD, SCHOOL, AND WORK

Wherever we were, our parents worked as a team and maintained strict rules. The emphases in our household were on doing things for others, spending our time productively, and always putting God first. In Alexandria, Dad worked at the sawmill for a few years and then at a gravel pit. He attended the local technical school and became a certified welder. Mom was a private housekeeper off and on during our childhood.

Dad had us memorize full chapters of the Bible; we had to stand before him and recite. That Psalm 91 is a long one to memorize, but it sustains me to this day.

I am grateful for it now. Our mother comes from a long line of great cooks. In our house, everything was made from scratch. She made the best cakes, pies, gumbo, fried chicken. I could go on. Eating from a fast food restaurant was not allowed. When we returned home for visits as adults, we never went out to eat. She cooked our favorite foods. Great food along with her wise counsel continue to be her greatest gifts to us.

As strict as they were, Dad insisted that each of us get a driver license when we turned 15. Being able to drive was part of another of my parents' character-building strategies. My driving was restricted to family errands, including chauffeuring elderly family members to doctor appointments and church services. Of course, I often ended up in places I was not sent, and I was punished for it if discovered! They often sent my brother with me on errands. He could not hold water. If I veered from the straight and narrow, he would "tell it" before he got both feet in the house. Considering Dad's old-school ways, I was surprised that when I turned 16, he allowed me to "receive" company. It was all very formal and, I suppose, a carryover from his and my mother's courting experience. Guys would come to visit me, typically on Sundays. We sat awkwardly on the sofa and conversed uncomfortably, knowing that we weren't completely alone. If the guy overstayed what seemed to be sufficient time for a visit, Dad walked through the house winding the clock. That hint that it was time to leave could not have been more obvious.

As was the case with most Black parents at the time, our parents focused on the importance of education and their desire for my siblings and me to escape the backbreaking work for those who did not seek higher education. To this end, going to school was as important as anything else we did. I never attended preschool or kindergarten. My mother taught me the alphabet and my numbers. I was ready for school. From the moment I stepped into Mrs. Castain's first grade classroom at South Alexandria Elementary School, I loved school. I loved everything it offered, especially a glimpse into a world foreign to my daily existence and the wonderful possibilities life held for me. School was my respite, my escape, my saving grace in a segregated system designed to subjugate me. I also wanted more from the life I had. School brought me both joy and hope. In elementary school, I loved geography and still remember being fascinated by Greenland and Iceland and wondering how anyone could live in such a cold climate.

We moved from the Sonia Quarters across one set of the tracks and near the Garden of Memories Cemetery when I completed elementary school. I enrolled in one of the two junior high schools, Lincoln Road, with all the kids I had attended elementary school, but I stayed there for only one semester because we moved into a neighborhood requiring my attendance at the opposing junior high, Jones Street. I was heartbroken because I did not want to leave my friends. However, I had no choice. The only good thing about the move was that my elementary school principal, Mr. Spottsville, had been promoted to principal of Jones Street, and he knew me. That gave me some comfort. I distinctly remember the assistant principal saying to me on the day I enrolled at Lincoln Road that I had made all A's at Lincoln Road but that would not happen at Jones Street because Jones Street was much more challenging. Who says something like that to a seventh grader? I have never forgotten his comment and have endeavored in my career as an educator to never say such a thing to any student. A distinct Jones Street memory for me is participating in Louisiana Interscholastic Athletic and Literary Organization (LIALO) oratory competition in eighth grade. Ms. Tabor, my English teacher, selected Poe's "The Raven" for me to recite. I competed against a young man who performed a dramatic recitation of Judas' remorse after the betrayal. I was certain he had won, but he did not. I took home the prize.

Despite my disappointment over changing schools, attending both schools gave me a huge advantage when we all ended up together in 10th grade at Peabody, the only public high school for Black students. I knew just about everyone in our class, having spent time at both feeder schools. As a matter of fact, I was voted "most popular girl" and "best all-around girl" in our senior class and president of the student council in my senior year. The longer I was in school, the better things became for me. Although I was busy with jobs, church, and responsibilities of being the oldest child in the household, I was active in high school. I participated in numerous activities and was given leadership opportunities, providing the impetus and experience for thinking about what I would do in the future. One of the ways I took advantage of high school activities and programs for broadening my educational experience was to participate in Bayou Girls State in Baton Rouge in the summer of 1967. Doing so was the highlight of my high school years. Separate but equal activities were still the norm in the country then, and Bayou Girls State was the Black version of a statewide program. Both were designed to acquaint students with how government works. It was a transformative experience for me. I spent a week with other Black girls from all over Louisiana, learned a great deal about Southern University where the program took place, lived in a dormitory, and participated in a process that provided discipline and knowledge about government that I would otherwise have never obtained. Being involved in this program broadened my horizons and my understanding of leadership.

Because of my experiences in the first 18 years of my life in Alexandria, I faced my future with confidence. I realize now that I moved along as a child on a mission under the pressure of the constant refrain from our parents: "I do not know what you are going to do when you are 18, but you got to get out of here." I knew they meant it. They forced independence. They instilled us with Christian values and a serious sense of right and wrong, and they expected us to make good choices for the rest of our lives.

Whether conscious of it or not, I think now that I was always living with a sense of urgency, always involved in something meaningful and engaged in multiple activities toward a greater purpose. That involved working, another of the values strongly held by my family. I started my first job the summer I turned 14, as a babysitter for a toddler, a white girl named Kelly whose mother worked outside the home. I don't recall much about that job except that the house was in disarray. All the mother wanted me to do was take care of Kelly all day, and that was all I did that entire summer. I started my first bank account with that job. It also was the first summer I did not spend all or part of with my grandmother in Marco. In high school, I got a job for another white family in town. One of my mother's cousins worked for them during the day. They had five stairstep children. I worked there on Tuesday and Thursday evenings and on Sunday mornings when they went to church. I was the evening and weekend "help" with responsibility for the two youngest children who were probably 18 months or so apart. They lived a privileged life that was truly foreign to me. I never "connected" with them, as would be expected in a situation where enforced racial and social segregation held sway. The job was a means to an end. I did what I was paid to do, and that was to add money to my bank account toward the end of that type of servitude.

While working for the physician's family, I became part of the federally funded Economic Opportunity Act's Neighborhood Youth Corp (NYC), approved in 1964 as part of LBJ's War on Poverty. There were 11 programs in the legislation, and I participated in two of them, NYC in high school and Work Study in college. NYC provided work and training for young men and women between the ages of 16 and 21 from impoverished families and neighborhoods. I certainly qualified when it came to poverty in financial resources, though I would like to think I was rich in other

*Sandra Williams, Kathlyn Giles, and me in our uniforms at Pinecrest State School, Summer 1967*

ways. NYC provided three important job training experiences: an aide at Pinecrest State School for individuals with intellectual and developmental disabilities; an aide at Huey P. Long Charity Hospital; and with my best friend, Jackie Mayeaux, a recruiter for the Head Start program.

## My Awakening

There were whites in the work environment in the first two jobs, but they now are a blur to me. However, I clearly remember the patients I encountered. At Pinecrest, I experienced children with disabilities of all kinds, including sweeping cases of babies with hydrocephalus and young patients in the hospital with terminal illnesses who were there on a Saturday I worked, and deceased by the next Saturday. It was more than I could take, but I survived. I was not the one suffering, and the least I could do was offer aid. I knew then that such work settings were not ones in which I could build a career. My empathy would override my ability to do the job. Those images and experiences have stayed with me my whole life and instilled in me an understanding I would not have had otherwise. The Head Start experience involved walking across the Pineville bridge from the NYC office and going door-to-door in Smithville and Pineville to sign up participants. That job involved lots of walking and interacting with people. We even worked in the program at Mary Hill once it started. That work was more appealing to me. My NYC work provided a variety of work experiences and a peek into the real world of work, and it provided steady income. Between the domestic work and NYC, I was able to take care of many of my needs, especially when it came to graduation expenses.

My experiences as worker with NYC and my jobs as a domestic represent my closest and longest sustained encounters with white people in my 18 years in Alexandria. Of course, I saw white people when I went downtown or rode the bus, but sustained contact did not exist. In those two situations, I spoke only if it was required. I had nothing to say and little was asked of me that required a verbal response. I did not have sustained contact with whites until 1971 when I fulfilled my student teaching requirement. These minimal interactions were a result of the racial hierarchy of the time.

I experienced the strange and unnatural feeling of avoiding communicating with another human being when I exercised my right to sit at the front of the city bus one day. Neither my parents nor I was part of any organized opposition to segregation. Little was said in our home about what was happening in Alexandria. However, we were aware of the national scene. Chet Huntley and David Brinkley brought the news of civil rights into our home every weekday evening. I knew what was happening or had happened in Birmingham, Little Rock, and other cities throughout the South. I knew federal legislation had passed allowing me to sit anywhere I wanted on the bus or eat at any restaurant I wanted to. I became bold enough to step outside the vacuum of my home environment.

On that Big Day, at age 14 and scared to death, I dropped my coins in the fare box opening, steeled myself, and sat behind the bus driver. Nothing happened. I rode through the Sonia Quarters and downtown to my stop. The driver looked at me through the rearview mirror but uttered not a word. I sat in the front of the bus from then on. My bus riding days, however, were drawing to a close because I got my license to drive the next year. I also remember vividly the day Jackie (Mayeaux), my best friend, and I finally got the courage to sit at the lunch counter at the W.T. Grant store. Jackie remembers our teachers encouraging us to do so. I remember the vivid newspaper and television images of other young Black teenagers risking their lives to give us the right to do so. We used to walk through Grant all the time and talk about "doing it." When we finally sat at that lunch counter one day and ordered hamburgers, we received no resistance.

We were inching toward integration, but I could not wait for a future escape from the segregated conditions that existed for too long in my hometown. I wanted to know more about a broader world. The segregated environment in which I was born was shaped internally by those who lived and led within it. We were with people who knew and understood us and knew what we needed to survive and even thrive and not be stifled and completely limited in our expectations for ourselves. They cared about us, saw the potential in us, encouraged us, and sometimes forced us to see beyond our circumstances what we could and would become. They knew that our hope was in becoming educated and in having experiences that exposed us to the broader world and not the racially oppressive one designed to keep us in subjugation to white people and their ways. They also knew that persisting toward that education required a toughness, a willingness to take risks, and endure discomfort. This discomfort extended even into the educational arena where, one would think, a more enlightened attitude toward equality, fairness, and a greater comfort level would exist. That, however, was often not the case.

## COLLEGE

At the end of my senior year, I had a scholarship to Southern University in Baton Rouge and was planning to be on campus in the fall of 1968. I had some trepidation about being a college student, but Southern was familiar to me as I had spent a week there as a citizen of Bayou Girls State the prior summer. As chance would have it, the Bishop College financial aid director (Mr. O'Bannon) who was from Oakdale, a nearby town, contacted one of the counselors at Peabody on a Saturday morning in June, indicating that he had full rides with a combination of financial aid and scholarships for six students. The counselor called six of us to his office where we were offered the packages, and all six of us accepted. What a turn of fate for us all. Jackie and I left for Dallas a couple of weeks later for participation in a summer program. The trajectory of our lives changed that day.

What a change to my life! Affiliated with the Baptist church, Bishop was a historically Black college founded in Marshall, Texas in 1880, and in 1961 moved its campus to Dallas. It was a beautiful, intimate campus in the southern-most part of the city with a student body of about 2,000 Black students from across the United States and a few students from African countries. The professors were a diverse group: African Americans, Black and white Cubans, American whites, and Europeans. This kind of exposure to others was a first for me. They all appeared to have a common interest in the success of Black students. For the first time, I met Black students from all over the country.

Prior to going to college, I had only been to cities in Louisiana and Mississippi to visit my paternal grandparents who would move to and from areas where highway work took them. I also had been to Houston to spend a summer or two with my mother's sisters. Meeting students from California, Chicago, cities in Texas, the East

Coast, other southern states, and the Continent opened a world for me I had not imagined. There was even a student from Pocatello, Idaho. How diverse we were! This new environment required adjustments for us all. The college was a safe place for me to continue my growth and development and to enter an even broader world a little at a time. Dallas offered the large city experience but was just as segregated as Alexandria.

I was as busy in college as I had been in high school. I participated in student government, joined a sorority, worked in the library at the time they changed the cataloguing system from Dewey Decimal to Library of Congress (LC). I remember that so well because my job was to replace the Dewey Decimal numbers with the new LC ones and to make sure the cards in the card catalogue matched the numbers I "burned" on to the spines of hundreds of books with a hot pen. I also babysat for professors and worked at the first Target in Dallas as a night head cashier while maintaining a decent grade point average. I still had that sense of urgency I felt in high school as I reflect on it. As a student leader, I represented the college at a national United Negro College Fund event in Detroit. What an experience for me! I had my first airplane flight and took a day trip to Windsor, Canada, my first international travel experience. I loved college as much as high school.

## MOVING BETWEEN TWO WORLDS

Racial oppression has long-lasting effects. Although I began my teaching career at age 21 in an integrated environment of Blacks, whites, and Latinos, it was not until I was 25 and in my very first graduate course at Texas Woman's University that I sat as a student in a classroom with others who were not Black like me. I admit that I felt some discomfort and questioned my academic abilities and seriously wondered if I could compete. I had similar questions and misgivings about myself, when, in September 1971, I was thrust into a student teaching situation in a predominantly white school with a white teacher who had apparently not experienced the likes of me in such a capacity. It was a first for both of us. I realize now that I had bought into the "inferiority" or "lesser than" hype that results from growing up in an environment designed to subjugate my people and me. I had been complicit in my own subjugation without my conscious knowledge. I doubted myself and my abilities because I had spent the first 18 years of my life in an environment designed by white people to lower my self-esteem. Every single day, their words (or lack of words) and actions supported that. Fortunately, family members, my one-race school classmates, and my church community showed me that I was valued.

Those years were lessons in contradictions to young minds taught patriotic songs that we sang with great fervor. The contradictions came with the realization that the words of those songs and others did not reflect my experience. My classmates and I never received new textbooks, only used ones with the names of white students we would never meet. In school we were taught principles of democracy, but we lived our daily lives in a "separate and apart" unequal world with its own set of rules designed for Blacks and whites. These practices, if one took the time to pay attention and let their effects register, were enough to drive one into madness. Thankfully, those around us would not allow us to take that path. They encouraged and urged us to live above the circumstances of our birth. I did not know of W.E.B. Dubois' notion of "double consciousness" as an elementary school student, but I certainly experienced the dilemma described by it. That was indeed my life.

As I was growing up, adults who cared about me wanted me to do better than they had done. Teachers were the only professional role models I saw daily, so I decided to become one of them. I spent my professional career in various educational settings. I advanced from being a teacher in a public high school in Texas to increasingly responsible administrative positions in higher education, ending as an administrator in a large community college system in California. Professionally, the move to California was fortuitous. In the fall of 1989, I participated in a national leadership program sponsored by the League for Innovation in Community Colleges with 16 other people of color from across the United States. The program gave me hope and exposed me to a world of possibilities. By the time it ended in June of 1990, I had a job in the San Francisco Bay Area. I had given my all in Dallas in service to the community and in my workplaces, but there was little opportunity there for advancement. I went West and encountered colleagues and a system different from the one I had experienced in the South, one more favorable in furthering my career goals but not necessarily favorable for my children who had to adjust to a life radically different from the one they had left. We persevered, however, to a better outcome for us all.

While moving between segregated and integrated worlds presented major challenges for me after I left Alexandria, my movement between two worlds was successful because I never lost my sense of self and the core values that shaped me. My life could have turned out differently, but I decided against internalizing the anger and hatred exhibited toward me on numerous occasions, for it would make me lose my center — my essence — and render me useless in a world that needed me whole to make a difference. I refuse to carry that anger and hatred within me. Witnessing how my grandparents and others in rural areas and Blacks in Alexandria were treated and how they responded to the injustices and indignities placed on them has stayed with me. I have endeavored not to have racism become a distraction in my life. Toni Morrison's words reverberate:

The function of racism ... is distraction. It keeps you from doing your work. It keeps you explaining, over and over again, your reason for being. Somebody says you have no language and so you spend 20 years proving that you do. … None of that is necessary. There will always be one more thing.

Thankfully, I learned this early and moved on with my life. I have devoted my life to education as a teacher and administrator, always paying it forward because of the help and support I received in my educational experience. As a result of my career choice, I have been in school since I was six years old and have loved it. I am reminded of the words with which Mr. Jim and many others closed their prayers back in the day. They express what I wish for myself at this point in my life: "May my last days be my best."

# AS I SEE IT

*"For I know the thoughts I think toward you, saith the Lord,*
*thoughts of peace, and not of evil, to give you an expected end."*

JEREMIAH 29:11

## Jo Ann Cotton Williams

As a Black person growing up in Alexandria, life was not easy. We were living in poverty and didn't know it; my parents worked hard to ensure we had what we needed. My dad migrated to Alexandria from Chambers, Louisiana, and my mom came here from Lamourie, Louisiana, both seeking a better life. After the moves, my dad eventually joined the Army, and my mom worked in a private home. My mom at the time lived on Wise Street with her sister who was married to an Army man.

My uncle was friends with my dad; thus, he introduced my dad to his sister-in-law. After a short courtship, they married in 1939. Once they began their family, they realized they needed a place of their own. They found a house on Mason Street. My dad was able to get a GI loan to buy the house, which was a miracle at a time when very few Blacks were able to buy a house. It blows my mind when I recall their mortgage payment, $27 a month, which was a lot back then. How things have changed!

*My parents raised eight children in that home, working hard to ensure we had food on the table and a roof over our heads. They led by example showing us that hard work pays off.*

My parents raised eight children in that home, working hard to ensure we had food on the table and a roof over our heads. They led by example, showing us that hard work pays off. After being honorably discharged from the Army, my dad got a job driving a delivery truck for Wellan's Department Store. He later took a job working for streets and parks for the City of Alexandria. He remained in that job until he retired. My mom continued to work in private homes until she began to substitute in the school lunch rooms for the Rapides Parish School Board. After several years of substituting, she landed a job working in the cafeteria at Nachman Elementary, a white school. She remained in that position until she retired.

I grew up during a time when you had to ride at the back of the bus even though there were seats available in the front of the bus and when you could only go to the Paramount Theater on Saturday between the hours of noon and 1 p.m., using bottle tops for admittance. We were seated in a designated area where we were constantly watched and blamed for things we hadn't done. Forget about sitting inside a restaurant or drinking from the same water fountain as whites or not being watched in

## Doll, Toy Fund Show for Colored Saturday

The colored people of Alexandria expect to add a considerable sum of money to the colored division of the Daily Town Talk Doll and Toy Fund by giving an amateur vaudeville show and a full length moving picture at the Ritz theater on Lee street Saturday morning at 9 o'clock.

The show is being sponsored by the Colored Federation of Church Women, and the entire receipts of the show will be given to the Doll and Toy Fund. The picture, the use of the theater and even the tickets have been donated by the management of the Ritz and there will be practically no expense in giving the show.

The young colored folks of the city will present the vaudeville feature, and as is well known there are a number of artistic persons in that group here who can present a very laudable performance.

*Article from Alexandria Daily Town Talk, 11.17.1940 when the events were separate.*

the department stores while their own stole them blind. Some things have not changed; we are still being watched.

I can't help but smile when I think about the Doll and Toy Fund. The program has been in existence for decades. Our local newspaper and the Rotary Club now sponsor the fundraising drive to ensure children in central Louisiana have a bright Christmas. In my time, tickets were given to schools, and teachers gave them to selected students. Events were held in separate places for white and Black students, the Casson Street Community Center being our location. We could pick any toy we wanted if you got there early and receive a bag of fruit and candy. Those were the days.

Today, the separate events are gone, and there is one event for all children. It is still a community event, sponsored by *The Town Talk* and the Rotary Club.

Back in the day, we had corner stores. You could buy a nickel's worth of anything in the store (flour, rice, meal, pressed ham, etc.). We certainly can't do that today. Even though we have large grocery stores, department stores and movie theaters, we are still treated with disrespect. We are still followed and watched until we leave. I don't think that white business owners have realized that their own are ripping them off.

I have fond memories of my old neighborhood. Everyone knew each other. We played, fought, got over it, and moved on. Back then, our streets weren't paved; thus, we played in the dirt. We didn't think anything of it. That was also the time when adults could discipline you, no questions asked. You knew by the time you got home your parents knew what you had done. I never could figure out how the news traveled so fast. It was also a time when we had neighborhood schools.

In the Sonia Quarters, there was South Alexandria Primary and Elementary; in Woodside, we had Lincoln Road, Peabody Elementary. Jones Street and Peabody were located on Lower Third. Today, those are no longer as we knew them. Peabody Elementary is now a magnet school, as is Lincoln Road (now Phoenix Magnet). Both are in Black neighborhoods and our kids have to apply to attend. In most cases, they are not accepted. Peabody Magnet is the same. I never thought I would see the day when white students would be bused into our neighborhood. Go figure. Before de-segregation came about in the early 1970s, our neighborhood schools had the best teachers in the parish. They made sure we learned what we were taught to ensure we would be successful in life. Those great teachers took those same values and concepts with them when they went to white schools. They were not readily accepted. Unlike their white coworkers, they showed up to do the job they were hired to do.

I started working when I was 14. My first job was that of an ironer, and I didn't last a day! I eventually was hired to work during the summer at the grocery store across the street from my home; that lasted two years. I began working in the meat market, and later became a cashier. I remained in that job until I graduated high school. That fall, I attended Southern University, Baton Rouge. I remained there for several years. I returned home and began substituting for Rapides Parish Schools. Because white teachers would not show up to work at our neighborhood schools, I worked daily. (Not to brag, I was a very good sub.) I was often requested. The second semester of the 1972 school year, I was asked to fill in for the business education teacher for the rest of the year. I was so proud to become a part of Peabody's faculty and staff. I was fully engaged, lessons planned, roll book completed, etc. I would say that my proudest moment was when I marched with the faculty on graduation day.

In 1974, I was asked by one of the assistant principals at Alexandria Senior High to apply for a secretary position. I applied and got the job. My first year on the job was the worst ever; nothing was ever good enough. Mr. Andrews, former band director at Peabody, encouraged me daily not to quit. Our break time was the best part of the day. Mr. Andrews told me a joke every day and because of his encouragement, I made it through the first year. I went on to do 18 years in various positions. I served as secretary in the front office, Library and Guidance Office.

The one position I should have ended up with was head secretary. I was not offered the job because it would not look right for a Black woman to hold that position at a prestigious high school. Though I did not want the job, I was angry that I was not even asked. The principal at that school realized a day later that he had made a mistake. It took me two weeks to calm down enough for me to tell him what I thought about how he handled the situation. It took him two years to apologize for denying me an increase in salary. He vowed to make sure that if there was any position I wanted in the parish, it was mine. I thanked him but declined his offer.

By the end of the year, I was recommended for a head secretary position at a new school the parish was opening. I interviewed for the job and walked away with it. My principal told me that I was being considered for a job, and he would release me to take that position. Though he didn't want to see me leave, I was the best he had. I was the front office "go-to" person when they needed a report done right and on time. I started the new position in 1991 and remained in it until I retired. I realized hard work does pay off.

Reflecting on the educational system in Rapides Parish over the years, I see a little change in how our children are being taught. To know that we have a few really dedicated teachers in the classroom, especially in our mostly Black schools, blows my mind. If our children are misbehaving in class and teachers are afraid, those kids learn nothing, especially when they are no longer teaching basics. Can you imagine a child graduating high school not being able to read? It is still happening in our schools today. Just a few weeks ago I heard a grandparent tell his granddaughter to always pay attention when the teacher is teaching and to sit close to the front to get the information that teachers are giving the white students. Our kids deserve better. Desegregation didn't do us any favors.

In 1974, I married my high school sweetheart, and like most couples, we desired to one day own a home. In 1978, we began our search for our dream home. After a brief search, we located the house we would call home. The house was across town in a mixed-race neighborhood off Horseshoe Drive. We just knew after we met the realtor and walked through the house that we would be set to buy the property, only to be told that we could not afford it. Imagine our surprise to be told that we could not afford it when we knew we could! We thanked the realtor for her time and left. We decided to call someone else to show us the house, and we left with keys to the house.

I wish I could say that things have changed. Racism is still alive and well. We are the last hired and the first fired. We are still denied when it comes to buying a home in certain neighborhoods, still being told we are over-qualified for a job. How about the one when there is a hiring sign in the window, you go in to apply only to be told that the job has been filled. Some things will never change. I am reminded of a time when the police showed up at our house demanding a receipt for a bicycle that we bought for our daughter the year before. A white neighbor's daughter had the same kind of bike, and hers had been stolen. The neighbor saw my daughter riding the bike we had purchased for her and called the police. We were asked if we could prove that the bike our daughter had was, in fact, hers. Well, I still had the receipt. Neither the neighbor nor the police apologized for making an unproven accusation. That did not surprise me. When I think about Alexandria, I find not much has changed; we have a long way to go still.

Do I wish things were different? Yes, I do. I wish all the work that has been done over the years would have made a dent in how we are perceived in America today? We will not worry, for change will come…

How do you see it?

# MY FAMILY LEGACY

*"They shall not labor in vain, nor bring forth
trouble, for they are the seed of the blessed of
the lord, and their offspring with them."*

ISAIAH 65:23

## Rose Dempsey Williams

MY STORY BEGINS in Alexandria, LA where I was born in June of 1950. I remember walking up the walkway to our new home located in the Lower Third area. I was a toddler at the time. I was happy and playful with Mom, Daisy Lee Hayes Dempsey, and Dad, Louis Dempsey Sr., holding my hand, as we entered our new home. I have no memory of our previous home. The houses were primarily single family and Black-owned. We lived in a tight-knit community where the children played together, and the neighbors looked out for one another.

I am the oldest of five children. We all attended the nearby schools, named at that time, Silver City Elementary, Jones Street Junior High, and Peabody High school. They were in walking distance from our house. Mom stayed home, and Dad was in the U.S. Army until he retired. After retirement, he was employed at Veterans Hospital until he passed away in 1990. In grade school, I remember Dad teaching me my ABCs and how to read. There were a lot of tears. Mom attended PTA meetings and was involved in school and church activities.

During summer break, I spent time with my grandmother in "the country," as we called it. We called her "Mama" and, my mom was "MaDear."

My grandmother was a strong woman, and I believed she could do anything. She owned a house and farm where she grew crops, and owned chickens, turkeys, and other farm animals. I saw her ring the necks of chickens and even kill a hog with a sledgehammer. The next time I saw the hog, he was hanging up and cut in half for the blood to drain. I remember thinking she must have had help with this.

Mama grew cotton as well as other crops. One summer Mama hired all her grandchildren to pick cotton. After working so hard in the sun and fighting bugs, my bag of cotton was only worth 25 cents. Needless to say, that was my last money-making effort with picking cotton. In addition to working her farm, my grandmother cooked and cleaned for some rich white people whom I do not remember meeting. I stayed in the house until she returned.

*As a result of winning the civil rights suit against the trade school with Louis Berry as her attorney, Mom advocated for civil rights and social justice for the rest of her life.*

*My grandmother, Mama,*
*a strong woman!*

One day I was at Mama's house with one of my aunts when a snake dropped from the ceiling. Of course, my grandmother had no fear of snakes, and I vividly recall her killing them with shotguns. My aunt, however, was deathly afraid of snakes. So terrified that she immediately packed our bags and got us on a bus back to Alexandria. I was 10 and completely unaware of Jim Crow, so when I boarded the bus, I simply sat in the front of the bus. My aunt, who was still shaken up by the snake, went on to the back of the bus. It was not until she sat down and got settled that she realized I was up front. She quickly snatched me up and led me to the back row. In a way, this incident has always haunted me because my aunt never explained to me what I did wrong. So, at the tender age of 10, I experienced racism, although back then I was unable to articulate it. I continued to visit my grandmother and spend time there during the summer months. Mama eventually moved to a house next door to us in Alexandria.

I graduated from elementary school and moved to junior high school and adjusted to the classes and routine. I joined the band and enjoyed it; my instrument was the clarinet. While there, I remember sitting in the school library when it was announced that President John Kennedy had been assassinated. I remember it being a sad period. When I returned home from school, my parents seemed pretty upset about his assassination. Kennedy was seen as someone who believed in civil rights, and he was dead.

After my promotion from junior high school, I attended Peabody High School. I have fond memories of my high school years, which included, friendships, social and school activities, boyfriends, and the prom. I was a proud member of the Peabody Warhorse 100 Marching Band. In 1968, Martin Luther King Jr. was assassinated. I remember coming home from school and finding my father sitting at the dining room table crying. That was the first and last time I ever saw him cry. I will carry this somber image of my father crying in my heart forever.

During our early school years, we were not very aware of racial discrimination. Our world was school, home, and church. My younger sister, Ruby, remembers, a few events. When she talks about these events, I always ask her where I was because I have no recollection of the events. When the popular movie *The Ten Commandments* was released, we lined up for a while to get into the theater. Once in the theater, Ruby wondered why all the white people were sitting on the first floor and all the Black people were in the balcony. I later found out this was called the "buzzard" section. Initially, I did not notice this because I was too young and was only interested in watching the movie. Ruby also remembers protesting with Mom when the school board discussed closing and merging some black schools. My mom joined with others to protest this affront to our community. My sister remembers holding signs and marching with the other protesters. The fact that I do not remember some incidents is perplexing, but maybe I was away at college when the protests occurred.

After her last child entered grade school, my mother decided she wanted to learn a trade. She was interested in secretarial training. Mom and her friend, Rosalie Pryor, took an entrance exam at the local employment office. They were sure they had passed the exam. When informed they had failed the test, they did not believe it and were angered by this blatant act of racism. My mom refused to let this one go, as she did not take failure lightly.

Louis Berry was the first African American permitted to practice law in the city of Alexandria. He was an Alexandria native, and he graduated from Howard University School of Law in 1945. After the passage of the Civil Rights Act in 1964, he worked with Black ministers in Rapides Parish to register African Americans to vote. In addition, he worked to have the civics test removed as a condition of voter registration. An article in the *Alexandria Daily Town Talk* in April 2007 described him as being instrumental in improving living conditions for Black people in Alexandria. Louis Berry was inducted into the Louisiana Political Museum and Hall of Fame in Winnfield, Louisiana in 1996.

Louis Berry is the man my mother chose to represent her. He took the case and fought for their rights and won. Consequently, instead of secretarial training, she and four other women decided to enter nursing school, but there were no schools available for Blacks in the area. Yet, once again with the help of Attorney Berry, she and four ladies entered the Charity Hospital Nursing School. She graduated in 1967 and began her nursing career that spanned 27 years at Central Louisiana Hospital. She retired to care for my father when he became ill. As a result of winning the civil rights suit against the trade school with Louis Berry as her attorney, Mom advocated for civil rights and social justice for the rest of her life.

*My mom and sign in front of building named for her*

My mom also used her tenacious spirit to advocate for our community. She was instrumental in organizing the senior citizen exercise ministry at True Vine Missionary Baptist Church. This program outgrew the space at True Vine, so she lobbied local governmental representatives for a building to house the program. Years of lobbying and persistence led to the building of the Broadway Community Resource Center, which was home base for S.A.G.E. (Seniors Aging with Grace and Energy). Mom was

S.A.G.E. board president. She and the women who helped form the board provided exercise, meals, health education, and screening for the community. The building was later renamed Wilborn-Dempsey Multipurpose Community Center. She also served as a volunteer for the Red Cross, the American Heart Association, Parish Fair, and several other organizations. My Mom always wanted to help people. She believed this was instilled in her as a child because my grandmother would feed any stranger who came to her door. In 1990, Mom was honored with a volunteer worker award by the Rapides Senior Volunteer Program.

I graduated from Peabody High School and enrolled in the Dillard University Nursing Program in New Orleans in 1968. Dillard University was not my original choice, I wanted to attend USL in Lafayette, but Mom insisted that I attend Dillard. You see, she was proud of a family member who had graduated from Dillard and felt that it was the right school for me. Mom and Dad had an impact on the direction of all our lives. We were not asked if we were going to college. It was expected. As a result of their dedication to education, all four girls graduated from college. I marvel now at how this was accomplished with their meager financial earnings at the time, but they found a way to make it happen, and for that, I will always be grateful. As a side note, my brother decided college was not for him, and he became a career serviceman.

Once at Dillard, I enjoyed campus life. There were occasional protests on campus around racial and social injustice in the world. I attended some of the rallies, wore the dashikis, and even wore an afro wig. I graduated from Dillard in 1972, married a few months later and began my nursing career. Three years later, I gave birth to my first child, a daughter, and, 18 months later, my son was born.

I decided to take a job at Charity Hospital in New Orleans because it afforded me the opportunity to have a portion of my student loans forgiven for each year that I was employed. Most of the patients and staff I worked with at Charity Hospital in New Orleans were African American. The hospital was dedicated to caring for the poor and indigent. I enjoyed my experience of caring for the poor and underserved community. Charity Hospital was a great place for the novice nurse and doctor to learn and grow in their profession.

About 10 years later, I left Charity and started working at Hotel Dieu Hospital. Hotel Dieu was a private hospital owned and managed by the Daughters of Charity, and although there was a racial mix of patients, I still had an enjoyable nursing experience. While working at Hotel Dieu, I was promoted to section Manager of the Inpatient Oncology Unit and earned a master's degree in nursing from the University of Phoenix. Ten years later, the Daughters of Charity sold the hospital to the State of Louisiana. The hospital was renamed University Hospital and later renamed The Medical Center of Louisiana. I was promoted to Section Manager of the inpatient Oncology Unit. I retired from the State of Louisiana in 2013 but continued working, as the hospital had changed management to Louisiana Children's Medical Center (LCMC), a not-for-profit health system.

Aside from the bus incident with my aunt, growing up I did not experience any signs of overt racism, yet there were plenty of subtle ones. For example, whenever I entered a store, I was greeted with dead silence, but when a white customer walked in, the white cashier would happily greet and chitchat with the white patrons. There was one time in particular that really made my blood boil. I went to the grocery store right after work, so I was still in my white nursing uniform when a white woman came up behind me and had the audacity to ask if I had the time to take in extra laundry. I found the question insulting and responded with a tone that verified that I was insulted. I did not pick up on the clue that it was racist. As I gave it more thought, I realized that it was racism and wondered if she would have asked a white woman in uniform the same question.

After 43 years of nursing, I resigned from my position at LCMC, and, along with my sisters, became a fulltime caregiver for our mother. It was hard watching and caring for this beautiful, smart, hardworking, vibrant woman, who cared for so many people slowly deteriorate. Mom and Dad taught us so many things, among a few were a good work ethic, independence, compassion, and service to others and the community. Mom and Dad rarely missed a day of work. They were committed to their jobs and taking care of us. This is where we received our work ethic. Dad wanted his girls to finish college so we could become financially independent. Mom cared for many relatives and friends, and we learned to care for others. My parents were dedicated to the church, and they passed their commitment and dedication to us, as we are all loyal servants to our Christian faith.

*Seated: Mom and Dad; Standing, from left: Lizzie Dempsey, Sandra Dempsey Doublin, Louis Dempsey Jr, me, and Ruby Dempsey Rozier.*

# THE LEAST OF THESE

*"Then shall he answer them, saying, 'Verily I say unto you, In as much as ye did it to one of the least of these, ye did it to me.'"*

MATTHEW 25:45

## Winnifred Lorraine Edwards Jett

I WAS BORN INTO the Eliza (Wilton) Edwards-Joseph Edwards family that originated in the late 1870s in the Natchitoches and Boyce, Louisiana communities. The family moved to Alexandria, LA in 1900. Myra Brent Wilton is my paternal great grandmother and the founder of a temple of worship in the South Alexandria area in 1905. She purchased the land, making the property available for the community's spiritual growth. The church's original name was Methodist Episcopal Mission and later was renamed Wilton Methodist Church by the Board of Directors in 1909 in honor of Myra Brent Wilton's act of kindness.

*Myra Brent Wilton is my paternal great grandmother and the founder of a temple of worship in the South Alexandria area in 1905. She purchased the land, making the property available for the community's spiritual growth.*

Myra Brent Wilton

*Wilton Methodist Church*

My father, Albie Whitney Edwards Sr., received educational training from St. James Catholic School and Grambling College, served in the United States Army from December 5, 1942, through December 9, 1945, thus serving his country during World War II as a Medical Technician. He often spoke proudly of the bronze arrowhead medal he received during his military service.

To the union of my father and mother, Mary Delia Carter Edwards, three children were born: Eulalia, Winnifred, and Albie, Jr. Our family valued religion, education, and strong loving relationships with family, acquaintances, and community. We were taught to practice honesty and to set goals and work steadfastly to accomplish our goals. Both of our parents worked in the community, and we began public service work as children helping older persons with grocery shopping, housecleaning, and yardwork.

As a family, we enjoyed being together and often cooked together. We would also take evening walks during the summer months from Hardtner Street, Mason Street to Fenner Street, and back home by walking down Overton Street. Oftentimes, other families would be sitting on their porches because few houses had air conditioning. We would exchange greetings and make connections with neighbors. I shared a close relationship with my maternal great grandmother, Ella Hopper, and grandmother, Viola Kerry. I was surrounded by love and support from grandmothers, cousins, and good neighbors.

Our teachers lived in our communities and were our neighbors, and they were supportive in helping us learn at our best. Sometimes, we borrowed their encyclopedias to complete homework assignments and would turn those assignments in to that same teacher who lent us the books.

My maternal grandmother and mother worked for a Jewish family who owned a local men's store in Alexandria. We had a close relationship with that family, which allowed my siblings and me to feel as if we were being raised in a blended family. We attended musical performances, plays, and other local arts activities. As a teen, I kept their children when the parents were working, traveling for their businesses, or vacationing.

*Our family*

Our family was active. My father was a master brick mason and was hired for jobs throughout Louisiana, Arkansas, and Mississippi. In the 1960s and 1970s, brick flooring and brick arches were popular in the interior and on exterior of homes. My father was an expert at constructing these structures. He taught other men to lay bricks. He also taught them to read. My father played on an all-Black city baseball league team that played other Black teams in the area. We enjoyed attending their games.

My siblings and I took piano lessons until we got to junior high school where we joined clubs and participated in sports. I was a member of the track team and ran the

440 and the 50-yard dash. I was a member of the Student Council, and a member of the dance group in both junior and senior high school. In 1967, my mother, Mary D. Edwards, graduated from Peabody High School with my sister, Eulalia, after receiving her Adult Education Certificate. That was a proud moment for our family. My mother encouraged about five other ladies, who were school lunchroom workers, to complete the Adult Education Program, as she had done. These ladies later became nutrition lunchroom managers until their retirement from the elementary and junior high school cafeterias.

We had to be alert in our neighborhood because of our proximity to the white neighborhood. My family lived only one and a half blocks from Lee Street, which separated African American families from white family homes. When white teen boys and/or young adult men got old enough to drive, they would ride by our house, try to make conversation (which oftentimes meant trying to lure you to go for a ride in their car). Their intentions were not honorable and sometimes led to girls being assaulted. As a defense, I would scream curse words that I would not normally use to scare them or tell them to take their mother or sister for that ride. We learned to travel in groups or with family only.

Two weeks after my graduation from Peabody Senior High School in 1968, I started summer school at Grambling College. By this time, my parents lived in separate residences, and my mother was my primary supporter. I was a young woman on a mission. For the next three years, I focused my attention on completing my undergraduate degree, which I completed in six semesters and three summers, graduating with a Liberal Arts Degree in Social Work in May 1971. In 1985, I graduated with a master's degree in Social Work from Louisiana State University, Baton Rouge, LA. In 1997, I earned a Board-Certified Social Worker Degree/Licensed Clinical Social Work Certification.

With my degree in hand, I returned to Alexandria certain that finding a job would be easy because I had just finished college. That was not the case in 1971. There was a Civil Service Test to be taken. I spent time calling different offices inquiring about employment opportunities and traveling by bus and walking to interviews. I was given a variety of reasons for the rejections: overqualified, no openings "at this time", or, only persons who score in the 80s or 90s on the Civil Service Test are hired. I knew African Americans who scored in those 80s and 90s who were never hired.

After searching for jobs for three and a half months, I took my first job in 1971, at the age of 21, as a teacher aide in a full year Head Start run by the CENLA (Central Louisiana) Community Action Committee, Inc. The office ran all the programs established as part of the War on Poverty. My duties included providing a comprehensive educational program for preschool children ages 3 to 5. I assisted students in developing a sense of security, good self-esteem, self-expression, self-creativity, and responsibility through varied educational experiences. After serving as a teacher aide for three months, I was promoted to teacher. A month passed working as a teacher, and I was promoted to the Central Office for Head Start.

The program served 800 children who were primarily Black. I was responsible for the operation of 12 centers in Rapides Parish. Our job was to take care of all the needs of our clients by working closely with the parents. We had to keep the enrollment at 800. The goal of our office was to have healthy children. We ensured that they had immunizations and physical exams annually. This job prepared me for the services I would deliver for the rest of my career. The work also helped to build on what I had been taught to do — serve others. It was an experience like no other, involving Black and white clients in need. Race made no difference to me. The families needed help and support that I could offer, and I did everything I could to assist them.

A few experiences come to mind. I stayed with a woman whose son had drowned and remained with her as authorities dragged his body from the lake. I stood by another mom who lost two of her children in a housefire and continued to support her, as she suffered the loss of her remaining children to protective services until they were returned to her. I also worked with numerous children who were the victims of molestation. I not only worked with teen mothers as young as 13, I followed up with many of them for years after they gave birth. In working directly with parents during visits to the center, I was able to meet with families in need, linking them to screening clinics and other community services.

I was newly married at the time, and my husband was away for six months at a time on his military assignments. I devoted considerable time and energy to making the lives of the children better. My grandmother had taught me sewing, and I took advantage of those skills. I would buy fabric and make an outfit to wear to work the next day. Sewing helped me to occupy my time alone when I wasn't helping others.

When I was promoted to Director of Social Services for Head Start, I supervised service caseworkers and social workers in coordinating and assisting them in circumstances involving preschool children and their families. I was responsible for recruitment and processing enrollment certifications for 800 children on an ongoing basis. I also handled scheduling for the children's required screenings.

In 1981, I left Head Start and worked for a nonprofit family counseling agency, heading their domestic violence program for five months. It was a better paying job, and from that job I learned the importance of a graduate degree. Most of the employees had master's degrees, and I was encouraged to get mine. I designed and implemented crisis counseling for battered women and their children and provided awareness of education programs in the community that would provide services for their family needs and safety. I even provided individual and couples counseling for couples with domestic violence histories.

It was not until 1981 that a semblance of equal opportunity arrived in the Alexandria Office of Family Services (OFS). The agency performed poorly on a federal review that revealed the agency did not have appropriate representation of African Americans on its staff. Prior to that review, African Americans with college degrees were hired as transportation workers, driving clients on long trips for services in New Orleans, while jobs they were qualified to hold were held by whites without degrees. Once the review mandate was made public, there were white employees without degrees grandfathered into social worker positions. The OFS was mandated to hire a minimum of five African American workers who met the job requirements. I had applied for several advertised positions between 1971 and 1981 and had been turned down every time. I was finally hired because I had an application on file and was one of the five prospective workers offered an interview.

It was then that my career finally took off, and I was able to do the work for which I was qualified.

For the next 25 years, until my formal retirement in 2006, I worked in a variety of jobs in which I was able to use my skills and help hundreds of people in need of social services. I discovered that there was a great deal of work to be done for people who were in dire need of assistance. When I encountered clients, they were surprised by the level of empathy the new group of Black social workers brought to their positions. Reception of Black social workers in the office was mixed. There was so much work that needed to be done, we chose to focus on doing our jobs.

By carefully reading and learning program policies, procedures, and guidelines, I overcame the challenges of discriminatory practices. The knowledge I gained empowered me to be the best advocate for the clients I served. I would make sure they took advantage of resources available to them through the state funds in the areas of education, recreation, housing, and healthcare. Foster children received eyeglasses, braces, musical instruments and membership fees for social clubs and tuition assistance for college.

Moving forward, I applied a strategy that worked for me. I had planned to work on a job for three to four years to enhance my skills and abilities in social work and to avoid burnout. Things did not always work out as planned, but I remained hopeful and committed. By the end of my 25-year career, I had succeeded. Today, I take pride in the breadth of my work and career with the agency. From my first position in 1981 as a social services worker, to clinical social work positions, to ultimately a social worker at Level 4, I retired with a feeling of accomplishment not only for myself but also for those for whom I provided services.

For the next nine years after retirement, as a private contractor for the State of Louisiana, I was able to work with families and parents needing support with foster care and adoption, including adoption of children within the United States and abroad in Russia, Honduras, Guatemala, and cities in Mexico. I am currently doing work with prospective adoptive individuals for families needing to complete the Adoption Home Study Process. I plan to retire in 2021.

I have had a successful career. I've always practiced positive thinking, maintained good humor, and treated others with respect even when they may not have deserved that respect. I learned at an early age to stay focused on my efforts, and if I happened to not have reached a goal, simply dust myself off and try again and again until I made it. I continued the volunteer efforts and community services training I received from my family all those years ago. I have served on the board of the Friendship House (a day program for senior adults), as well as the Central Louisiana Arts Council for the promotion of local artists and a variety of plays for family entertainment. I also have served on former State Representative Israel B. Curtis' Youth Programming Activities Board, and I am a lifetime member of Delta Sigma Theta Sorority, Inc.

Life is good. I enjoyed a seven-year courtship with Joseph Ray Jett that began at Lincoln Road Junior High through Peabody High and Grambling College. We celebrated our 50th wedding anniversary in 2021, and we are blessed with two children, two loving grandsons, family, and friends.

Two sayings have guided my steps and kept me focused when dealing with life matters. The first is a quote I saw in a neighborhood diner on the corner of Mason and Turner Streets: "It's nice to be important but more important to be nice." The second is the scripture found in *Matthew 25:45*: "Then shall he answer them, saying, 'Verily I say unto you, inasmuch as ye did it to one of the least of these, ye did it to me.'"

# THE ROAD LESS TRAVELED

*"Threescore years and ten are the length of days."*

PSALM 90:10

## Elaine Ford Provost

*I liked the changes when segregation began to ease. There was no problem spending money on nice things at good stores. My skin color didn't matter then, only the color of my money.*

MY MATERNAL GREAT grandparents, Mose Henderson and Jannie Jones Henderson, made their journey from Frogmore near Jonesville, Louisiana, and settled around the Magda Echo area known as Poland, Louisiana. They were sharecroppers trying to provide for seven children. One of the girls was named Mary Magdalene, but as soon as she could, she changed her name to Mildred. All my aunts stayed in the Alexandria area, along with two of my uncles. One worked for the railroad and the other moved to Port Arthur, Texas. My aunts and uncles helped to care for their parents until their deaths.

My maternal grandparents, Steve and Isabella Henderson Mitchell, left the farm after they married. Steve started working at Rapides Meat Packing Company, and Isabella stayed home until all the grandchildren were in school. She did go to work as a cook and babysitter for Dr. and Mrs. Maxwell. As a treat, sometimes we rode with my grandfather to pick up my grandmother from work. My grandparents had two children, Leon and Lowrece, my mother. Uncle Leon was drafted into the U.S. Navy, and my mother worked on

*Mose & Jannie Jones Henderson*

the farm. She also pressed (straightened) little neighborhood girls' hair. My grand-mother kept marriage and birth certificates in an old family Bible locked away in the chifforobe.

My paternal grandfather, John Henry Ford, came from the Marksville area in a place called Hickory Hill. Calvin Ford and Mamie McIntosh had 14 children. They were Catholics. My father, Roosevelt, lost his mother, Mamie, at an early age. My grandfather vowed he would not remarry until all his children were grown. Grandfather moved to Magda and later to Alexandria with 10 children. He made good on his promise and stayed with his family until John, the youngest, graduated from high school. My grandfather then moved to LaMarque, Texas to start a new life. He obtained employment in the school system there as a janitor. He later married Ms. Zola.

*My brother, Levy, and me (1956)*

My mother's parents were proud home-owners, living at 2909 Seventh Street. It was a clay, muddy street when it rained. Those were the types of conditions that existed back then for Black people. I didn't think life was bad there because I was comfortable being with my family and community members. We lived by the canal, which meant crawfishing and good eating. I didn't really venture out too much. I lived a sheltered life.

My parents, Roosevelt and Lowrece, had two miscarriages before I was born. We all lived with my grandparents until my parents built a house next door because I made it clear that I did not want to leave my friends and established relationships. Moving from my grandparents would have meant a new home, new school, new neighborhood, and new friends. I could not survive the resulting "crisis." My brother,

Levy, who was seven years older than me, attended Southern University for three years before being drafted into the U. S. Army. Because of him, I became aware of Leesville, Louisiana, where he was stationed at Fort Polk. Levi (Levy used previously) then went to Vietnam, and oh, how my family prayed for his safe return! My parents were disappointed that Levy did not return to college. He married and moved to Chicago, Illinois until my grandmother passed.

Life at home was good. My mother was strict, but my father was a little more relaxed. They were hard-working people. My Dad had two jobs. One was in construction, and the other was at a food company. My mother didn't want to move so that my Dad could get different work, so we stayed in Alexandria. My mother was a domestic in the home of a doctor that my grandmother cooked for. I would go to work with my mother, and I played with the white children who lived in the home, but never considered them to be my friends. I used to wear hand-me-down clothes from the white children, but once a year I got a new, anniversary dress.

I never liked that my parents had to call their employer Mr. and Mrs. while they called my parents by their first names. My mother's name was odd, so her employer called her "Sister" like the rest of my immediate family. It seemed like their middle daughter, Ann, was closer to my grandmother than to her own mother. Ann was a middle child with problems, but she became the most educated. I never liked her relationship with my grandmother. The Maxwell family came to visit my grandmother after she retired, and they were surprised to know she was a homeowner with an inside bathroom and a well-furnished house. They had no idea "Negroes" lived such a life. My family tried to protect and bring us up as children with the knowledge that we had more opportunities to live better lives than our ancestors.

My first plane ride was to visit Levy in Chicago. I was afraid to fly by myself, but once I was in the air, I enjoyed myself. I had breakfast on the plane, and I ate well. It reminded me of when I was younger and used to have two breakfasts.

Changes came to Alexandria in 1968. It was a historical year. My parents knew about the things that were happening in the Civil Rights Movement, but they didn't participate in any marches nor were they active in any other manner. They talked about what was going on, though. The town had been segregated for so long that I just didn't pay too much attention to the way things were because that was how life was. I only went to town when I took the bus there to pay a bill, and I knew where I could and couldn't go. Mr. Norris was the white bus driver for my route, and he was a mean type. When he died, I was not worried.

Certain people discriminated against Blacks. They did everything to make us feel bad. We knew we had to be waited on after whites were served. One time I was in a store and a white lady told the clerk she could wait on me first. The clerk was horrible to me, like most of them were. My father didn't take nonsense from white people once integration came to town. He was quite outgoing and friendly, and he wasn't uncomfortable around whites. He never expressed anything about negative incidents with white people. My mother was more cautious and protective of me. To be honest, I really didn't think about white people much. The most exposure to them I'd had before desegregation came from the doctor's house where my mother worked. I liked the changes when segregation began to ease. There was no problem spending money on nice things at good stores. My skin color didn't matter then, only the color of my money.

After desegregation, I had more interactions with white people. You could say I became "friends" with a couple of the women I worked with at the school. We would go to lunch together sometimes, but it wasn't a friendship that meant going to each other's homes. These relationships were sometimes difficult for me because I am shy and introverted. It was more like talking with each other to share information and small talk. It was never easy for me to make friends anyway. The best friends I had came from my school years.

Several unforgettable things happened as I was growing up. One of the most memorable was the time my brother and cousin, Gloria, were debating if the curtains would burn in the house, so my brother set the curtains on fire, and, of course, they burned. He tried to put out the fire with a big attic fan, but that made it worse. My grandfather who was supposed to be watching us was across the ditch talking to some lady when the fire happened. Needless to say, they "caught a good switching licking." That evening I told everything, and my brother and I caught a good Madear whipping.

School memories hold an important place in my life. Elementary school had some glorious times mixed with some bad days. I attended kindergarten at Augustana Lutheran Church. Classmates Carolyn Milton, Shirley Paige, and Houston Benjamin also attended. Houston jumped out of a swing and broke his arm. Many months passed before we could play on the gym set again. Kindergarten prepared me for first grade. My grandmother placed me in her friend Mrs. Lillie B. Chambers' class. She was so very kind. I learned to count money selling donuts from Johnson Bakery. Donuts cost only five cents, and then 10 cents.

My time in elementary school was sad in the second grade. My friend Franetta King lost her mother. Mrs. Duell, our teacher, took us to the funeral. I wondered about the loss of my mother and who would take care of me. In the fifth grade, I caught the red measles. I was out of school for a week. It's a very contagious infection caused by a virus, and my body was covered with a rash. Dr. Evans, my doctor from when I was a baby, explained the cause of the rash. In the sixth grade, Donald Owens, Elga Senviel, and Jeffrey Washington were academic students. This honor enabled them to skip the curriculum of one grade in school. I looked at them as very intelligent. I could tell later that something was happening in their hearts more than the knowledge in their heads.

Junior high opened a new world for me. I was a thumbsucker until the seventh grade. Discipline was maintained in our schools through corporal punishment in elementary and junior high. Mr. Thomas, our homeroom teacher, vowed that anyone caught sucking their thumb would be punished. I caught many whippings from him. After so many hits with the board from Mr. Thomas, I finally decided it was time to stop this habit. My second encounter with "the board" was in my physical education class when I caught a popup ball and refused to give it up, allowing runners to score points. I got licks with the board for that behavior. I was active in the arts in junior high. I participated in the choir, appeared in two plays, *No Suit for Bill* and *Amelia*. I had a very important scream in *Amelia* that I missed. I got on stage and never screamed. In junior high, Mrs. Smith and Mrs. Walls chose me to deliver the closing speech at the ninth-grade graduation. My speech was entitled, "The Road Less Traveled."

Singing in the choir was my favorite activity. My brother told my parents I had a good singing voice when I was in first grade because of my performance as a sunflower in a school activity. I joined the choir when I entered Peabody in 10th grade. Mrs. Willie B. Morrison was the choir director. Singing was not my goal. Our choir was just phenomenal. "Battle Hymn of the Republic" was Don Sibley's specialty. Johnny Freel wrote the lyrics to our class song to the tune of "Try to Remember". I enjoyed singing, but it was mainly in church. My first church solo was "I Must Tell Jesus". Later, I thought it was my singing that was making the people shout and faint in church. I didn't understand that it was the Holy Spirit moving in the lives of my great-aunt Ruthie and cousin Rebecca in the Daughter of Zion Baptist Church in Magada, Louisiana (now known as Poland). The church still stands today. It was in a community of three Baptist churches and one United Methodist church. It was a unity of Christian people in fellowship.

I did not attend college my first year out of high school. I went to a business college in Dallas, Texas, and I worked in the Sears & Roebuck mailroom sorting and separating mail for forwarding to the right department. My mother came to get me on my 19th birthday. When I returned to Louisiana, I started at the University of Southwestern Louisiana. My mother became ill and had been a patient at hospitals in Alexandria and in Pineville. Someone, by the grace of God, paid all her medical bills. We were so, so grateful. The person did not want to be identified or recognized by the family for their wonderful deed. After that, I enrolled at Louisiana College in Pineville. It was a Baptist college, and although I did well at the University of Southwestern Louisiana, things were different at Louisiana College. I was made to feel that I was unqualified and didn't belong there. People acted like, "How can you afford to be here?" I was in a five-year music program, but I got through in four-and-a-half years. My father put me through school for two years off his own sweat and hard work. I never thought of his circumstances or his love for his only daughter. I did not work until my senior year in college when I got a job in lumber management at the State Forestry Center in Pineville. Thank you, Dad. I graduated from Louisiana College summer 1974. Mrs. Jerry (Ivory) Brown and I were the only two Blacks in the graduating class.

I obtained my first job after graduation as a kindergarten to sixth grade music teacher at England Air Force Base School. It was not like anything I could have imagined. It was a state-of-the-art school. When the enrollment ratio changed at the school, I was moved because I was not certified in music. Later, I taught music in junior high for a while. I bought my first car but couldn't drive! My mother had to take me everywhere. I met Mrs. Anna Oubre at work, and she would transport me back and forth home. When I finally took the driving test, I failed it twice before I got my license. I worked for the Rapides Parish School Board system for three years. After that I began work in the mental health field where I helped people find jobs. I taught a preparation class each week to help people learn interview skills and how to dress and speak during interviews. The years I worked in mental health have been rewarding as are the friendships I made along the way.

My life was not all work and no fun. I entertained myself with friends playing dominoes and bid whist. I enjoyed activities in my Alpha Kappa Alpha Sorority, Inc., too. My faith remained important to me, and I sang and played piano in church. I focused on acceptable religious music, such as the "Lord's Prayer", not secular songs. I enjoyed singing at weddings and other functions. As I continued with my life, I attended Northwestern State University for a while, but marriage and a baby took preference, and I didn't complete my studies there. At age 30, I married Melvin C. Provost, a surgical technologist. He commanded the room with his presence. He also felt strongly that no one was going to mistreat him. He was not going to accept it.

The year 2020 has been a living experience. COVID-19 is affecting everyone in many ways, from school closures to changing descriptions of our job duties to diminishing incomes and church closings. We are encouraged to continue to keep abreast of the pandemic, as we move forward, as new activities emerge. It's the same steady way that I feel I transitioned from living in a segregated community to being part of an integrated one. I believe I did well in adjusting to that, and I feel my life now is a satisfying one.

PART TWO

# OUR COMMUNITY:
# SEPARATE AND UNEQUAL

*"Any law that degrades human personality is unjust. All
segregation laws are unjust because segregation distorts the soul
and damages the personality. It gives the segregator a false sense
of superiority and the segregated a false sense of inferiority."*
— DR. MARTIN LUTHER KING SR.

THE 1896 LANDMARK U.S. Supreme Court case, *Plessy v. Ferguson,* established the separate but equal doctrine declaring that racial segregation laws were not a violation of the U.S. Constitution as long as the separate facilities were equal. Well, the white people in power implemented the law, and they defined equal. They created one of each facility: white public schools and colleges and Black public schools and colleges, white recreational facilities and Black recreational facilities, white libraries and Black libraries, white public restrooms and Black public restrooms, and the list goes on. Throughout the South there was a deeply embedded, unfair separate and unequal daily life for Black people to which they, of course, adjusted for many years.

Despite separate and unequal circumstances, Blacks lived with dignity, creating a place for themselves in which they felt comfortable most of the time. In Alexandria, by the 1940s and 1950s, there were three movie theaters, two on Lee Street and Silver City on Lower Third Street. There were churches for every persuasion, schools, in-home daycare services for children, Black-owned businesses (laundries, tailor and shoe shops, mechanic shops, barber and beauty shops, nightclubs, grocery stores, fish markets, funeral homes), and social clubs. The community also boasted Black physicians, attorneys, dentists, and its own separate baseball team, the Alexandria Black Aces, pictured below in 1956.

The writers in this section share insights into the variety of aspects to Black life in Alexandria in the 1950s and beyond. The impact of poverty on daily living is well described as well as important connections with whites who empathized with the plight of African Americans. Writers also share their experiences with desegregation as adults and experiences in the military. The steps whites took to enforce the separate but equal doctrine are well documented.

## OUR COMMUNITY: SEPARATE AND UNEQUAL

Because of the small number of Blacks in Alexandria before the Civil War, the enslaved were not segregated in one part of town. They lived in households of the slaveowners for whom they worked or in separate dwellings on the property. From 1860 census data, Seip concludes, "There is little reason to suspect that segregation of an individual or residential nature characterized Alexandria race relations in the decade before the War." Despite Seip's conclusion, it is hard to theorize that even with the small number of freed Blacks living in town, they would be mixed with the whites. The Civil War changed the dynamic. With the coming of industries to Alexandria, more Blacks from nearby rural areas moved to town for work, and the distinct neighborhoods emerged.

Fredrick Marcel Spletstoser's book *Talk of the Town: The Rise of Alexandria, Louisiana, and the Daily Town Talk* provides information indicating that a division of the neighborhoods appears to have been created in 1893 with the establishment of West Alexandria as a separate entity. Parcels were sold to establish a community free of "disease, crime, and fire" as an exclusive residential area for whites. The parcels sold, and West Alexandria came into being. West Alexandria merged with Alexandria in 1899 by a vote of the residents.

West Alexandria was above the city's Lee Street, presumably named for Confederate General Robert E. Lee, and west of the Texas and Pacific railroad tracks. To this day, Blacks continue to live east of Lee Street, though some of the formerly all-white neighborhoods are now mixed. Spletstoser does not point to race as the motive for creating a West Alexandria, but it is a reasonable obvious deduction based on how the town's neighborhoods have evolved over more than a century.

Alexandria's Black neighborhoods emerged and developed after the Civil War in the late 1800s, and those neighborhoods eventually became home to a variety of industries, trapping residents in undesirable, stench-laden, and toxic environments.

- Lumber-related companies, including a pressure treated wood product (creosote) plant and an oak flooring company, located in the Sonia Quarters, Sam Town and Woodside.

- Cotton-related businesses (at least five cottonseed oil companies), situated in Lower Third, Upper Third, and the Oil Mill Quarters, the latter aptly named for the Red River Oil Company.

- A chicken processing plant (J&M Poultry), located in the Sonia Quarters (named for Sonia Oil Company), where hundreds of workers were employed.

- Five meat packing companies, one of which included a livestock yard, and another that focused on animal rendering, all in the heart of Lower Third.

- A cotton Gin, Falstaff Beer Distributors and an iron yard/junkyard, also taking up real estate in Lower Third.

- The foundry and machine shop that operated from 1908 to 1985, formerly one of the most toxic industrial sites in the nation, again, positioned on acres in the Sonia Quarters.

- The iron yard and the point at which all the railways (used by Texas and Pacific, Southern Pacific, Kansas City Southern, Rock Island, Louisiana and Arkansas and Missouri Pacific) merged, staged next to Rock Island Quarters.

- The Black business district located close to downtown and encompassing five or six blocks served as home to a variety of entertainment and services available to Blacks. It was the one section of town in which Blacks lived and worked that did not house large companies and industries.

On the outskirts of Alexandria, plantations and other farming businesses required workers. Blacks worked in tenant farming communities into the 1960s as sharecroppers on white-owned property.

- Plantations on the southeast edge of town and dairy farms housed Black families on their property as sharecroppers and agriculture workers.

- Whites and Blacks lived in Bayou Rapides, a rural community, north of town. Some blacks were sharecroppers, others owned their own farms.

Companies and farmers employed hundreds of Blacks who worked numerous hours for low pay at a time when they had no choice. Many left Alexandria for larger southern cities like Houston and Dallas. Others moved to cities on the West and East Coasts, but many stayed, endured the hardships, and built families in a system that perpetuated dependence and flaunted the Jim Crow traditions of the Old South. Blacks working in rural areas moved to Alexandria in the 1940s and 1950s to escape the economic entrapment of the sharecropping system in exchange for a life with slightly better economic opportunity.

Lee Street served as the center of the Black business district with its neon lights, juke joints, and various businesses, all catering to the African American community. It served as the social hub and gathering place for a good time and met some of the service needs of Blacks. The north end of Lee Street began at the Red River levee and ran through Alexandria, dividing the east side from the west side. About four or five blocks of Lee Street, as well as adjoining streets to its east, were dedicated to the Black community. There was a hotel, a movie theater (The Ritz), barber and shoeshine shops, funeral homes, nightclubs, churches, cafes, pool halls, clothing and shoe stores, homes, and apartments. Three baptist churches (Union, Rose of Sharon, and Shiloh) were within a few blocks of each other. The Black Catholic church (St. James), school, and rectory were nearby as well. The area was an active place where Blacks from surrounding communities would come to have a great time. World War II Black soldiers stationed at the nearby three military bases (Camps Beauregard, Claiborne, and Livingston) frequently visited the area. Depending on who is asked, Lee Street was the place to be back in the day.

Because military bases were so close to Alexandria and the armed forces were replete with Black soldiers and even an all-Black regiment, soldiers often would come to Alexandria on weekends. As many as 3,000 Black troops would come to the town on weekend passes. January 10, 1942, was such an occasion. Contradictory reports exist in the newspaper and in eyewitness accounts recorded by others on what really happened

that day. There appears to be general agreement among the various accounts that a riot
erupted in reaction to the arrest of a Black
soldier by a white military policeman, as
the soldier exited the Ritz Theater. What
ensued was a clash between military police,
city and state police, and white civilians on
one side and several thousand Black troops
on the other with Black civilians trapped in
the melee. It was a bloody battle, especially for the Blacks involved. The police and
the Army initially reported that 28, 29, or 30 Black soldiers were shot, and that there
were no deaths. The event received national coverage. Baltimore's Black newspaper, *The
Afro American*, as well as the National Association for the Advancement of Colored
People, and others insisted that the riot was racially motivated by whites and demanded
a full investigation. They also insisted that deaths had occurred. The city and the U.S.
Army denied that anyone was killed and maintained that those claims were exaggera-
tions based on unfounded rumors. The Army released a final report three months later
with details of the injuries. It is believed by many Blacks in Alexandria to this day that
the city and the Army covered up the truth. A historical marker in February 2021was
placed on Lee Street to memorialize the event.

From slavery's Brush Arbour revivals, when slaves crept away to the woods to craft
a "lean-to of trees" as a natural house of worship, religion has been a staple of Black
life. Noted sociologist and author, E. Franklin Frazier, held that the "The church is
the spiritual face of the black community." Inarguably, the church has always been a
stabilizing force in the Black neighborhood, providing hope, solace, and inspiration.
Alexandria's Black churches in the 19th and 20th centuries served as the center of the
community, engaging parents and children in various religious activities designed to
build spiritual character and provide educational opportunity.

Central Louisiana Academy Education of Colored Youth under the direction
of the Eighth District Baptist Association for Colored was located in a building on

the square back of the Shiloh Baptist Church. It enrolled 115 pupils in 1909, according to an announcement in the *Town Talk*. It appears that the Eighth district Association also ran Alexandria's first Black newspaper, *Louisiana Baptist*, established in the late 1800s.

In addition to regular Sunday service, churches offered weekly prayer meeting, auxiliary involvement, Bible study, and annual soul stirring revivals. During the summer, large and small churches offered Vacation Bible School programs, not only for children in their membership, but throughout the neighborhood. Bayou Rapides boasts the oldest Black church in Rapides Parish, First Evening Star, celebrating 172 years of existence in 2021. First Union Baptist Church on Lee Street, established in 1866, is the oldest Black church in Alexandria.

*Picture day for Rose of Sharon Baptist Church Vacation Bible*
*School, 1953, in the Black business district*

*Vacation Bible School final day program at St. Lawrence Baptist*
*Church in the Sonia Quarters, circa 1958*

The Casson Street Community Center was several blocks from Lee Street and connected the various neighborhoods in Alexandria. Located in the former United Service Organization (USO) building erected by the Army for Black soldiers, the center provided and hosted a variety of activities for the Black community. Events included Friday and Saturday nights roller-skating, the annual Doll and Toy Fund distribution, beauty pageants, live entertainment highlighting nationally known rhythm and blues performers, and boxing events featuring local talent. The center also served as a meeting place to address political issues affecting the Black community, especially in the 1950s and 1960s. After the war ended, the library in the USO facility became the Carver Branch of the Rapides Parish Library. The library also provided book mobile services in the Black community.

State Library of Louisiana (http://www.state.lib.la.us)

*1940s. Rapides Parish Library. Interior view of the Carver Branch at the
USO building located at 8th and Casson Streets in Alexandria, La.*

The gathering place for Black teenagers in the 1950s and 1960s was Cheatham
Park, fondly called "The Park". No other place was like it for Blacks in Alexandria.
(Of course, there was the white counterpart with more acreage and amenities.) The
Park was a public square for social gatherings and included a recreational complex
equipped with an outdoor swimming pool, a tennis court, two baseball fields, a Dairy
Queen, swing sets, seesaws, a concession stand and a covered pavilion for cookouts.
The Park was situated within an educational and recreational complex, for Peabody
High School and its huge auditorium, football, track and baseball fields were all
situated in the same area. The high school used the tennis courts as part of its physical
education program. An elementary school and one of the junior high schools also
were part of the expanse. The physical arrangement exists to this day and continues

to offer educational and recreational activities for the Black community. Peabody's annual homecoming festivities are held in the same area and carry on the tradition of The Park as a gathering place.

*1950s. Carver Branch of the Rapides Parish Library. Miss Hazel Harris,*
*branch assistant, at the desk, checking out books to a group of children.*

The Park attracted people from all parts of town. During the summer months, it would be so crowded one could hardly find a picnic spot, especially on the 4th of July. Young men could be seen riding through the park in their hoopties with a "gangsta lean," one arm hanging out of the driver's window and the other on the steering wheel with their sweethearts so close you could hardly distinguish one from the other. The swimming pool was typically filled with youth, and there were games at both baseball fields. Minor league teams from other Southern cities played our hometown favorites, the Alexandria Black Aces in the larger baseball park across from the Peabody campus. Baseball was a big deal back in the day, and folk would come from miles around to watch the games.

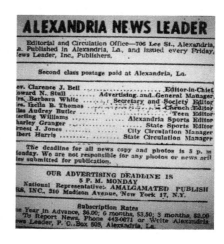

The concession stand (located in The Park) and the Shack (a few blocks away on Seventh Street), both opened on weekends and sold snacks, soft drinks and offered the opportunity for teenagers to display their dancing skills. Twenty-five cents deposited in the juke box would play a few of your favorite records. The Shack opened a little later than the concession stand, and when one closed, the crowd naturally flocked to the other. The concession stand was an open-air pavilion. Conversely, the Shack was a large room converted to a dance floor — a shining example of African American ingenuity. At times, there were so many revelers in the Shack the floor shook, and it's a small miracle the foundation didn't collapse. The Park offered wholesome, safe, and enjoyable activities for youth of all ages.

Black newspapers were vital to the Black community in the South. *The Louisiana Baptist* was the first Black newspaper published in Alexandria. The dates of publication are not exactly known as only a few copies remain. It reported local, regional, statewide and national church news with plenty of details. Its topics also included concerns about the race. Advertisements were featured from a variety of businesses. It referred to itself as the Louisiana Baptist, Colored Division. The second Black newspaper, *Alexandria News Leader,* was not published until 1963 and ended its run in 1975. Rev. Clarence Bell, pastor of the Progressive Baptist Church, served as the editor and wrote editorials on important issues of the day for Alexandria's Black community. The paper also provided national, state, and local news, as well as other relevant community, cultural, and social stories and events at the time not published in the *Town Talk.*

# A ROCK ISLAND QUARTERS STORY

Sherman 12 2020

# ANALYZING AND FIXING THINGS: A ROCK ISLAND QUARTERS STORY

*"Of all the gifts life could send me, the greatest*
*gift life could send me was my mother."*

## Sherman Fulton

*"Most of the time, it was me by myself. I was a loner. I would spend the whole day at the canal catching crawfish. Analyzing tadpoles.... Everybody knew I was that weird kid who was always fixing stuff in the backyard."*

I HAD THREE BROTHERS and one sister; Willie, two years younger than me; Henry, four years younger than me; Robert, next; and my sister, Mary Ann, the youngest. I lived in the Rock Island Quarters. The Sonya Quarters was to our west across the railroad tracks slightly to the north, the Oil Mill Quarters was to our west. Also, slightly to the south, we were separated by a maze of railroad tracks.

The main area to the north of us was the Alexandria Scrapyard. It went all the way down almost to Third Street, and behind the scrapyard was the compress. It housed bales of cotton. It did not stretch as far as the scrapyard. The train track to our south, standing at Ninth Street going west, went all the way down by the Kellogg sawmill and beyond. To the east, the track went all the way to Third Street where it terminated. To our east was Third Street.

I lived at 725 Maple Street, Alley 1954, a row of shotgun houses facing Ninth Street. In the middle area were water faucets, one on each end and one in the middle. There were bathrooms built like small houses. Each one had four toilets on each side. There were four of these units, two households per unit. Each household had its own key, and each household had to make sure they cleaned up after using the toilet so the next household would have a clean unit. Everyone was good about cleaning. Our Maple Street house had rats, and when you woke up in the middle of the night to use the slop jar, the floor looked jet black because of them. When you turned up the kerosene lamp, they would scatter, and you could see the brown wood floor again. If you jumped out of bed too quickly, you would be stomping on them.

## SURVIVAL IN TIMES OF POVERTY

My father left my mother when I was a baby. She told me he wanted to take me away with him. My mother said she would not let him, so he left and my mother, said she never saw him again. He was Puerto Rican, a conductor on a train, coming down from New York to the South. Anyway, during those days, trains were the main source of transportation. My mother came from St. Landry Parish. She came to Alexandria at a young age all alone, the youngest of two sisters and three brothers. She only had a third-grade education.

We were very poor, on welfare. We got clothes from the Salvation Army. My mother would sew patches on the clothes that were raggedy, so they weren't so bad. Food was another story. When my mother would get her welfare check, we would go to Mr. T's grocery store around the corner. The house part of the store was where Mary Clifton, one of my classmates, lived. When the food ran out, my mother would borrow flour from neighbors to make flatbread pancakes for us. There were times my mother would give me a note and send me to Lena's Grocery Store. It was at the end of the alley. I would give Lena the note, she would read it, go over to the shelves and get some canned goods, put them in a bag and give it to me. She would say, "Tell Lola to come see me." I would say, "Yes, Ma'am." My mother would get food from Lena on credit to make it to the next welfare check. She always paid Miss Lena, and Miss Lena always helped us out by giving my mother credit. I will always remember what Miss Lena did for us.

Sometimes when the food ran out, we would have to go three days without eating, just cups of water. I knew I could go three days without food, but one time it was longer. I remember that night. I was on the floor in the kitchen, playing with my little pet chicken. In shotgun houses, the front area is the front room. The middle area is the bedroom, the end is the kitchen. My mother's bedroom was the front room. My mother said, "Son, it is time to go to bed." I said, "OK, Madear." I put my pet chicken back in the cage I made for him. It was made from chicken wire. I kept a little cornmeal to feed him. I patted him on the head before I put him back in the cage. It was what I did every night. I closed the cage door.

My mother tucked me in bed. I think my brother Willie, who was 3, and my brother Henry, who was 1, were staying with other people. When the food ran out, my mother knew they could not last three days without food. She knew I could. She asked as she tucked me in, "You hungry, son?" She heard my stomach make sounds. I said, "Yes, ma'am." She told me not to go to sleep, and she would get me something to eat. I wondered to myself what store was open so late? After a while, I smelled chicken frying. It smelled good. If I had gone to sleep, I think I would have died. That's why she told me not to go to sleep. She knew I always listened to her.

This was around 1955. She came to me and said, "I have something for you to eat." She helped me out of bed because I was weak. As we got closer to the kitchen table, I could see the chicken on the plate, but something wasn't right. She sat me down at the kitchen table. I looked at the plate. I had a bad feeling about all this. I looked over at my pet chickee, the cage door was open, and he was not there. I started scream-ing, "No Madear! NO, NO, NO!" I was crying so bad the water out my eyes had my raggedy shirt drenched. From my out-of-control crying, she had to hold me down in the chair because I was kicking and screaming. She kept saying, "Son, you have to eat. Please son, please, if you don't eat you gonna die." I said, "Madear, I can't, I can't." She force-fed me. She took a small drumstick and held it to my mouth and told me to open my mouth. She had to pick me up and carry me to the bed. I was weak from the emotional trauma of everything. After a few days, I came around. We got the welfare check, and my mother got food for us.

Chickens were all over the place. There was this time in the quarters I called killing day. Everything about it was a community effort. It was most of the time Sundays. All the people would come together and start killing chickens. Neighbors would grab them by the neck and twist the chicken in the air until the neck popped. There were areas with a block of wood or tree stump with two nails to allow a space to place the chicken neck, and with an ax someone would chop the chicken's neck off. If someone tried to pop a chicken's neck, and it would not die, the chicken was running wild all over the place. One of us kids had to catch it and give it to an adult. Blood would be everywhere. The stench settled in the air, as chickens were placed in the hot boiling water, making it easier to pick the feathers off. The odor remained when they were cut open to be cleaned. You had to have a stomach for it. My job was picking off the feathers. Me and some other kids. After the chickens were gutted and cleaned, everyone got a chicken to fry for Sunday. The best part of the whole day was when the chickens were being cooked, and the air was filled with good smelling fried chicken.

The pigs did not belong to anyone and were everywhere. One day, a wild boar somehow got in our chicken wire fence. My mother saw him, got a butcher knife and chased after him. She had me sit on the back step. She ran after that boar all around the yard. The boar ran past me, then my mother right behind him. I did not know my mother could run that fast. She ran a bit ahead of him when he made a turn, and she stuck him in the neck with the knife. I heard the boar moan, my mother stabbed him two more times, and he went down.

## PROTECTORS AMID THE BULLIES

My mother met a man who shall remain nameless. He would beat my mother, and I would hit him, and tell him to stop hitting my mother. He would hit me, knock me against the wall. My mother would go after him with an icepick. He would come to the house when my mother was gone and ask me to fix him some food. I would tell him we did not have any food. He would get mad at me, hit me or knock me against the wall. When I would tell my mother, she would get on him about it. She'd tell him, "Don't be laying your hands on my son!" The fighting between them would start again.

The man got hurt on his job, and he was to get a $3,000 payment for that. My mother was very happy. We were going to have food. When he finally got that money, he left my mother for another lady in the compound. My mother was hurt. One day not so long after he left her, I heard a sound in the front room. It was my mother. She was sitting in a chair crying. I stood there for a second. As soon as she saw me, she jumped up, pretended everything was OK. She said, "Son you want something to eat? I'll fix you something." I said, "No Madear. I am OK."

As a kid, I was always fixing things. I would find stuff, take it apart, put it back together, or fix it if it was broken. I was always looking in the grass or bushes for stuff to take apart or fix. I was always analyzing stuff trying to figure out how things worked. One day when I was working on something to take apart, a big dark shadow came over me. I said, "Oh lordy no, not now." It was the compound bully. She bullied everyone. She reached over, took what I was working on and threw it against one of the toilet walls, and said to me, "That will fix you." I got up and went in the house. She bullied everybody, and nobody liked her. I don't even think her mother liked her. My mother did not like her at all. All of the boys and girls stayed out of her way because she was bigger than all of us.

Cousin B, my mother's good friend, would keep me when my mother had to go somewhere. She always made sure I got to eat. When I went outside, she told me don't go far. When it was time to come in, she would call me. She treated me like a son. One day some kinfolks of hers visited. I was on the front porch, and this girl, maybe kin to Cousin B, around my age was sitting on the porch. We just looked at each other. There was a blanket on the clothesline. Don't remember whose idea it was, but we went under and between the blanket and started hugging each other. It was a good feeling. This went on for a good little while, and we both decided to stop before someone came out. When everyone got ready to leave, we waved goodbye. I don't remember her name, and I never saw her again. This was around 1954 or 55.

## SIMPLE TIMES, RICH MEMORIES

During the summer we would sit on the front porch at night and look at the stars. Sometimes my mother would have sugarcane sticks from Kellogg's Mill way down the railroad tracks. Sometimes she would have a bag of roasted peanuts. We would sit all night, laughing and talking. She would always have a rag to fan the mosquitoes away. Sometimes me and my brother, Willie, would fall asleep and she would wake us up to go inside. Sometimes it would be around 3 a.m. We had fun just talking and laughing as a family. My mother always tried to make us happy and make sure we had food to eat.

Sometimes I would visit my marraine's (godmother's) house. She lived in the shotgun houses behind us, all the way to our right looking out the back door. My marraine had a wooden fence around her yard. When you went inside, it would be like another world. There were pretty flowers everywhere, and the smell of the honeydew was enough to make you want to stay there forever. Wherever I smell that smell it takes me back to my marraine's backyard.

My mother and my marraine used to tease me about this and burst out in laughter. When I would see a truck, I could not say truck with the "t", I would say it with an "f". Everyone would fall on the floor laughing. When I saw another one, I would say, "look, that's another F___k!" They would laugh even harder. It was not until I got older and was thinking back that I understood why they were laughing so hard.

During the summers, we would go down to the canals to fish for crawfish. Coming back, we would pick the wild blackberries along the railroad tracks. They were everywhere. Some were black, some were red. My mother would bake blackberry pies and boil crawfish. We would get pecans from the pecan trees and my mother would make pecan candy.

One day, a beer warehouse burned down. My mother got cases and cases of beer that was thrown out because the cans were burned on the outside. They could not sell it with the name burned off. My mother must have had about 40 cases in the front room stacked all around. She told me and Willie not to touch them. One day when she was at work, one of us decided to try one. I drank a little, gave it to Willie. He drank a little, and before long we were test drinking all the brands to see which was best — Jax, Pearl, Miller, Falstaff, Pabst Blue Ribbon, Milwaukee, so many more. Well, we started getting a little tired, we thought, not knowing we were getting drunk. When my mother got home, we were laying on the end of the porch. She said, "Sherman, Willie, what's wrong with you?" She looked at us, saw we were drunk, and we got ass-whippings.

On Friday and Saturday nights I loved listening to the radio. It was a wooden radio with a large battery. I loved hearing all the music. I imagine it was like being in the café clubs. At night, I would draw pictures by kerosene lamplight. At first, we didn't have electricity in the shotgun houses. When the houses were wired for electricity for the first time, I could not believe how bright it was. I could see everything!

## MONEY ISSUES AND OTHER PAIN

On Sunday mornings I remember James Lawson would come to collect the rent. I believe he was Victoria Lawson's (another classmate) dad. I remember my mother paying $7. I can't remember if it was for the month or the week. I remember my mother letting me go to Mr. T's store one day with a friend. My birthday was coming up, and I wanted to buy a water pistol. My mother had given me 6 cents. I was excited. At the store, my friend got what she was sent to get. I got my water pistol. It was yellow. When I went up to pay for it, my friend said, "Sherman, you don't need to pay for that." I told her I had the money. She grabbed the water pistol out of my hand and stuck it in my pant pocket and said, "Come on, let's go."

She had paid for what she got. We walked past Mrs. Pauline, Mr. T's wife, and walked out. As we walked toward the railroad tracks, I heard something behind us. It was a big car. I looked, and it was Mrs. Pauline. She stuck her hand out the car window and said, "Give it back." I put my hand in my pocket and gave her the yellow water pistol. She took it back and said, "Sherman, I am surprised at you," and she drove off. She did not warn me that she would tell my mother. Her and my mother did not get along at all. When I got home, I told my mother I forgot to get my water pistol. She said, "You seemed so excited about getting it." I told her that tomorrow I would go and get it.

Mr. "T" was there when I went back the next day. I told him I wanted to buy that yellow water pistol. He got it and gave it to me. I handed him the 6 cents. He said, "No son, you don't owe nothing, it's a birthday gift." He knew my birthday was a few days away. I walked out the store, I stopped, looked at the water pistol, and thought, "I stole this, and then someone gives it to me anyway? For free?" I told myself that I would never steal again or allow someone to make me steal. I felt sorry for what I did.

My mother got me a pet dog; his name was Butch. He was dark red. He would follow me around wherever I went most of the times. The compound bully stayed away from me when Butch was around. One day, the next-door neighbor called the dog-catcher and said my dog Butch tried to bite him. My mother told the dogcatchers that wasn't true. The dogcatchers took my dog Butch away. I remembered Butch pulling back, while they were pulling him to get him in the back of the truck. I was crying. Butch never bit no one. My mother said James just didn't like him. That's all. Butch would bark at anyone who came too close to me. He was a happy dog, and he loved to play catch ball. I missed my dog Butch. He was the only close friend I ever had.

## A HARD LESSON LEARNED

I loved the summertime, growing up in Alexandria. It had a sort of magic about it, fun stuff to do. Things I can find to fix. One day I was going across Ninth Street to see what I could find to fix or take apart. I always looked in the grass or weeds. As I was making my way to Ninth Street along one of the shotgun houses, I jumped back, after spotting the "compound bully" on the porch. Her back was turned to me, and she was playing jacks. I forgot this was where she lived. I started to walk away quietly. I saw a brick near me, and without thinking, I took that brick, threw it as hard as I could, dead center at her back. I took off running so fast the brick was still in flight. I heard screaming so loud people in the nearby Oil Mill Quarters could have heard her.

I was running so fast, and by the time I reached the edge of a row of shotgun houses where we lived, I almost fell when I made a sharp left turn. As I got near my house, I jumped up on the porch, and walked in real fast, hoping my mother was not around to ask questions about why I was in a rush. I went to the left corner, got my marbles and pretended to be playing with them. The screaming from the bully was so loud, I heard people coming outside. I was hearing people say, "What happened? What's going on?" By now, my mother had come into the front room asking, "Sherman, what's all that noise I hear? "It seems to be coming from the back." I said I didn't know. My mother came back and said, "Somebody did something" to the bully. I heard the people saying, someone hit her with a brick."

I was scared, thinking, suppose I missed and hit her head? She may die or be hurt really bad or crippled. My mother came back in the room and said she had been hit in the back with a brick and split her back open. She said they were calling an ambulance. I heard people asking, "Anybody seen anything? Anybody heard anything? Anybody seen anyone running through here anywhere?" I heard the sound of the ambulance and my mother telling me that the cops were on the way. Lordy, I am a dead duck, I thought. I heard people outside saying the cops were on the way and that they would find out who did this. This was way bigger than me. What I'm gonna do if someone saw me? What if she is crippled and in a wheelchair? The cops asked everybody questions. They knocked on our back door. My mother answered it, and I heard the cops ask my mother did she see anything or hear anything. My mother said no. They left.

I was still in that corner pretending to play marbles. I picked one up and I looked at it and I said to myself, "Sherman, maybe you losing your marbles." Pulling something like this. My mother came back in the room and said, "They said she will have to have a lot of stitches to sew up her back because of that brick. It split her back open." My mother went on to say, and these are her words, "See that, Sherman, I told you one day someone was gonna get her for being so mean and nasty to you kids. Because she had so many people who didn't like her it could have been anybody." I said, "Oh."

When she got out the hospital, she seemed scared, always looking around. She stopped bullying us. One day I was looking around for something to fix or take apart. I looked up, and she was coming towards me, I thought, "That's it. She found out. I am dead." But she walked by me, didn't say anything. Usually, she would call me a name or hit me, as she went by. She did look like she was worried about something. I didn't take pleasure in what I did, I felt bad, and I told myself to not ever do something like this again. The outcome may be bad, really bad. I made sure I never did anything like that again in my lifetime. I got lucky. Luck don't come twice. I think this was a test. I failed the first part, but I think I passed the second part by learning from this and never doing this again.

## In Good Old Spring-Summertime

That summer was bad! But spring and summer times mostly were fun. Growing up in Alexandria during those times of the year was absolutely the greatest. It didn't get any better. Lots of time to learn how to make things and explore parts of the city. In

March, we made kites out of newspaper, strings and sticks, we used flour and water to act as glue. We would fly those kites so high I would swear it was higher than an airplane. We would make bows and crossbows during the summers also. The bows were strong enough to kill rabbits or possums. To do this, we would put a soda bottle top on the end of the arrow and hit it with a brick to fold it over the arrow shaft. To sharpen the end, we would rub the ridged end of the bottle cap against cement. Now the arrow was able to slice through the skin of a rabbit or possum. I didn't kill any rabbits or possums because if you killed anything you had to take it home to skin, gut and prepare it to eat. I did not like possum or rabbit.

The wild game in those days were in a wooded area on the other side of the tracks at the end of the last shotgun house, which was where Miss Lilly stayed. The wooded area went from there looking west to Ninth Street, and in the other direction it went east almost to Seventh Street in a wooded area. Because of all the different types of wood, we had everything we needed to make bows, slingshots, china ball guns. We called it "the woods" because rabbits, possums, armadillos, wild boars and snakes were there.

Way across the woods was the area where my Peabody classmate Carolyn Gaines lived. I don't know if she lived over that way in the early 1950s. And, somewhere along that area was a café called The Mombo. My mother told me about it because that's where she used to go sometimes when she went out with her friend. Going toward the east of the woods across the other side was where my cousin Pearlie Lewis lived, and at the corner at Seventh Street was the club, Green Frog. There was a row of warehouses over there beyond the woods. I just know from growing up in Alexandria.

In the summers, I learned early how to make and build things. James Lanhart and a guy named John taught me how to make a zip gun. It fired a .22 caliber bullet. I learned how to make one and fire one when I was 5. The zip gun was more deadly than my bow. I decided not to make another one or teach anyone how to make one. John and James Lanhart were older than me, and they taught me how to make a lot of things. They were very smart. James looked like (former rapper/actor) Ice T. They could be twins. They sound almost alike, move their mouths the same way.

James Lanhart showed me how to make a boomerang, too. We got the wood from a tree in the woods. He showed me how to shape it. He said when I throw it, it will come back to me. I could not believe this, but I knew James was not joking because he never really smiled. When we finished, he showed me how the boomerang worked. He stood in one spot, he drew back with his right hand, threw it slightly down. It came up, came around to the right, and he held his right hand up and caught it. I said, "WOW!" I never saw anything like that before. I threw it like he showed me. It came around, but I missed it. "Don't move. It's coming back to this spot," he told me. I threw it again, and it went around to the right, came back around right to my hand. I caught it!

In the Rock Island Quarters, around Eighth Street, we would become blood brothers. It was an agreement between two people who had high respect for one another. Me and my friend James Lanhart decided to become blood brothers because he had taught me how to fix stuff, how to make things, and he saw I was smart and not afraid. To become blood brothers, you need a sharp razor blade. You have to cut your thumb. It was my right thumb. James cut his thumb also. While the blood is coming out, both thumbs are touched, and the blood is transferred between the two people. Once the blood stops, the thumbs are removed from contact, and after it was done, we became blood brothers. Blood brothers never fight one another, never betray one another. We always respected one another, and we never argued with one another.

We used to make what we called the bullwhip. We took a piece of lightweight wood about 12 inches long and cut a hole at one end. Used the kite string or some thick string, ran it through the hole with about 2 ½ feet in length on both sides, cut it. Tied the ends together. The object is to twirl it around your head like a helicopter, and it will catch the wind, and with that piece of wood spinning it will produce a sound like a roar of wind or a bull. You can change how it sounds by twirling it slow or fast. The length of the string can be shorter for a small person or longer for a taller person.

In the summer the girls were doing the hula-hoop. We guys would be in groups playing marbles. The girls would play skip rope. The guys would play with our wooden tops. I loved spinning my top on the porch. Some of the guys would play with yoyos, doing all sorts of tricks like walk the dog. Some of the girls played hopscotch, and others would be on the porches playing jacks. Some of us played hide and seek. It was an unwritten law. No one hides in the woods because none of the girls were going in there.

## MOTHER'S WIT AND GRIT

My mother was smart and strong. She taught me how to balance an egg on its small end on the table. When she first showed me how, I said, "Wow!" She told me to try it, and I could not balance it. She told me she had put salt on the table first. She put the egg on it. Blew the salt away, and the egg was balanced on its end. That part I didn't see until she showed me. She also showed me how to take a clothespin, cut a notch in it, put a piece of small thick string across it, hanging on each side. Put it on the end of your index finger, and it would not fall and be in balance. My mother also taught me how to make a button spinner, but I only remember how to start it.

My mother was strong. I remember going to pick cotton with her when I was around 8. We got up at 3 a.m. The bus picked us up at 4 a.m. We rode with others in that old bus for a long time to get to some plantation cotton farm. We all got big cotton sacks and were led to a row. My row was next to my mother's. I looked down that row of cotton because you can pick from the left side and the right side. But the row was so long it looked like it stretched all the way back to Alexandria. We started picking. The older people were singing all sorts of songs. Some were church songs. We had one, I believe, 10-minute break to get a drink of water or soda. Later around 12, a 15-minute or 10-minute break to eat a sandwich. My mother asked me how I was doing? I said OK. The sun was hot. Picking the cotton, I could see people's hands on the other side. My mother was at my left side. When I stood up, I could barely see over the top of the cotton plants, but I could see all the people everywhere.

We knocked off at 5. I did not finish my row. My mother said it was OK. We had to bring our sacks over a scale to get the weight. They emptied the sacks on a truck with a large compartment. They took a percentage for the transportation and a percentage for the owner of the cottonfield and what was left was our take-home pay.

Well, I held my hand out, and the guy gave me a dime and two pennies. My mother got, I believe, 75 or 80 cents. People who made big money got a dollar.

As a person who analyzes all the time, I knew I better stay in school. My mother and I went out to pick cotton a couple more times, and I remember going out to clear fields to be ready for cotton to be planted. It was so hot when I got home, the sun had pulled all the water out of my skin. I had stuff stuck on my face. I didn't know what it was. My mother said it was salt. My body was hurting so bad I thought a train ran over me. I love working and people have called me a workaholic, but this was a bad balance. The amount of work outweighed the amount of money.

## DEAR OLD GOLDEN RULE DAYS

My first day of school I remember well. My mother took me to Peabody Elementary School in 1956. I remember being in the lunchroom area. She signed some papers and was talking to the teachers. I remember her saying, "I have to go, son. I'll be back later to get you." I wanted to go with her, and she said I had to stay. I started crying at the window for her to not leave me. One of the teachers took me from the window and said, "It's OK, she will be back." I looked around and all the other kids were looking at me. They probably said to themselves, "Who's the dummy?"

One weekend in the quarters, when I was in first grade, a bunch of us wanted to play ride the horse. We used long sticks for that. There were some in the makeshift shed in the backyard, so I got on top of the lumber to get sticks for everyone. Walking back and forth on those wooden lumbers, I lost my footing, and I grabbed at a board that was part of the wall. The board had a rusted nail at an angle. My right arm went right down on that nail because I was falling and could not stop myself. The nail went in my right arm and protruded out my thumb. James Lanhart was there. He tried to get me loose. He couldn't. He ran to get my mother who was running out the door because of my loud screams. I was hanging in midair, and all the wood had fallen down. Blood was squirting everywhere. I was screaming louder than the compound bully was when I hit her in the back with that brick. I guess what goes around comes around. My mother got up there and tried to unhook me, but she could not figure out how to get me down. She had to hold me a little higher to have more room to work the nail out my arm. It was more painful coming out than it was going in.

The ambulance came. At the hospital, I got stitches. Everything healed OK. They took the stitches out when the time came. I was OK for a while, but something, I can't explain what, happened. I remember walking through the middle room to get to the front room, and my legs began to get stiff. With every step my legs got stiffer until I could not move any more. I called out to my mother who was in the front room. I told her I could not walk. My legs got stiff. She tried to help me take steps, but I could not. She said, "Sherman, stop clowning around." Because she knew I was always clowning around making everybody laugh. She saw I was trying to walk but could not, so she knew I was not playing around, so it was an ambulance again to the hospital. This was about a month after the nail in my right arm and wrist, as far as I can remember.

## RECOVERY, AND THEN SOME

I don't know what the doctors told my mother in detail, but this is what my mother told me. I had some sort of lead poisoning from that rusted nail in my bloodstream. The doctor said I was going to be in a wheelchair. The nurses at Huey P. Long Charity Hospital in Pineville told me I could use my wheelchair to go to the toilet. They showed me how to get in the wheelchair from my bed and wheel myself over to the toilet, move from the wheelchair to the toilet stool and back to my bed. There was another boy in the room with me. He was older maybe 10 or 11. I was the only 6-year-old. Whenever I needed to use the toilet, I would wheel myself over and back again.

My mother would come visit and bring me cookies or candy. Sometimes she would fall asleep in the chair or lying across my bed still sitting in the chair. One night when the nurses were not around, I was sitting in my wheelchair, getting ready to go over to the toilet. It was not far away. I remember it was beyond the end of my bed and a few steps to the door, which was always open for me and the other boy in the room. I came to the conclusion I could crawl all the way to the toilet. I didn't feel any pain in my legs, so I crawled all the way to the toilet, but getting on the toilet was a little harder. I felt a little stiffness in my legs, but I managed to succeed.

I continued to crawl, going to the toilet to when the nurses were gone, which most of the time was at night. One time the other boy in the room looked at me and said, "They gonna be mad if they see you doing that." I said, "Well, I just won't let them see me doing this." I did that for a while and decided I could maybe try to walk alongside the bed and crawl the rest of the way to the toilet. I was able to in small steps because I could feel my legs were still a little stiff, but there was no pain. As the days went by, I was able to take bigger steps, and after more days went by, my legs got stronger, I guess? All I know is I could walk from my bed to the toilet and back as many times as I wanted.

Once, when my mother came to visit, I told her I could walk to the toilet and back to her, and she hugged me and started crying. My mother told the doctors, and I believed they did some kind of tests. I remember them checking my legs and asking if I felt pain in response to stuff they were doing. After being there six months, they released me and gave me crutches. I told my mother I did not need them because they were for people who were crippled. When we got home, my brother, Willie, was at the screen door, and our mother asked him if he remembered me. He had a puzzled look and went into the middle room. After a while, he came back, and we started playing. He remembered me.

I had less than three months to pass first grade. They gave me a lot of tests, but I passed first grade and had Miss Jackson in second grade. I was able to walk to school with no problems. My mother said just don't run. I used to walk to school with a friend of mine named Ernest Buckner. I do not know what happened to him.

## WATER, BEGONE!

Like I have explained, summers growing up in Alexandria always were fun. I was soon back at fixing stuff in the backyard. I saw a shadow come over my left side. It was a small shadow someone my size. I looked around, and it was Little Beaver, that was his nickname. His name was Charles Lee Austin. He asked me to go swimming with him and his friend, Dunee, who was teaching him to swim. I said no because I was fixing something. Over the days and weeks, he would come by and tell me how good a swimmer he was.

I made a wheelbarrow to make it easy for me to go around the compound and find stuff to take apart, analyze, fix, and put back together. Everybody knew I was that weird kid who was always fixing stuff in the backyard. One summer day in the backyard after hauling stuff, I was taking something apart when a shadow came over my left side. It was an adult. I could tell. It was my mother saying my name. I put down what I was doing and turned around. My mother said my name in two ways: when everything was OK and when something bad had happened. This was a something bad happened sound.

"Do you remember Charles Lee? He drowned in the Red River," she said. I jumped up and asked, "What? How?" My mother said an undercurrent got him. My mother took me to the funeral. I was 7. Charles Lee was 7. I remember the long line of people, as we walked up to his coffin. I remember him lying there like he was sleep. I also remember telling myself if Charles Lee was a swimmer and water did this to him, what chance do I have? I am no swimmer. I said right then and there I better stay away from water. I know now that I was traumatized. That was the first funeral I had seen. I was very saddened by it all. For weeks, Charles Lee was my friend.

In the fourth grade, Miss Walker's class, Lane LaCoure, I think he was French, was my best friend. He was always talking about being a carpenter. I would tell him I wanted to fix airplanes. I remember one weekend someone brought news to the quarters that Lane was dead. They said he was taking a bath and an electric lamp fell in the bathtub when he was getting up, and he was electrocuted. I was really sad. I could not believe it. I remember that week in school we were laughing and talking, having fun. He was a fun guy. Always happy. Always laughing, very nice to everyone. Always upbeat. He was my very best friend, and I missed him dearly.

This was in 1959. I did not go to his funeral. I was too traumatized. I would not do anything for a while. I would just sit in a chair and stare out the window for hours. Nothing to look at except the house next door. My mother would tell me to go outside some time, or to get stuff I like to fix on in the backyard? I would tell her I didn't feel like it. The next day as I sat staring out the window, I said to myself I need to analyze all this. I just sat there not making a sound. Just thinking. After a while, I spelled out to myself. W A T E R, it was W-A-T-E-R that killed my friend, Lane. It was electricity and water combined but water played a part. This did not help my relationship with water at all. I hated it even more so. Here it has killed two of my friends and left me traumatized. I am not even 10 yet.

## A NEWER BEGINNING

We moved out of the Maple Street Alley in 1960 to 8008 Eighth Street. It was near the Alexandria Scrapyard. We were still in the Rock Island Quarters, but I remember that early morning move. I was in the truck with all our furniture. It was early morning and my mother walked ahead of the truck, as we followed behind her. I remember she had two kerosene lamps. One in each hand. The lamps had to be carried by hand in the truck or they would be broken.

I remember my sixth-grade classmate Janice Marie James Joseph. She was cute, funny, wore glasses, had dimples. She told me Marie James was her middle name. We knew her as Janice Joseph. She moved to California. One day our teacher asked me to help with something. As we were walking down the stairs, my teacher said, "Sherman, you not going to be nothing." Those were the exact words. I remember them well. I was very hurt by this and coming from a teacher made it the worst. I thought a teacher would or should help you gain confidence. I know I lacked confidence in stuff at school, but I also know why. I already analyzed that. I didn't have a father figure. Most all the students had a father and a mother. Also, because we were so poor, I was on free lunch. All these things made me feel different and inferior to the other kids.

I remember a Father's Day program at school where all fathers of the students would come in and the students would introduce their fathers, and the fathers would tell what job they did and a little about themselves, and students could ask them questions about their jobs. I know I wasn't the only one who didn't have a father there, but it was hard for me to sit through that. Very hard.

## MORE SUMMERTIME FUN

Again, summer days were my favorite in Alexandria. My mother would give us a big slice of watermelon and I would sit on the back steps and eat all the watermelon I wanted. I always had near me a wooden airplane to build that I would play with later. One day I was sitting on the back steps and a group of other kids were riding by on bikes. I saw this really cute girl go by. I jumped up and wondered, "who was that?" I had never seen her before. She was real pretty, but she had on these raggedy clothes that did not bother me because I grew up wearing raggedy clothes myself. I had not seen her before, but we were fairly new in this area.

During the summers on Eighth Street, we would build go-carts. I learned how to build go-carts from a guy named Bennett Riser. He had a younger brother named Curtis and his older brother was Bow. I believe Bow was around my age. Bennett was the best go-cart builder in the Rock Island Quarters, and I listened to everything he showed me on how to build a good go-cart.

During the summer days I would go to the canal back across Ninth Street because we lived on the corner of Eighth Street. The scrapyard was on the side of us. We were separated by the road and a large ditch. You could see the canal from the back door of our house, looking toward Ninth Street. Most of the time, it was me by myself. I was a loner. I would spend the whole day at the canal catching crawfish. Analyzing tadpoles. This was a small canal near our house. The big canals where we all would go as a family was at the railroad tracks off Ninth Street going west towards the Kellogg sawmill near the Oil Mill Quarters.

This small canal area was my little getaway. There was an area of green grass, a little field, I would lay on and look up at the clouds. I would see all types of shapes. But to get to this little field I had to cross the canal. It was shallow, just a small stream unless it rained. If it was a lot of water, I would not be there. Sometimes while I was down there the train would pass and the engineer would blow the horn and wave. This happened a lot because I was always at that canal at least three days a week during the summers. The train engineer I learned later to be my Peabody friend Leon Lefear's dad, Leon, Sr.

I was most of the time at the canal by myself. Nobody seemed to share my adventurous nature. Oh well, did not bother me none. As it got a little dark, I would get what crawfish I had and catch lightning bugs, put them in a jar to bring back and watch in amazement how they light up like that. I loved summers in Alexandria because I loved catching all the different butterflies and grasshoppers and bugs to analyze. Unlike my mechanical stuff, I did not take any of the lightning bugs apart or cut them up. I just watched what they did. Analyzed their movements, studied their design, wondered why they do what they do. Now, my crawfish, I cooked and ate them. It was just enough for me. If my brother Willie or Henry wanted any, I would tell them they could go with me next time. We never wore shoes during the summers. I was always barefoot. This was between 1960 and 1963.

My mother would send me to Mr. T's Grocery Store to get meat or kerosene for the lamps. The guy behind the butcher counter was a guy everyone called Tiny. He would always give an extra small piece of meat after everything was weighed. If I came for kerosene there was two stops on the tank. One for 6 cents and one for 12 cents. If I asked for 6 cents worth of kerosene, he would take the container, set the tank stop at 6 cents and pump it in, and he would flip the stop out and pump a little extra kerosene to help us out because he knew we were poor, but we were not the only ones poor. What I saw in Tiny and Lena helped make me the person I am. To see them help someone in need not only made me admire them, I wanted to be just like them.

## PLANES, BIKES, CLUBBING STICKS, OH, MADEAR!

From time to time, I would think of my friend Lane Lacoure who was always excited about being a carpenter when he grew up. He would ask me what I wanted to be when I grew up. I would tell him a mechanic, and when I saw and became obsessed with airplanes, I would say I wanted to be an aircraft mechanic.

With a scrapyard being across the street from the house, I could go over when they were closed. Sundays was best to get anything I wanted to analyze and take apart. I found all kinds of toys I would fix up - cranes, trucks, buses. Most just needed wheels or something fixed. I would use my pliers. I found a lot of tools to help me fix stuff.

I wanted to build a bike because there was a lot of bike parts over there, so I started finding what I needed and soon I had everything to make a bike. I learned by trial and error how the mechanics of everything went together until I learned every area and what was needed. I learned how to add or take out links from a chain to make it tight or loose depending on how I wanted it. I learned how all the guts, as they were called, went in the rear and front rims. The guts for the main crank, as well as the front fork. But you had to find a good frame first. I believe the larger bike frame was 28 inches, but I learned to put everything together to make a nice size bike. A friend showed me how to get the tire and innertubes and how to patch holes in it. He had a pump. The last thing was a rubber piece that went around the rim before the innertube. Once everything was put together, you had a nice bike, and it did not cost you anything.

During the summers I enjoyed making airplanes. The body would be a piece of pine about two inches wide. I would cut one end down at an angle. The wing would be wood from a window shade. A smaller piece of the shade wood would be the elevator. I used mud to make the rudder. I used tacks to nail the wing to the main pine body and elevator. The wheel base was mud. The wheels were made of mud, and I put it together with match sticks. The propeller was a popsicle stick. When I was finished, it looked like a real Cessna. I was obsessed with airplanes.

One afternoon some of us were in the scrapyard looking around. It, I believe, was a Sunday. But I heard someone yell, "The roaches are coming. The roaches coming." That was the name for the cops. Everyone was able to get out. I was too far in. They all made it to the fence on the west side and climbed over fast. I ran around the shallow three bay hopper train that was there before the fence and jumped in as quick as I could. I could not climb the fence; the cops would have seen me. Maybe yelled to me to stop or they would shoot. I stayed as quiet as I could because they came over to the fence. One of them said, "They climbed over the fence and went through that wooded area." I stayed low until they left. I waited a while before I came out. I climbed the fence went around by the canal and came out at Ninth Street. Went straight to the house, came in through the back door. I just loved Louisiana summers. So much fun and excitement.

My mother gave my brothers and me an allowance on Friday nights when she got paid. I got 25 cents, my brother Willie got 15 cents, and my brother Henry got 10 cents and my brother Robert was only 3. Mister T, the grocery store owner, had a son we called "Brother". I do not know his real name, but he had a side area built on the store, and he sold snow cones out of it. We all went crazy over them. My favorite was cherry. I believe they were 6 cents. We would buy one, and if we had more money go get another one. Everybody up and down the quarters was always eating snow cones during the summer.

Sometimes, my mother would make popcorn balls, and she would sell them to the kids. She used syrup and something else to make them stay together. I loved pecans, and my mother also would make pecan candy for us. There were pecan trees all around Alexandria. The main tree we would go to was beyond the railroad track by the train station. We had an iron rod we would throw up and hit a branch and it would rain pecans. At one point I thought I could get some and sell them, but you needed a ton just to get a couple dollars. So, I always got the pecans for my mother to make pecan candy for us. She taught us how to make it and taught me how to cook. My mother was a good cook. She worked as a cook at the café by the train station. At one time and also the café on Orden and Third.

## BETTER LIVING, COMFORT AND JOY

Things started to get a little better for us. We had electricity in the house. We still had to go to the toilet in the area in the center of the shotgun houses in the back. We got a black-and-white TV in 1962. I enjoyed watching TV and all the programs and cartoons on Saturday mornings. Christmas was getting a little better for us, too. Cowboy guns was the top thing for Christmas for boys back then. I got a Rifleman rifle one Christmas. It looked real. My mother would put stuff on layaway. Another Christmas I got the Have Gun Will Travel Gun Set. Christmastime growing up on Eighth Street was a good time. My mother always made sure we had lots of food for Christmas.

We moved to 529 Nolan Court in 1963. It was still in the Rock Island Quarters. I met Allen Lavalais and Douglas Moran. They lived nearby. One day Allen was walking by, and I was in the street, and he had a white something in his hand. I asked him what it was, and he said it was a swinger. I asked, "What's a swinger?" It was a camera. (Polaroid Swinger had just come out summer 1965.) He showed me how to use it. When I see the final product, a picture that was taken only seconds earlier, I was hooked that moment in time. I loved photography.

*My mother on Nolan Court, 1971*

During the summers, we would ride our bikes all around the quarters but when Miss Nancy came around, it was like high noon in a western town. She was a big red woman with a loud, loud voice, and she used a walker. She would fuss at us kids saying we up to devilment and she going to tell our mothers. She would look down every alley way between those shot gun houses to fuss at whoever she got to where I was. Once I was just working on my bicycle, and she said, "Sherman your long skinny ass not fooling me. I know you up to devilment. I'm gon' tell Lola on your ass. Those were her words. That was Miss Nancy.

Shortly after the move, I got to see the pretty girl with the raggedy clothes. I was somewhere near the train station. We got to share an ice cream cone. I only had enough change for one, but we shared. She seemed happy around me for some reason. The very last time I saw her was on the tracks down from the train station. We walked over there and just sat talking. It was the tracks up on the hill. I said we have to be on alert because we are on the tracks. I had to keep checking with my hands to feel the track to see if there was a vibration, so we needed to know in advance. I told her I like her and one day I will marry her. She said, "You don't even know me. You don't know nothing about me and in five years you won't even remember my name, and besides you could leave and go off somewhere." It all came true.

## LEISURE IN THE JIM CROW REALM

There was a program where we would go to the Paramount Theater Downtown. We got coupons for free RC soda and other stuff. We went in through a side door. The white people went in the front door. We sat in the balcony section. I think we had the best seats. I remember seeing *Jason and the Argonauts*. I also remember when we went downtown passing Walgreens. We had to look straight ahead because if we looked in and made eye contact with a white customer sitting in there eating, we would get in trouble, maybe arrested, I was told. Most of the time, I would be going around the corner to the bookstore to buy a comic book. Whenever I went to Walgreens, it was to get something for my mother.

I can't forget the train station at Third Street that had water fountains, "White Only" on one side and "Colored" on the other side. And, I remember that on Lower Third Street at the front top center on Peabody Elementary School's old three-story building you could read the words, "Peabody Negro School." Thinking about school, I loved going to school to see all the pretty girls and to get my education, but I did not like "board" meetings in Nap Johnson's class if I forgot to do an assignment. During my time going to school, I received free lunch because the family income was low. I always went to school without breakfast or anything to eat. I was hungry by lunch-time, and I was able to do better in my classes after I had eaten something.

## ACCOUNTABILITY IN REAL TERMS, REAL TIMES

When we did something wrong, my mother would get the belt and give you a whipping, but there were times we would do something and she would just get mad, and we would think that was it. But, late in the night the cover would be pulled back, and you could feel the air and you would get what I called a delayed late-night whipping. I didn't like those. Just give me my whipping in real time so I can get it over with and sleep in peace at night.

Riding trains or jumping trains was one thing some of us in the Rock Island Quarters love doing. If we hopped on from the scrapyard side, we had to get over to the other side quickly before the train got to the yellow bridge crossing over third Street. I am sure most everybody going into downtown on Third Street saw it. It was yellow, and it had printed on the side "New Orleans, Shreveport, Kansas City". Back then, Third Street took you into town. If we were on the train station side, and jumped the train, we had a little more time, but we had to get off before that yellow bridge.

This day we were going to jump. I was showing Chris Berville how we did it. Me and Chris got along good, but Chris had a cast on his arm from something he broke, so I told him to just watch what we do. To do the jump you have to run along beside the train and match the speed of the train. Next, you grab the second or third step with both hands then focus on putting your right foot on the last step. All the while the train is moving the left foot will follow. We all hopped on and had limited time to hop off before the point of no return — that yellow bridge. I heard what sounded like Chris. I looked back. He was holding onto one of the steps and his feet were dangling all around that train wheel. I yelled to Chris to push away and let go! He did.

The track is uphill gravel, so I saw him roll down into the gravel. He was ok, but I realized as I looked up and ahead, everyone had jumped off, and because I was distracted, I had passed my point of no return. I could not jump off. There were all kinds of glass that would cut a person to ribbons. You cannot jump off on the bridge from a moving train because it's too narrow. Plus, you will come down on a railroad tie, the wooden piece the track sits on, and break a leg or get knocked into the train wheel. You cannot jump off after the yellow bridge because it's about two stories down. Next stop — Red River. I wasn't happy about the situation, but I knew I had to stay on until the train crossed Red River. I did not want to look down. Me and water are not friends. I was hanging on the side with nothing below me but water. I kept looking ahead. My only worry was if the train picked up speed. You cannot jump off if it's going too fast. It did not increase in speed, and as soon as it reached Pineville, and I saw a good spot, I jumped off.

As I was able to come to a normal walk, I looked around. It was a city dump. I looked to see if I could find something to take home to take apart, analyze, and fix. Most of what I found was a little too big to carry back. I could see the train disappear out of view. I made my way a little bit toward what seems like the way out. I saw some books. I looked around a bit and I found a *Playboy* magazine. I said I better put this in my back pocket and cover it with my shirt, so my mother won't see it. I knew it would be starting to get dark by the time I got back, so I had to make my way to the bridge to get back to Alexandria. I made it home, went in through the back door and went straight to the middle room closet to put the magazine inside my clothes.

The next day I saw Chris. I fussed him out about doing something that stupid trying to jump a train with a cast when I told him just to watch us. He said he was sorry. Chris has a lot of respect for me because I treated him as my equal, and I taught him how to fix stuff.

## IN THE MONEY

Mr. Dooley was a substitute teacher at Peabody, and recruited me and others to work in the Neighborhood Youth Corps. I could not say yes quick enough. The job was for the City of Pineville. They taught us how to use sling blades to cut grass. Our job was to go into an area and clear it of grass. We had to have a certain number of feet distance on both sides of us to be safe from hitting the other person. Levi Smith and Allen Lavalais were on the work program also. We did not get paid until the next Saturday. For the one day, I received a check for $9.56 after taxes. Right away, I knew I would be able to get my class ring and yearbook. I worked every Saturday. I was a workaholic. It did not bother me at all because I knew this was easy and more money. I bought me a Timex watch, some clothes form Bailey Clothing Store, got a swinger camera and got into taking pictures.

During the summer when school was out, they said we could work four days during the week and Saturday if we want. Didn't have to ask me but once. There were not many people working during the summer. Just myself. I didn't know anyone else. Levi and Allen worked a few days but that was it. I worked the whole summer. I remember the check I got working during the summer. It was for $34 and some change. I thought I was rich. I received one for $42. I helped my mother with stuff she needed help with. I remember going to my homeroom teacher, Mr. Brady, and telling him I can pay for my lunch. I don't have to get the free lunch anymore. Mr. Brady told me I would still receive free lunch because the family income did not change. At the time, I could not understand that.

During my last two years of school, before graduation, I took typing over auto mechanics because I knew how to fix most anything so auto mechanics would not get me anything new that I didn't already know. But typing, I did not know. Because of the times we lived in back then, I would wait until the halls cleared before I went to my typing class. I was the only guy, and I became one of the fastest typists in the class. My typing teacher Ms. Anna Williams asked me if I wanted to enter the state competition. I said no. She said just think about it a week or so. When she came back and asked again, I said no. I didn't have confidence. I could do some of any and everything in the Rock Island Quarters because I had high confidence. I was like two people. This daredevil in the Quarters and Clark Kent in school.

During my senior year, working for the City of Pineville was great. One day the boss had us clear a field. He left for a while, but I continued to work. I remember working that sling blade and thinking about buying more clothes and film for my camera when I get paid. But I noticed that there were not too many people at my left or right side. Soon, I didn't see anybody. I looked back and everybody was over by the truck either smoking or just talking and watching me work. It didn't bother me none. I just kept working.

After a while I heard what sounded like my boss. I looked up, and he told me to give him the sling blade. He then told me to go sit on the truck. I said to myself, "Oh man, I am in trouble." He had all those guys get the sling blades and start clearing that field. As they worked, he had me sit on the back of the truck and watch them work. I sat there a long time. The boss stood by the truck and watched them. He didn't say anything. When they finished and got on the truck to go in, I thought they would be mad at me or say something nasty to me. But no one said anything to me at all.

One Saturday we went out on the truck with a guy named Price. He got to the area we were to clear. He said you boys get out the truck, clear that field. Nobody liked being called boy. I remember someone saying, "What? Who you calling boy?" We all refused to work. He took us in, and all of us left and went home. The regular boss was out that day. He was a good guy who respected everyone. The next day Mr. Dooley came to my house. He was laughing. He said, "Sherman you guys cannot just walk off the job like that." I told him we didn't like being called that. It was the same as being called "ni—er," and we all stuck together. Mr. Dooley said he got us all reinstated. We reported to work the next Saturday. Mr. Dooley said try not to walk off the job again. I said if they treat us like humans and there's no name-calling, we won't.

When I worked some Saturdays and Levi and Allen didn't come in, I rode my bike. Lunchtime, I would ride across the bridge to Alexandria to the café on the corner of Ogden and Third where my mother worked as a short-order cook. She would make me a hamburger and give me a coke. That was good.

## MOVING TO ADULTHOOD

I took shop in high school because I wanted to learn how to work with wood, and I also took art because I wanted to learn more about drawing before I graduated. I was also getting prepared to go into the U.S. Air Force. I had most all my paperwork done. I passed the mechanic part of the test with flying colors.

I was an usher at Pilgrim Rest Baptist. One Sunday Leon Lefear came in. I was at the back. He spoke and stood for a little while, then he left. Pilgrim Rest was just down from True Vine and Rev. Gus Kennedy was our pastor. Some Sundays we would be there until 11:30 at night. All the churches would be long gone. But I wouldn't mind sometimes.

As we got close to graduation, my job with the City of Pineville ended. I got another job after school at a community center on Lower Third as a janitor. On Sundays in summer 1968 some of us would get together and ride our bikes down to Morock Ford Town to test drive the cars. They left the keys inside in those days, as long as you didn't drive the car off the lot, but the lot was big. It was at the end of Third Street at the end of town. If you went left you would be heading to the traffic circle and England Air Force Base. If you went right, you would be heading to Shreveport. This particular Sunday there were some white teenagers on the lot test-driving the cars. So, we all waited across the canal until they left, then we went over. There were six of us, me and my brother and two other guys and their brothers. We picked a car, got in and drove it around, but didn't drive it off the lot because that would be considered car theft.

I was parking one of the cars, and I heard someone say to me, "Is this your car?" I looked, it was a cop. Someone called the cops on us. No cops showed up when the white boys were test-driving. I told the cop it was not my car. He told me to cut the engine off and get out of the car. I got out, they got all our names and addresses and let us go. I had graduated from Peabody in May, and this happened around the third week in June. All my air force papers were in and ready to go. When the cops let us go, I thought that was it.

My mother was excited about the Fourth of July. She had lots of food and water-melon. I remember waking up on the Fourth, I heard my mother talking to someone at the front door, and I heard my name mentioned. My mother came in the middle room. She said, "Sherman, what you done got yourself in now? That's a policeman. He said for you to get dressed and come with him." I got dressed, and as I was heading to the door, my mother reminded me about the knife in my pocket that I always carried. I threw it under the sofa as I got to the door. The cop kept rushing me like I was going to take off somewhere. When I came out, the shirt I had on was blue and it was raggedy. I didn't have on any shoes. The other guy was in the backseat of the police car where they put me. The three brothers were 16 years old. They didn't arrest them. We were booked into the Alexandria jail downtown. Later that evening, the other guy was brought in. He turned himself in.

I analyzed that. They waited until the Fourth of July to arrest us, knowing judges, court people would be on vacation, causing us to be locked up for a good week or so. The jail section we were in had three bays. Each bay had four beds, an upper and lower on each side. There were two other Black guys in the bay on the end. We were in the middle bay and in a bay at the other end, there was an older man. He looked homeless. He was laying on the floor, he went on himself. Each bay area I recall had its own toilet but the two guys from the other end would come over during the course of the day and poke fun at the old man and laugh at him.

It didn't take me long to have my fill of that. I told them to leave the guy alone, he wasn't doing anything to them. One of them grabbed me by the collar and slammed me against the window that had a small set of bars. It hurt my back. I said again to leave the man alone. He said, "You little ni—er. You don't tell us what to do." I was 18, about 98 pounds. They were around 25, 26 years old. Way bigger. He dropped me down. I went to my other two friends and asked why didn't they help me? There's three of us. Without them saying anything, I could tell my two friends didn't want any part of this. I knew I would have to do this alone, but it didn't matter. I was not going to let them poke fun at and harass and humiliate that old man. I learned from my mother, Lena, and Tiny, that life isn't all about us, it's about us helping one another. Better to stand for something than die for nothing.

The next day I was ready for them. I waited. They didn't go over to bother the old man at all. Now I knew it was not because they were afraid of me. Something was up. We had to go over to the cell door to get our food through a square opening. We all got our food and sat at the wooden tables like picnic tables. As I was getting ready to eat, someone reached over my shoulder took my tray of food and said, "You not going to be getting any more food we going to take it from now on." I sat up straight. I said to myself, "Ok. Good." They not going to mess with the old man any more. My two friends said I could have some of their food. My mother always brought me something to eat. When she came, my mother told me to tell the police they were taking my food. I told her it's a jail thing. The old man can rest. I still get to eat. They happy taking my food. I achieved that goal.

As it came time to go before the judge, my mother brought me a good shirt and shoes. That day we walked into the courtroom before the judge. My pastor, Rev. Gus Kennedy, was there. He talked to the judge and got us off with clean records. We all left. My two friends left in the car with their parents. My mother and my pastor asked if I wanted a ride home. I said no. I wanted to walk home.

## THE END AND THE BEGINNING

I left for air force basic training July 23, 1968. I finished aircraft mechanic school as an aircraft hydraulics mechanic technician December 1968 with the highest average in the class. I served in the military for 7½ years. I spent time in the Philippines with two temporary duties in Viet Nam. I worked on C-130s, B-52s, and KC-135s.

After the military, I got an associate degree in electronics and worked for Motorola. I studied photography at the New York Institute of Photography and became a professional photographer. One of my wedding photos was published in *Jet Magazine*. I have continued to analyze and fix things. I have never needed a repairman.

Of all the journeys we take in our lifetime, the most difficult journey of all is one into ourselves. All these events are true, as best I can remember, and they happened in and around the Rock Island Quarters in a town called Alexandria a long, long, long, long, long, ago. Once upon a time.

# SAVED BY THE PROMISE

*"Blessed are the peacemakers."*

MATTHEW 5:9

*"Violence is the last refuge of the incompetent."*

ISAAC ASIMOV

## Kathlyn Giles Stewart

## WHAT GROUNDS ME AND SAVES ME

*"Knowing I had little to no money, poor was not a word we used to describe our circumstances. I knew I just did not have a lot. Families made choices. I learned the importance of choosing, commitment, and consequences. Not having all my desires met made selecting what I needed from what I wanted the key to the joy I experienced as a student."*

THE MOST IMPORTANT part about becoming me is the one constant relationship I have in my life with Jesus Christ. My first encounter or introduction to Jesus was with my Aunt Effie Belvin. She was my kindergarten Sunday school teacher and my uncle's wife. Soft-spoken, quiet, yet faithful, she could be stern without raising her voice. She was small in stature and the mother of two boys with my Uncle Cleophas. I was considered their little girl. She was proud of me and told me so. I recited Bible verses on the Fourth Sunday in church. It was a tradition. Every time I visited my grandmother in Louisiana, it was my aunt who would take me to church. It was because of her love for me and her persistence that I came to know Christ and attend church every Sunday. It was through her teachings that I learned scripture. I love Sunday school because I believed. Jesus was just like me, "a child of God".

My family's church was Shiloh Missionary Baptist Church, on Washington Avenue in Alexandria. I grew up in the church, married in the church, and learned to love God and learned to know God loves me. My awareness of learning to love God has been continuous, but knowing the love He has for me truly has been the adventure in this journey of life. Through His salvation and grace, I have learned He is always with me.

For a period of my early childhood, my family lived in Houston. During that time, when I was 9, my father owned a juke joint there at the corner of West Montgomery in Acres Homes. On the same side of the street at the next corner was a small white steepled church. One Sunday morning I heard music coming from the church. It was louder than the music coming from the juke box, and I was drawn to it. When I arrived,

I realized I wasn't dressed for church, so I sat outside in the grass listening to the music of guitars, cymbals, drums and voices in praise of God. It was beautiful. While the services continued, I kept sitting and thinking about missing my church in Louisiana. After a while, the doors of the church opened, and tall beautiful black and brown women dressed in white blouses and skirts and white gloves and white shoes approached me with a glow of the sun and sky. They reminded me of angels. As they marveled over me, they started asking questions. "Where did you come from? Who are you? Why didn't you come in?" And then the "angels" began to pray over me and call on Jesus to protect me. They wanted to take me home, but I pleaded for them not to. I feared my father would get angry. By then, my father had started to physically abuse me.

At the time, the abuse continued, and my home life was getting worse. I began thinking of running away. The day I made my attempt to leave, God interceded. My mom shared that she was also unhappy and had been staying in her abusive marriage for her children. The next day we left for Louisiana for safety. Going back to Louisiana meant I could go back to Shiloh Missionary Baptist Church. It meant a return to Sunday School, Vacation Bible School, choir, testimony Sunday, and joy. Wanting to know God and knowing that He's with you and that you want to Be with Him is a testimony. Every time evil would come for me, God's salvation was always at hand. (Psalm 27: 1)

## In the Beginning Were Rhoda and Robert

In identifying the origin of my family, I utilized ancestry.com and stories told to me by my family. I chose to focus my interest on the women in my family and the stories they shared. The lineage of my Louisiana roots begins with my great-great grandparents, Rhoda Smith (b.1855) and her husband, Robert Smith (b.1854), both born in Louisiana, near Cotile (Boyce) in Rapides Parish. It appears the two met and married around 1873. Rhoda has been described to me as "half Indian". She was hard-working. Two girls were born to this union, Elizabeth (b.1876) and Rosa (b.1875). Rosa, the link to my lineage, was the eldest daughter of Rhoda and Robert.

On or about 1894, Rosa Smith met and married William Taylor (b.1874). After marrying, William and Rosa moved to Township 3 of the Chickasaw Indian Territory in Oklahoma and worked as farm laborers. William was identified in the Dawes Genealogy Records of the United States, claiming his rights to Indian land and compensation. This Indian slavery agreement compensation established by the United States recognized slave and free men's roles in the five tribes of the Indian nation. The Dawes commission was authorized by the United States Congress in 1893 to allocate land to tribe members and free persons for the dissolution of the reservation system, according to the Oklahoma Historical Society and Ancestry.com. Indian slaveowners were cruel and often inhumane to Blacks even though many married Blacks and had families together. While working as a farmer laborer in Indian territory in Oklahoma, Rosa had three miscarriages before giving birth to three children, Robert (1897), Isaiah (1901) and Azalee. Azalee was my grandmother, born April 21, 1903.

Between 1900 and 1910, there was prosperity within the Cherokee Nation, but things were about to change. The United States no longer wanted to recognize the sovereignty of the Indian territory. A campaign began to remove the land from the control of the Indian nation through land leasing, land grabbing by whites who lost land during the Civil War. Struggles occurred with attempts to assimilate the tribes with the establishment of Indian boarding schools and with the establishment of Oklahoma as a state on November 16, 1907. It was on or about 1910 when Rosa and William returned to Rapides Parish to escape the harsh treatment they experienced at the time.

Whites in Oklahoma envied the prosperity of the Indian nations and established Black townships such as Greenwood in Tulsa, which was destroyed by whites in 1921. Until recently, the June 1, 1921, tragic event there had been largely ignored and buried with the hundreds of souls lost, many whose bodies were unclaimable in the vicious attack. For the first time in its 100-year history, on June 1, 2021, the mass killings by whites that day in the all-Black community was brought to the forefront on the international stage by President Joe Biden. Though long overdue, the president visited the site of the crimes to honor the dead and officially commemorate the centennial.

In a speech on the hallowed grounds, the president solemnly and plainly said, "This was not a riot. This was a massacre."

I feel strongly that the segregation of Blacks and Native Americans made us prosper. Whites thought the isolation would keep us down because they believed they could restrict our resources. Envy turned into jealousy when we owned our own cars and dressed better than them. Robbery was at the forefront of the massacre. We are a resourceful people, and we can make what we need. When whites killed the hog for ham, they gave us the chitlin. When they killed the cow for steaks, we got the tail. My family saw the natives trying to hold on to what they had, and the anger of Blacks trying to share in it because the government said so was where things were going bad for my kin. So, they returned to their Rapides Parish home.

William began farming, and Rosa continued to grow the family, adding three more children with Ollie B. (b.1911), Adelia (b.1913) and Paul E. (b.1915). Shortly after the birth of Paul, Rosa died of consumption, tuberculosis (TB). She was 31 years old. After Rosa died, Azalee had just turned 12. When Azalee spoke about her mom, she shared her favorite memory from when she was 5, traveling on the train with Rosa. Before the train pulled in, her mom was coaching her to say she was 4. Five-year-olds had to buy a ticket. When the train pulled up, the Black porter looked at Azalee and told her how pretty she was in her beautiful coat dress. She was so excited to hear she was pretty, that when he asked her about her name, she said with pride, "My name is Azalee Sadonia Ann Juliet Taylor, and I'm 5 years old." Her mom's smile left her face, and in that moment the porter and her mom began to laugh. My grandmother was happy and proud on that day. The porter helped them both on the train. It was a beautiful day. "To this day I still miss my mom," my grandmother shared with tears in her eyes. When Rosa died the family got split up. Azalee's grandparents, Robert and Rhoda, took the younger three children: Ollie B. (4), Adalia (2), and Paul (6 months). Azalee, 12 at the time, and Isaiah, 14, stayed with their father, William, on the farm. Robert was on his own at 18.

Azalee Sadonia Ann Juliet Taylor, my grandmother, had a secret. She shared it with me when I was 20. She had been a victim of incest for which she later forgave her attacker. After the death of Rosa in 1915, six years later, Paul died of consumption, tuberculosis (TB). I never heard anyone speaking of him. He was listed in ancestry. com as being the last child of Rosa and William. I found no photo or obituary regarding Paul. After Rosa's death, Azalee and Isaiah worked on the farm with their dad, William, who began to use his middle name, Shedrick, according to the 1940 census.

Azalee would often visit her grandparents, Rhoda and Robert, to play and help out with her younger siblings. Rhoda taught Azalee how to crochet, mend and sew to help pass the time. She developed her skills, and they came in handy when she worked as a washer woman. In the summer of her 16th year, Azalee met her husband, William Belvin. William was born in Boyce, Louisiana, on March 26, 1895. He served in the United States Army in World War I. He served in Company D of the 524th Engineer Division. Upon his return home, he met a skinny dark-skinned Black girl named Azalee. The story of how they met was a common story for girls in her day, seeking freedom from their families. You had to be married to leave home.

This is my grandmother's story. She was hanging laundry when she saw William. She ran up to the top of the road and watched him pass. She did not say anything to him because she was shy. After William passed by, Azalee, would run back down the hill to finish the laundry. Later that week, she saw him pass again. William was tall and fair skinned, handsome according to my grandmother. After a few more spying adventures, William finally asked her name. It was after that they began to talk. She learned he passed by every day on his way to his job at the sawmill. They started meeting and seeing each other on top of the road every day.

Then one day, he asked her out for a date, but she did not have anything to wear, so he gave her some money to buy her a dress. Later that day, her father saw her with the money and took it away from her. She didn't know how she was going to tell William what happened. The day of their date, she met William at the top of the road, crying, sad and ashamed, and she told him what happened. On the following week, William went to meet Azalee's dad and asked him if he could marry Azalee. Her dad said no. "I need that gal to help me bring in the cotton," Azalee's dad explained to William. After several days of negotiating, an agreement was made. William and Azalee were married in 1920. To this union, seven children were born. The first to arrive was Dewitt (1922), Nathanael (1924), Gladys (1926), Cleophas (1928), twin girls, Rosa Lee and Ruth Lee (1930), and Annie Mae (1935).

After several successful years at the sawmill, The Great Depression caused the mill to close. William was no longer able to work in Boyce, so he took the family to Alexandria to live. They moved to a home off Lower Third on Leonard Street. Azalee began to work as a domestic or housekeeper for a prominent family. She added to her skills by becoming a beautician and a seamstress or dressmaker. To provide for the family, my grandmother planted vegetables, fig trees and peanuts in the yard to provide snacks for her children during The Great Depression. During the mid-1930s, President Franklin Roosevelt created the New Deal to change the jobless situation caused by The Depression. One of the programs was called the Civilian Conservation Corp. It operated from 1933 to 1942, putting unmarried men 17 to 28 to work in rural areas on roads, in forestry and service camps, etc. These men traveled across the country.

Many Black men boarded with Black families in the area. My grandmother boarded several men during this time. One of the young men was named Thomas Lee Williams, Jr. (1898). He was about 5 feet 6 inches tall, a small framed, dark-skinned man. My grandmother's story to me about Mr. Williams was that my grandfather took a liking to him because after he would come into the house after his government job, he would play with the kids and help my grandmother with chores. My grandfather convinced Tom to come back when the program ended. It took a while before my grandmother would agree to this gentlemen's agreement. On January 21, 1942, William Belvin died of an

*Residents of 1617 Applewhite Street*
*Azalee Belvin & Tom Williams*

aneurysm, and Tom Williams returned and remained with the family until his death in 1981. Mr. Williams was the only grandfather I knew.

When Tom returned after the death of William, Azalee decided to buy a home for the family. They moved to a big white house located on the corner of Applewhite and Seventh. Shortly after moving in, Nathaniel contracted the highly contagious tuberculosis from sharing cigarettes with friends. Nathaniel died the summer of 1943 at age 20. Shortly after Nate's death, Dewitt enlisted in the military and served in World War II. At 19, Cleophas went to work at the meatpacking company where he met and married Effie Joffrion on December 23, 1947. My mom, Annie Gladys, called Gladys, and nicknamed "Dot" and "Red" by her siblings, was 5'7" tall, slender and high yellow with black hair and brown eyes. She was "a looker." At 16, she was sent to Houston to help her Aunt Adellia care for her new baby. That is when Gladys' secret began.

## WHAT A LIFE IN HOUSTON, TEXAS

Gladys was viewed as quite shy, and very respectful. She had been taken away from her sisters and thrown into a world in Houston with cousins she did not know. The problem wasn't with her cousins, it was with her Aunt Adellia's husband, a man who fancied himself as good looking and a woman teaser. He was also a heavy drinker and somewhat abusive. He kept coming at Gladys in the absence of her aunt. After several failed attempts to return to Louisiana, she was given permission to live with her Aunt Ollie B. She had daughters.

While attending beauty college in Houston, my mom met my dad at the age of 17. Every day she would take the bus to and from school. One day at the bus stop, a young curly haired, dark-skinned college student appeared in a tailored suit and overcoat in July. Mom learned he was pledging Omega Psi Phi Fraternity at Texas Southern University, the historically Black college nearby. His name was Cornell Corles Giles. He was the youngest of six sons of George and Caroline Giles of Yoakum, Texas, and a veteran. No, it was not love at first sight for mom, but my dad was persistent. She was everything he wanted — a high yellow educated girl to take home to meet his color struck mom. Cornell and Gladys married in 1947. Shortly after, Gladys gave birth to a daughter, Rosalyn Giles, born July 1948. She died several hours later. The following year, another daughter, Kathlyn Renee Giles, was born December 23 to Gladys and Cornell. Nathanael Giles was stillborn in 1951. Darryl Patrick Giles was born May 1952, and Corles Andre Giles was born December 1954. The family was then complete with one girl and two boys.

*Dad and Mom*

When Cornell came home from the war, the G.I. Bill afforded veterans many opportunities. First and foremost, an education, and, the second, an opportunity to own a home. My father took advantage of it, all to the delight of my mother. However, on the delivery of the G.I. Bill to Black soldiers, many states in the South created Jim Crow rules to prevent them from getting their full benefits. After their service, many Black soldiers were disillusioned to find the South still showed them no respect. This

Kathlyn　　　Darryl

would impact my father and our family for many years. My father graduated from Texas Southern University with a degree in mathematics. He wanted to be an accountant, and when he applied for accounting jobs, companies were not hiring Negroes. The "boy" label frustrated my father. He was a man and wanted to be treated as one. He went to some of the finest restaurants in Houston seeking a position as head maître d, only again to be denied. He was told to go home and be a teacher and teach math to his own kind. That did not sit well with my dad. His older brothers did teach in high school and vocational schools.

Dad went to work for the United States Postal Service. My home in Houston, The Princess Palace, purchased by my dad, was a beautiful brand new three-bedroom brick home with a big kitchen and a big backyard with a swing set. It was a dream home in an up-and-coming neighborhood. All our neighbors were Black college educated or Black war veterans going to the nearby Texas Southern University. Our address was 3107 Webster Street in Houston's Third Ward. Our next-door neighbor was a college professor whose wife ran the daycare center on campus where I attended kindergarten. They were very kind to me, and I liked them. Mom was happy. She had a home she could be proud to show her mom, Azalee. She had set up Gladys Beauty Salon in the back. She had a thriving business and three beautiful children she could watch grow. One Easter when I turned 5, my grandmother and Mr. Williams came to Houston for a visit. My grandmother had made me a blue organza dress and my older brother Darryl a matching blue linen suit. My dad took lots of pictures that Easter. I felt like a princess.

By the time I was in third grade, my mom had been sending us back and forth to stay in Alexandria to protect my brothers and me from what was going on. Daddy began to change. He started spanking and slapping me and my mom. The year I entered fourth grade, things got worse. That year, Daddy decided to leave our beautiful home and Mom's business to open a juke joint in Acres Homes, an African American neighborhood northwest of Houston, and then unincorporated. He promised it would only be for a year. We traded my castle for a three-room, rat-infested shotgun house with no bathroom or running water. I looked and dressed like a pauper. I was not happy. My mom tried to keep us together, but eventually my baby brother was sent to live with my grandmother. By that time, Gladys had experienced a broken home, a lost career, abuse, declining health, and an unhappy daughter ready to leave and return to Alexandria to grandma's house.

Leaving my "family's palace" was heartbreaking, but dad offered the consolation prize, our first dog. We named her Queeny. She was a beautiful German shepherd. She had her own doghouse, but she was always chained. It was my responsibility to feed her and keep her area clean. She loved me, and one day she would prove how much. When that day came, a schoolmate decided she wanted to fight me after school. To avoid her, I went another way home. The girl knew where I lived, so she came to the joint. She came pushing and shoving me, and eventually shoved me to the ground and got on my back. We were rolling in front of Queeny. The dog barked and barked and barked until she broke her chain. She ran to me and was pulling the girl off me with her long sharp claws. She didn't bite her, but she scratched her up. My dad had to take Queeny to the country. That was the last time I saw my dog.

The juke joint was a success for my dad. He served beer, alcohol and barbecue, sausages, potato chips, and all kinds of hostess cupcakes. Banana Twinkies were my favorite. After a while, the food would make me sick, and I would throw up all the time. Dad thought I was pregnant at 10. It turned out I was anemic due to poor nutrition. When I was a princess, I was happy. Dad remembered me being talkative and laughing, but now no more. Sadness had quieted me. The people in the joint scared me. They were loud, ugly and smelled of sweet alcohol. I was really frightened of one man, Mr. Jones. He would walk up and down the street cursing while sweat poured down his face. He was angry. He would often stop in the joint, stand and watch the patrons. I would hide from him. One day Dad told me to get a tall glass of water and give it to him. I was so scared the glass shook in my hand. And, then, he spoke to me in a soft low toned voice, smiled at me and said, "Thank you, honey". I lost all my fears in that moment. I asked my dad later, why he was always cursing and looking crazy. He told me Mr. Jones lost his wife and family in a fire when he was at work and that he was more sad than mad and that kind of loss can make a man crazy. He told me to try not to judge him because you cannot always judge a man by looking at the cover. He told me not to be afraid of people I don't know. We are all strangers until we get to know each other. Lesson learned.

## WISHING UPON A STAR

When I was 10, I kept dreaming of fleeing my abusive father and his alcoholic environment that frightened me. I remembered that one day a man touched my hair in a way that frightened me, when another man told him, "Don't touch that girl. That's Giles' daughter. Her daddy is crazy, and he will kill you." The man apologized and left the joint. I realized I wasn't the only one afraid of Dad. Mom was, too. Then one

Saturday in a ruckus occurring outside the joint, a man was beating his wife. At first, all the men stood and watched, but my dad ran out with his gun and broke it up. The bloody woman was crying and screaming, "Why? Why?" as they picked her up and put her in a car to take her to the hospital. Then I heard a man say, "that n———r is jealous as hell," and I realized I had to learn the meaning of that word. *(JEALOUS: envy of someone, fiercely protective of possessions, unfaithful.)*

Working around the joint was hard, cleaning and stocking and peeling potatoes. I had fun when I would sneak away with my friends to see the Saturday night shows that would set up their traveling performances on flatbeds to entertain audiences. I got a chance to see Pigmeat Markham and other artists passing through. After their performances, they would go to my dad's place to eat, drink and dance. The joint was popular, and then came a problem my dad did not see coming, the police payoffs. Big white cops would walk in and want a piece of the action.

Because Dad saw himself as a man and not a boy, it was a challenge to get away from the intimidation of whites. Dad became angrier when he felt he was disrespected. Soon he started gambling and losing. The violence picked up, and at that time I had to leave. I just had to figure out when. The day I made my attempt to run away, God interceded. I almost got hit by a car, and the man driving swerved and shouted he was going to tell my dad. I ran and hid in Queeny's old doghouse. That evening, they were calling for me, but I didn't answer. Then my mom started crying, so I revealed myself to her. I told her I was unhappy and scared all the time. She said she wanted to leave, too. She did not want to take me from my dad, but if I wanted to leave, she would take me. We left the next day.

## HOME SWEET HOME (AGAIN), AT LAST

I loved it when I arrived at my grandmother's house at 617 Applewhite Street. I arrived with feelings of safety and sadness after leaving my abusive father in the dead of night because traveling at night was the safest way to travel from Texas to Louisiana. I was only 10 when I knew leaving my father meant that my family would no longer be the same. My mom was returning home to Azalee, her mom, with three children and little else. Her friend dropped us off and returned to Houston the next evening.

I have a distinct memory of the house. There were four doors exiting the home — two on the front porch and two exiting to the back porch from the bathroom and living room. At each entrance to the home was a photo of Jesus Christ praying. This was to bless those who were coming and going from the home. (Psalm 121: 8). Inside of the house, there were four big rooms, two served as bedrooms with two queen sized beds in each room. In the front bedroom stood two large chifforobes near a door that led to the front porch. It was Mr. Williams' room, and we slept in a bed across from him. The second bedroom was near the kitchen where my grandmother slept, and my mother slept in the bed across from her. There was a large living room. The kitchen had two big windows that looked on to Seventh Street and onto a fig tree and small garden full of peanut flowers. Azalee, my grandmother, sat in her favorite chair, looking out the window and drinking her coffee every morning; there is nothing like the smell of fresh brewed Community Coffee. Off from the kitchen, was the bathroom Uncle Buddy built. It also served as the laundry room on wash days. A door from the bathroom led out to the back porch and into the fenced in yard. In the yard stood a big pecan tree that would become my hiding place and my sanctuary for my talks with Jesus. Mama said Jesus knows all about me, and I can tell Him all about my troubles, and I did.

A few days after we arrived, my grandmother went to work purchasing three bolts of fabric from the Woolworth's Department Store. When the next day came, after a bath and washing and braiding of my hair, my grandmother had sewn me beautiful pajamas, a robe, two short sets and a dress. New clothes for a new me. Clothes made for a princess. In the fall, I enrolled back into Peabody Elementary. Happy! I even got a chance to teach the third-grade class, reading stories to them until they could find a substitute teacher. I felt special that they chose me. After a few months of settling in, my mom went to work filing for divorce. She worked several jobs to make ends meet, including working as a maid.

When the movie, *The Help*, came out in 2011, I was drawn to it, recalling a time in my life when my own mother was a maid. How did I forget? A few years after my mom left my abusive father, and her divorce was finalized, Mom went to work as a domestic worker for a white woman. I was 15. It was around that time that my mother also bought her own home for her family. We moved into our new place, down across the street from Grandmother's house on Applewhite, after staying briefly in Cousin Maggie's shotgun house on Douglas Street. For the first time since the move back, I had my own room. I was 16. Every morning, Mom would leave for work, and my brothers, and I would go to school. When we returned home, she was not there. She came home later. As she continued her position, she tried to explain to me she was working for a nice woman named Barbara Rogers. She had two daughters that often reminded her of me. Not knowing enough about her job, I would ask Mom to take me to work with her so I could help her. She said, "No. Kathy, you do not have the talent to be a maid. You are more like a decorator."

"I could be a maid," I pleaded. She told me that a maid can clean a house and leave everything in its place, but a decorator would decide that an item would look better somewhere else. The homeowner would not know what happened to her item and accuse you of stealing, and you would lose your job. She was right. I enjoyed making things, and decorating was in my blood. I changed my bedroom often. One time the bathroom was needing wall treatment, and I wall papered it with sheets of *Life* magazine that depicted the war in Vietnam. It was colorful and sad. Mom grew to appreciate the papered wall, as the cries of peace were being made to end the war the year I graduated.

My mom looked forward to payday and the weekend. Each payday she would stop at the drugstore or Woolworth on the way home to buy us gifts. Fridays were the days we looked forward to. But things changed. After several months of working, my mom became ill and was taken to the hospital. I was scared and angry. I blamed my mom's job as a maid. She worked hard and was tired a lot. I did not notice. She spent several weeks in the hospital. She returned home. The hospitalization led to the discovery of a heart condition known as mitral-valve insufficiency. From then on, my mom was bedridden.

## To High School with Love

*"Oh, we love dear old Peabody*
*that surrounds us here today...."*

We learned our school song in the first assembly our first year at Peabody in 10th grade. Those first two lines are true for me! I arrived at Peabody from Jones Street Junior High School in 1965, excited to finally be there. Peabody was really a big school to me at first, but the longer I was there the smaller it got. I was taken in by loving teachers who gave me 100 percent and above their attention. Their support gave me the confidence to be me. Peabody was such a caring and encouraging school. It promoted students' dreams and creativity. It provided opportunity within its walls and outside in the community. The school environment gave my fellow classmates and me the strength and courage to participate in the world that was changing around us. A world that gave us a voice. A world in which I was encouraged to speak and not be quiet. I became "Chatty Kathy." The true power of a Peabody High School education was in the mastery of our teachers who sought to invest in their students' success through love, compassion, challenges and thirst for lifelong learning.

Upon arriving at Peabody, I was recognized by my neighbor who lived down the block from my house, Ms. Hazel Harris, Peabody's school librarian. She immediately took an interest in my becoming a successful student at Peabody. Ms. Harris was small in stature, barely four feet tall. She knew a lot and encouraged my curiosity by teaching me the value of research. Ms. Harris' favorite quote, mirrored that of my Dad's: "Anything you want to know can be found in a book." The library became my second home. Ms. Edna Jones was my biology teacher and a feminist before I knew the term. Ms. Jones graduated from Leland College, Baker, Louisiana, and received her master's from Columbia University in New York City. She was a beautiful, stately woman who impressed upon her female students that a lady did not need a man to succeed. She encouraged me to look at my own capabilities to solve problems and make informed decisions. Ms. Jones encouraged me not to wait on the handsome prince for my rescue but to rely on my own abilities. In my earlier years, I thought Ms. Jones was wrong, but because her words stayed with me, I learned she was right.

Ms. Doretha Anderson, my thespian coach, showed me that my imagination could serve me in the future if I let positive thoughts play out. As a thespian, I enjoyed the competition of theatre, and I caught the acting bug during our state competition. In my senior year at Peabody, Ms. Anderson chose me to play the lead actress in our senior play, *Sidney, The Story of a Tomboy Finding Her Feminine Side.* I was acknowledged as best actress in our yearbook along with Vivian Johnson. Cicely Tyson was one of the first Black actresses I remember. Telling my mom that I wanted to be like Ms. Tyson was met with a strong "NO". Mom said, "It is not the life I want for you," so in my adult life I became a patron of the arts. I continued my love of theatre. Ms. Foccia, my Civics teacher, was another down-to-earth woman who encouraged me. She taught her students to stay current and interpret news for ourselves. I learned to love civics, politics and fighting for civil rights in the midst of our high school experience. The teachers living in my community, including Mrs. Raby and her twin sister, Mrs. Stewart, and every teacher that taught me in the three years I attended Peabody, left their threads of wisdom with me. Their teaching styles moved you to think your way through.

Knowing I had little to no money, poor was not a word we used to describe our circumstances. I knew I just did not have a lot. Families made choices. I learned the importance of choosing, commitment, and consequences. Not having all my desires met made selecting what I needed from what I wanted the key to the joy I experienced as a student. I was hungry for every experience Peabody offered, from the debate team to marching in the homecoming parade, being a booster to the cheerleading squad, to acting in school plays as a thespian and attending the Warhorse's homecoming game, to being a member of the homecoming court my junior year.

As I approached 16, music became my thing, and all the soul music groups were coming out, the Four Tops, Temptations, The Miracles. My friends Charles and Tiny and their brothers would gather and sing. We could only get Black music every evening after 9 from WLAC radio station out of Nashville, Tennessee, featuring DJs

John R and Billy "Hoss" Allen. I hosted a lot of house parties on the weekend under the watchful eye of my mom. We had good times. I kept my dating life under the radar because all of the guys were just good friends: Charles, James, Don, Duke, Billy, Ray, Michael, and G.D. The latter I married.

Everything about Peabody was transitional from school to community. As the Civil Rights Movement grew nationally, President Johnson implemented the Economic Opportunity Act that created the Neighborhood Youth Corp that expanded the opportunity for high school teenagers to work in 1964. During my junior and senior years, I worked for the program at Charity Hospital and the Louisiana State Hospital. I also joined the NAACP. I participated in Bayou Girl State, a leadership training program for girls held on Southern University's campus in Baton Rouge. In attempting to provide activities for youth in Alexandria, two interracial dances occurred at Wellan's Department Store downtown. The first dance went without any problems, but after the second dance, the attempt ended. I graduated from Peabody High School with honors in 1968. I left my mother, grandparents, brothers and friends. I left Alexandria and Peabody with the last verse of my school song in my heart.

"And we will not forget, though we be far, far away."

After leaving Peabody, I joined my father in Houston, Texas. Despite the difficulties my father and I had earlier, by the time I graduated from high school, he had become a much better human being. He had suffered many losses and transformed himself into the father I was proud to have. He and my Uncle Russell enrolled me at Texas Woman's University in Denton, TX the summer of 1968.

## COLLEGE GIRL, AND AGAIN, GOD'S PRESENCE

The weekend after my second semester in college, I returned home. I was 19. I wanted to go out with my friends. My mother gave me permission, some cash, and five nickels. Only one nickel was required to make a call from a pay phone. My mom requested that I call her every time I left one place and tell her where I was going next, and I agreed. My mom trusted me. Well, I thought I was cute. I wore a halter top with a matching skirt my grandmother had made for me. I can say it was fabulous. I looked so cute. That night someone from my church who was popular was paying attention to me. I couldn't believe it. I was naïve. He was a gentleman.

After spending some time with me, he excused himself. I saw him with a few of his homeboys. They were looking in my direction. I thought he was showing me off. (Another naïve thought.) When he returned, he bought me a coke. Mom's home training reminded me never to drink from a glass you did not get yourself when you go out. I thanked him and finished the coke I already had. (Rule followed.) As the evening wore down, further conversation led my church friend to ask if he could take me home. (Mom's rule: Remember, go home with the person you came with.) (Didn't follow that rule.) I trusted him. We grew up in church together. (Naïve!)

Upon leaving, I could not find the payphone. But he was taking me home, and my friends knew. (Mom's request not followed.) As we were driving off, he said, "Look, let me stop at my house. I want to give you something." I said OK. He said it was on the way home and said he would not be but a minute. Arriving at his home, he invited me in through the garage entrance of his home. As I waited on the couch in a room with the view of the kitchen, I could hear him looking for whatever it was, and in that same moment I heard a car pull up. Coming through the door were the same guys my church member had been talking to at the party. Before I could panic, I could hear my church friend calling me to the front of the house away from the guys who entered without invitation. As I rose from the couch, the guys began to partake in the cannabis that was conveniently placed on the coffee table as an invitation to try some.

On entering the room, my friend quickly closed the door behind me, swinging me against the wall and making it apparent to me, as he snatched away my halter top, that he wanted me. He had no gift, only the gift of rape. Pinned to the wall and considering my fate, I suddenly found myself silent and consulting my brain. What do you do now? What can you do? Who can you call to help?

I called on the only One I could, I called on Jesus. As I began to pray, I prayed for God's intervention, and I prayed for my friend who was now my attacker. I continued praying out loud and just like Daniel in the lion's den, the hunger went out of the beast. The beast began to declare his sorrow, clothed me and began to plot our escape. When we entered his car, the sound of the car starting awakened the other beast to give chase to no avail. My journey home with my church friend was silent except for his constant plea to me not to tell my mom. Arriving home, we both entered, and the courteous church boy gave his salutation to my mom and left. I never told Mom, but I thanked my Lord and Savior.

Yes, there have been numerous times living this life that God has saved me. He has saved me from bad relationships, snowy spinouts and near accidents, unbearable pain both physical and mental, deception, cancer scares, and other dangers seen and unseen. There have been times I have felt unworthy of His wonderful love, but He has let me know He still loves me. " I am a child of the King.

*My children*

After high school and college, I had kept in touch with several Peabody classmates, including G.D. He was attending Southern University in Baton Rouge, Louisiana. After his graduation from Southern, we married in 1973. After four years of marriage, I gave birth to a daughter the day after Mother's Day in 1977. A

C-section was performed, and after I became critically ill with toxemia. During my hospitalization, Pastor Luis Henry Evin and his deacons of Christ Temple Church in St. Paul, Minnesota surrounded my bed and prayed for me. (Prayers Answered) My grandmother, hearing how sick I was, sent my aunt from Texas to see about me in Minneapolis. She also sent my brother from Louisiana and my cousin from New York. They stayed with me until I recovered. I was surrounded by love and grace. Three years later, I gave natural childbirth to our second daughter, and in 1988, I legally adopted my godson. At the beginning of 1990, my family was complete.

## INDEPENDENCE AND RACISM AWARENESS

I guess I was unaware of the implications of racism at first because I lived in an all-Black community that never mentioned being Black was an issue. Everybody in the family looked different, black, brown, red, light, and damn near white. I had an aunt that was so black they called her black girl, an uncle so white he passed for a white man, while we lived in the Black community. And, my mama was considered "light too scared to pass" when she was young and wanting to see a movie. One popular expression used in particular in the Black community regarding skin color remains branded in my mind: "Black get back, to brown stick around, to light just right." Living in an all-Black community, I was aware of color preferences because black people came in all shades, and some people liked people because of the shades of their skin. Within family, though, you were just accepted.

The juke joint period, however, fortified my courage about dealing with people of all colors, and Psalms 27:1 took away my fears. I began taking risks with saying what I thought. In our community, white people entered the Black community. They were not our neighbors. They entered to sell us something, buy from us or intimidate us. One day, after coming back to Louisiana, changed, I did not fear white people, and I would prove it to my grandmother, Azalee. During my visit, a young white man, about 20 or 30, got out of his car and asked if Azalee was home? He had come to collect on her life insurance. Upon hearing him address her in that manner, I approached the door and told him that Azalea was not in, but Mrs. Belvin was home. As my grandmother emerged from her bedroom with her change purse ready to pay her $12, she invited Mr. "Unable to Remember His Name" in. As they both sat for their transaction, Mr. U.R.N. slipped again and called her Azalee. I again reminded him that he was in the home of Mrs. Belvin and to address her by her first name was disrespectful. Then, my grandmother told me to go sit down "child", as I stood in his face looking wild and unpredictable. The next time he returned, he asked my grandmother was I there, and I appeared, as he addressed her as "Mrs. Belvin". After he left my grandmother said, "You cannot talk to white folks like that. You got to go up North to do that."

The older I became, and the more trips I took outside of my community, the more awareness I gained about racism. I first noticed practices of discrimination at 16 when I started the job in the Neighborhood Youth Corp program as a nurse assistant at the Charity Hospital in Pineville. My first day of new hire orientation, I noticed the white assistants had their surnames on their badges, and all the Black people had only first names on theirs. When my badge was being created, I told the writer my name was Giles. She asked me my first name. I reconfirmed that Giles was my first and last name. Yes, I saw "Colored Only", signs, but they often confused me. One day I challenged its purpose. Before entering the grounds of the hospital, a long rectangular building stood out front. It was a restaurant and waiting area. It had two doors, one labeled "Whites" and the other, "Colored". The room was divided by a short partition where you could see both sides of the waiting area. I decided to enter the whites only side and walked up to the service counter to order. I asked for service. The man said I was on the wrong side, and if I wanted to be served, I needed to be on the colored side. I explained I did not understand. When the food is coming from the same kitchen, and the price is the same, why not serve me? The man threatened to call the police while the Black patrons coaxed me to come to the colored side where I belonged. They accepted it, I questioned it, and I never entered the building again. It was clearer that there were barriers and separations and discrimination.

Entering college in fall 1968 at predominantly white Texas Woman's University, located about 30 miles north of Dallas, had its flashpoint. The Ku Klux Klan entered the freshman dormitory row at TWU in a pickup truck and fired buck shots into the area of the campus where Black girls were lodging. I was one of them. Racial intimidation. The discriminatory practice that affected me most was the one involving the loss of my mother. Her illness had become an even greater concern for me by the time I left home. She and I talked every day about her symptoms. She had arranged to see the doctor Friday, November 8. However, on that day she became so ill, she called her sister for assistance. Upon arriving, my aunt called for an ambulance, 15 minutes later the police arrived and found my mom in distress. Thirty minutes later, the ambulance came, and my mom was non-responsive. The police stated that they didn't send an ambulance to the Black community until it was OK'd by officers on site. Critical loss of time led to the loss of life. Discriminatory practices. I was angry.

I remembered my grandmother often saying I needed to go North because she feared my mouth would get me into trouble in Louisiana. In September of 1973, following my marriage, I went North to Minneapolis, Minnesota. I experienced "Minnesota nice", a term I soon associated with the words of the OJ's song from 1972: "They're smiling in your face, all the time trying to take your place, the backstabbers." I also learned the difference between talking nice and telling the truth. Motto: "Damn what they say, watch what they do". I have learned you can never forget who you are. Black. No matter what shade you are. If you forget, a form of schizophrenia can change your reality.

(Read: *The Rage of a Black Middle Class* by Ellis Code, 1993.) In a Black woman's world, I have survived segregation. I must learn about the games of discrimination, Jim Crow, the law, the reality, the fantasy, the dream, the power of prayer, anger or madness, calmness, stupidity, bitter or sweet, ache or pain, love or lust, an associate or friend, different are unique, real or fake, trust or must, do or die, mind or mine, tiny or big, fat or thick, gay or happy, straight or crooked, hit or miss, Colored or white, brown or light, faith and forgiveness. Racism unpacked. In a black woman's world, confusion is a mystery to my dimensions. "Ain't I a Woman" (Sojourner Truth), "I Am a Phenomenal Woman" (Maya Angelou).

## ADVOCATE FOR NONVIOLENCE

In reviewing my life's work, I realize that the abuse and violence I experienced in my life shaped my career path. For the last 40 years, I have been an advocate for ending violence in the lives of women and children.

In the early 1970s, the women's liberation movement gave rise to the battered women's movement. Shortly after I arrived in Minnesota in 1973, I was introduced to several Black women looking for volunteers to work at a women's help center called Chrysalis. I was a phone advocate. It was during my time there that I received valuable training in helping victims of sexual assault, domestic violence, and drug assessments. The training and skills were limited, working with a few women of color in the beginning, but as the need grew, so did Chrysalis outreach and services. I was able to expand my training to include children of alcohol and drug-addicted parents.

In 1977, Minnesota became the first state to legislate funding to battered women's shelters. The bill was introduced by State Senator B Robert Lewis and State House Representative Phyllis Kahn. In the late 1970s, I joined with women of color, as we organized for better representation in the battered women's movement and more resources in the community. In the mid-1980s Black Indian Hispanic Asian (BIHA) Women in Action was initiated. I became the first Black woman director of the State Coalition of Battered Women Services, 1986-1987, and Chris Sam was named the first Native American president of its board. This was the time I embraced my feminist side to advocate for justice for women and children.

This also was the time prejudices and racism entered the script of ending violence and sexual assault in the lives of women of color. Racial stereotyping began to affect advocate services and how women of color were viewed by whites. White women continue to be unable to answer Sojourner Truth's question, "Ain't I a woman?" The board began to initiate racial awareness training for all women's shelters and services. Racial awareness training was the beginning of change, but it was not enough. In the third year of my leadership, violence came in the form of Black-on-Black crime. It had me asking does Black life matter?

Do Black Lives Matter?

In the summer of 1988, I was planning BIHA workshops on racism in shelters. Our keynote speaker was Angela Davis. In late July, my brother Darryl called to say his children were spending the summer with him, and he was sending his oldest son to attend a basketball camp I had been bragging about. My nephew was due the first week in August. On my nephew's arrival, the girls and I were so excited that we took him shopping for the supplies he needed for camp. On the day before he was headed to camp, my father called to say my brother had been shot and taken to the hospital in San Antonio, Texas. Dazed and confused at the news and how to tell my 15-year-old nephew who was full of anticipation to attend camp that his father had been shot was difficult. After hearing the news, my nephew cried and pleaded to go home. We left the next day.

Upon arriving at the hospital, I found my dad consoling my brother's family, as a decision was confronting them to relieve him of life support. As I witnessed him lying there, the boy I grew up with, danced with, and dreamed with was lifeless and non-responsive to my pleas to wake up. I could not accept that a 38 bullet had taken him away from me. Listening to my father describe the violent incident that brought us there was unimaginable:

*Two boys from Curero, Texas, stopped at your brother's job and was trying to harass him, but your brother ignored them, and they left. Later on, in the evening your brother stopped off to catch a beer and a pickup pool game before going home. One of the men got into an altercation with your dad and a gun was discharged, hitting a patron, and your dad tried to keep him from leaving before the police arrived* (noting my brother was once a bouncer and security guard in the local Minnesota bar scene.) *While detaining him in a headlock in the bathroom, the second brother entered. The detained brother shouted, "Shoot the nigger, shoot the nigger!" And he did. The two men fled and were later arrested and blamed my brother. Within the 72 hours that I left Minnesota with hope, my brother was dead and five children were without a father, and I was without my brother, and my dad was without his son. Senselessness, jealousy, envy and wrongdoing. We buried my brother in August of 1988 at the age of 37.*

In light of continuous senseless deaths by police at the forefront of this new movement and having participated in "stop the violence" and "take back the night", I continue to struggle with Black-on-Black crime, recognizing it is a crime of opportunity and proximity, but I do ask Black people, "*Do* Black lives matter?" Then, stop killing our own and police our own and say something. What are we waiting on? We are killing our own at a higher rate than the white population. We are killing our wives, our children and our own brothers "as Cain and Abel" testament.

In 2018, a national report was released, stating that offenders were the same race as the victim 70 percent of the time for Blacks and 62 percent for whites. This statistic for me is awareness that I lived with the loss of my brother. We have a problem that cannot be ignored in our communities because we want to rid ourselves of the wolves (police) in sheep clothing who have perpetrated lawlessness for generations. When George Floyd died, we made noise, but when a young mother sitting in her car was shot and killed, it was barely mentioned. I want to continue this fight for justice in all unnecessary killings. We are being attacked violently from the outside and within, and all attempts to silence our voices should be met by screams of "Stop the Violence" because BLACK LIVES DO MATTER.

Today, I teach and speak up; fear is not an option.

The sorrows in my life have been balanced by the joys. Sorrows came with the passing of my grandparents Azalee (1979) and Mr. William (1981); parents, Mom (1974) and Dad (1989); and my brother, Darryl (1988). Joy has been found in the graduations and marriages of my daughters and son, and the birth of my grands, and numerous family celebrations. I am grateful to Jesus for teaching me how to build family from the villages in which I travel, live, and grow. As Jesus continues to guide my path, I am grateful for the love I have found in family and friends. I am grateful for their presence and investment made in me and mine. As I continue my journey with Christ, I am thankful for His promises and assurance that I am a "Child of the King". Thank you all. Glory to God.

# NAVIGATING AND SURVIVING PREJUDICE AND INJUSTICE TO GROW INTO A PROUD BLACK MAN

*"We must accept finite disappointment, but never lose infinite hope."*

THE REVEREND DR. MARTIN LUTHER KING, JR.

## James Goff

*Black men in Vietnam formed a bond like no other I have witnessed. We greeted each other with a special handshake called "DAP," which stands for "Dignity and Pride." The DAP handshake represented the pact that we Black Vietnam soldiers made to commit to looking out for each other.*

I WAS BORN AT Huey P. Long Charity Hospital in Pineville, Louisiana, on October 27, 1950; however, our family residence was in Alexandria. During my time in Alexandria, we lived in three different sections of town: Woodside, Sam Town and Sonja Quarters. I am the youngest of six children (three sisters and two brothers).

I remember attending what was called "kindergarten" in the homes of Mrs. Atkins in Sam Town, Mrs. Simon on Houston Street, and Mrs. Johnson on Overton Street, before starting first grade in public school at South Alexandria Elementary. While in the first grade, I voluntarily participated in the Louisiana Interscholastic Athletic and Literary Association (LIALO) State competition. Although the LIALO, which was established in 1928, was focused primarily on sports, the goal of the organization was to help African American students in secondary schools achieve success. Each year, LIALO sponsored an academic competition at Southern University in Baton Rouge for students from Louisiana's African American (colored) schools. I, along with a classmate, took the test in mathematics which consisted of addition and subtraction of multiple columns of numbers along with some multiplication and division problems. The first time I participated in this competition, I wasn't even aware that it was a Statewide competition; nevertheless, I didn't get one problem correct. The test was way too advanced for my knowledge. Thankfully, this would not be my last competition, and it was the beginning of my determination to excel in mathematics.

Around 1959, two junior high schools, Jones Street and Lincoln Road, were built and opened for Black students in grades seven through nine. I attended Lincoln Road Jr. High from 1962 to 1965. There, I continued my love for mathematics and was introduced to Algebra in the ninth grade. In 1965, my ninth-grade year, I once again was selected to compete in the LIALO competition, taking the test in Algebra, but I did not qualify at the District level to compete at State. After graduating from junior high school, I attended Peabody Senior High, where, during my senior year, I once again participated in the LIALO competition, this time in Advanced Mathematics, and there was a very different outcome. At the District level, I finished second and, thus, qualified to go to Southern University to compete at the State level. At State, I tied for third place. In addition to my love for mathematics, I had also been working to learn skills in bricklaying since I was 12 years old. While at Southern University for the LIALO math competition, I was offered the opportunity to compete in the bricklaying competition. Without any formal classroom training, I was able to finish in second place in this event at the State level.

During the years, I remember following the news of the Civil Rights Movement, and two events from that time really stood out for me. The first was local, the second, national. The first occurred in 1962 in Poland, LA, a small rural community outside Alexandria. A young Black teenager named David L. Dunbar, who attended my stepfather's church, was accused of robbing and raping a 66-year-old white woman in Poland. While he was in the Alexandria city jail awaiting trial, my stepfather visited him to administer communion and prayer. In May 1963, the Ku Klux Klan (KKK) burned crosses at the church and at the young man's aunt's home in Poland. It was believed, but never confirmed, that the KKK did a drive by at our home in the Sonia Quarters.

## Home of Dunbar Aunt Site of Cross-Burning

A cross was burned at 9 p. m. Friday in front of a house occupied by the aunt of David L. Dunbar Jr., a Negro on trial for his life on charges of aggravated rape.

Sheriff's deputies said a makeshift cross was constructed on property owned by Stafford Whatley and burned there, across from the house occupied by Nell Butler, Dunbar's aunt.

Negroes at the house said they saw three white men make the cross and set it on fire on Whatley's property on the old river road. Whatley called the sheriff's office.

John B. Honeycutt, chief sheriff's deputy, said a complete investigation would be made and anyone arrested would be charged.

*Alexandria Daily Town Talk, May 18, 1963*

Dunbar was convicted in May1963 after pleading guilty to rape in exchange for a life sentence in lieu of the death penalty. He was 15 at the time of the crime. In1984, he was still in prison.

As a result of current events, I'm often asked by friends who grew up in different areas of the country, how it was growing up in the South. I always respond with: "We knew our place." The David Dunbar incident was an example. I don't think it mattered to the KKK whether he was guilty or innocent. Black kid — white woman — he had to pay, and the KKK had to send a message. That's how it was. I knew at a young age how to respond, where to go and where not to go…i.e. I knew my place. I guess, as sad as it may seem, I just knew that this young man didn't stand a chance, and that taught me to try never being in a similar predicament.

The second vivid memory I have of the Civil Rights Movement was watching the marches in Birmingham and Montgomery, Alabama, led by The Rev. Dr. Martin L. King Jr. I remember seeing the police unleash dogs and spray water from fire hoses on peaceful Black marchers. It was a horrible scene to witness. In November 1966, Dr. King visited Alexandria and gave a speech at the Rapides Parish Coliseum. I don't remember who I went with or how I got to the coliseum that night, but I do remember being there and being inspired by his speech. He called upon everyone to be the best at their chosen endeavors. He said, "If you are going to be a street sweeper, let it be known that you were the best to ever have swept the streets."

Another vivid memory for me is the day I learned Dr. King had been assassinated: Thursday, April 4, 1968. I was returning home after getting a haircut around 6 p.m. I was dismayed to learn that Dr. King had been shot and killed in Memphis, Tennessee. I watched the news as riots broke out throughout the nation. Large cities like Los Angeles, Chicago, Washington, DC, Philadelphia, New York, and many more were burning out of control. Black folks were enraged with anger all over America. I remember walking to school the next morning and small snowflakes began to fall. I said to myself, "Snow in Alexandria in April - WOW." It was an unbelievable time.

In June of 1968, upon graduation from high school, five of my high school classmates and I were offered scholarships to attend Bishop College in Dallas, Texas.

Coming from the small town of Alexandria, I was amazed when I began meeting students from places such as Paris, China and Italy — but was really dumbfounded to find out these were cities in Texas. I wanted to pursue a degree in mathematics but was unsure of a specialization. Unfortunately for me, my focus and interest turned from the classroom to the Student Union, playing dominoes and bid whist, and I found myself dropping out of college after completing one year of college in 1969. That summer, my mother remarried and moved to Texas City, Texas.

I always said if I didn't make it through college, I would go into the U. S. Air Force. So, with the war in Vietnam at its peak, I thought it best to move on with my military plans. Of my six closest friends who had been raised together, one had volunteered for the U.S. Marine Corps and already served in Vietnam. Four others had also served in Vietnam after having been drafted into the U.S. Army. All had made it through the war and returned alive. Being a math minded individual, I realized the law of probability said the next one to go to Vietnam in the army would not make it back alive, and I had heard that there was a low probability of losing your life there if you were in the air force. Therefore, in February 1970, I visited the recruiting station in Houston, Texas to enlist in the air force. Upon completing the air force entry examination, I qualified with my highest score in electronics. However, I was told they had reached their quota for recruits for the next six months and there was a waiting period. Since I had lost my military deferment from the draft when I dropped out of

college, I did not have six months before the army would draft me. I returned to Alexandria to live with my sister, and from the air force recruiting station there was able to join in six weeks. I enlisted and was inducted in April 1970.

I arrived at Lackland AFB, San Antonio, Texas, to begin Basic Training. This was my first experience staying with so many white guys. It was really a different environment from the segregated South I had been raised in. It was like a protected environment where everyone was treated equally, and we all wondered what our lives would be like after completion of training. I soon found out that I was assigned to technical training at Shepard AFB in Wichita Falls, Texas. This would be the beginning of my career as a telecommunications operator.

After completion of tech school, my first duty station (along with five of my classmates) was in Saigon, Vietnam. The one-year assignment in a warzone was quite an experience. My job as a telecommunications operator was to provide messages to the men and women fighting throughout that country. I worked side-by-side with whites and stayed in open-bay barracks. We called each other by first name or by rank and last name. I did not experience racial tension during this assignment. Saigon was pretty much a safe area, serving as a rest and recuperation center for many soldiers and marines.

The number of Blacks serving in Vietnam was far more than the 12 percent that populated America. We congregated outside the workplace — gathering at the Non-Commissioned Officer (NCO) and Airman Clubs during nonduty hours to socialize, playing cards and dominoes. I met young Black men from around the United States, fighting and dying for a country to obtain freedom that we ourselves didn't enjoy back home. Black men in Vietnam formed a bond like no other I have witnessed. We greeted each other with a special handshake called "DAP," which stands for "Dignity and Pride." The DAP handshake represented the pact that we Black Vietnam soldiers made to commit to looking out for each other. The movements of the handshake translate to, "I'm not above you, you're not above me, we're side by side, we're together." The DAP provided a symbol of solidarity and served as a substitute for the Black Power salute prohibited by the military. It is still used today to symbolize solidarity.

When my tour in Vietnam was over in October 1971, I was assigned to McChord AFB in Tacoma, Washington. Upon my return to the States, I got married in Houston, TX, then headed west to Washington state. This was a new experience for me. I was now in a new city where I did not know anyone. On the second day in Tacoma, my wife and I were driving back to the AFB when I noticed a Black guy walking across a bridge holding hands with a white woman. I was completely in shock. This behavior was unheard of in Louisiana. I became frightened thinking there was going to be a shooting, and I did not want to get caught up in the gunfire. It took me a while before I was comfortable with the fact that I was no longer in the segregated South. Tacoma was a beautiful city with no ugly slum areas. Even though racism wasn't as prevalent on base as it was in the community, racism was still evident, and there was still plenty of need for concern.

In the early '70s, the air force initiated a program called Race Relations. This classroom training was mandatory for all air force members. Its main purpose was to try to help whites and Blacks understand and accept each other. The classroom was mixed with students of all races. I remember one day in class a beautiful young Black female was seated between me and a young white guy. The instructor asked the young lady if she would go out with the guy next to her. She turned and looked at me and sighed, "probably." The instructor said not him, the white guy. She said, "Heck no." When asked why, her response was, "Because he's white." The instructor then asked the white guy if he would take the young lady out on a date. His response was, "I guess not." When asked, "Why not?" His response was, "She won't let me." The class laughed out loud. The Race Relations program was soon expanded to a new department called Social Actions, which also included classes in Drug and Alcohol Abuse and Sexual Harassment training.

By 1984, I had been reassigned to the Pentagon in Washington. I had moved up in rank and been selected to attend the NCO Academy in Biloxi, Mississippi. While driving through Alabama on Interstate 65 South, I was listening to the citizen band (CB) radio. I heard that a recreational vehicle (RV) had run out of gas at a mile marker a couple of miles ahead of me. It wasn't long before I passed the RV on the side of the interstate. About a mile beyond the RV, I saw a white woman walking with a gas can in her hand. It was obvious that she was from the RV walking to get gas. As I slowed down to give her a ride to a gas station a thought went through my head, "White woman, Alabama, I don't think so." Needless to say, I kept going without rendering assistance. I often think about that incident knowing I should have helped. However, I still vividly remembered how many Black men in the South had been killed for even looking at a white woman.

I retired from the air force in May 1994 and took a job working as a telecommunications center operator for the federal government at the Department of the Treasury. Basically, I was doing what I had been trained to do during my early years in the air force. The communications center staff was 95 percent Black. After four years, I joined the Secretarial Support Team. Our mission was to provide communications support to the Treasury Secretary and the Executive Staff when they were on travel overseas. The executive staff and advance teams were comprised mostly of young white political appointee personnel. This was an amazing assignment, as I got to travel to many countries for 10 to 12 days at a time. I traveled with the teams, taking trips to Africa, including Maputo, Mozambique, Abuja, Nigeria, and Kampala, Uganda. After we returned from one trip to Mozambique, Congresswoman Maxine Waters heard that a large delegation from the Department of Treasury had traveled to an African nation with only two Black employees on the trip. She raised a big flack about this, so on the next trip to Abuja, Nigeria, the Treasury tried to get any Black employee who wanted to go included on the trip.

In 2002, I left the Secretarial Support team to join the Office of Intelligence and Support (OIS) as a Facility Security Officer. My responsibility was to maintain security for a highly classified facility. In 2004, OIS was dissolved into a new organization called Office of Intelligence and Analysis (OIA). By 2016, OIA had expanded its mission and personnel, and the number of security facilities grew to 27. I oversaw the construction and management of all these facilities. The communication skills I obtained in the air force helped me achieve a successful career at the Department of the Treasury. I articulated tasks so that all staff, no matter the ethnicity, understood the goals. I retired from Treasury in June 2017 as Director of Special Security Programs.

As our country prepares to enter a new administration, we are still experiencing blatant racism. Racism has just taken a different form. Donald Trump has brought it out in the open. White folks still don't understand why Black folks are angry with all the killings of African Americans by police officers and the lack of accountability for the killings. Everyone knows that had the January 6, 2021, deadly events been led by members of Black Lives Matter or any Black organization, the response and the results would have been a lot different.

In the words of D.L. Hughley: "All these people getting arrested and losing their jobs for storming the Capitol building are realizing why their grandparents wore hoods."

# MY GRAND ADVENTURE

*"And I will sail my vessel,*
*Till the river runs dry.*
*Like a bird upon the wind,*
*These waters are my sky.*
*I'll never reach my destination*
*If I never try,*
*So I will sail my vessel,*
*Till the river runs dry."*

GARTH BROOKS

## Phyllis Hamilton Venable

S INCE LEAVING ALEXANDRIA in 1968 for Southern University in Baton Rouge, I have lived in New York City, Richmond, VA, Dallas, TX and back to Alexandria. Yes, I have come full circle and been on a grand adventure that has provided me a range of experiences that led me back home where it all started for me with a loving mother.

My mother, Ruby Boatwright McGago, was born in Abbeville, Alabama in 1923. She was third of 17 children. She had a fair complexion, what we would call "high yellow" in the South, and straight black hair. My sister and I, her only two children, did not look like our mother. We were quite the opposite and consistently disrespected by white people. When my mother took us out, whites constantly looked at us and would demand to know if we were really my mother's biological children. My mother did not miss a beat and would proudly tell them, "We are family." With that, my mother will always be my hero.

*"When I look at my generation, we were determined to change our way of life. I will not give up hope (for this generation), and I will continue to talk to them and tell them about our struggles."*

*My grandparents and mom as the youngest child, 1923 or 1924*

*My mom, my sister, and me*

In the mid-1940s, my mother was accepted to the Tuskegee Institute in Alabama and graduated with a double major in Elementary Education and Home Economics. Throughout my childhood, she would share her experiences with me. Many decades later, those stories of discrimination are simply still too painful for me to discuss. One high point, though, was when she attended Tuskegee. The esteemed Booker T. Washington was the president of the college, and the legendary scientist George Washington Carver was heading up the science department. How cool is that?! She always talked about their intellect and accessibility. After graduation in the late 1940s, she accepted a job at Peabody Negro School, later renamed Peabody Elementary. Despite being college-educated, she still felt the harsh sting of racism and Jim Crow.

I started grade school during the 1950s, and, to be honest, my elementary and junior high school years are a blur. I do, however, remember the turbulent times of the 1960s. I vividly recall when President Kennedy was assassinated. I was sad over this because it was probably the first white man that I could remember who appeared to want to help Black people. In 1966, my mother thought it would be a good idea for us to see Dr. Martin Luther King Jr. when he visited Alexandria, and that was definitely the experience of a lifetime. He was a great orator, and he carried a powerful message of peace. I will never forget listening to him inspire our generation to keep working to dismantle racism in nonviolent ways.

*Four generations: Me, my sister, Momma Hattie (grandmother), holding my niece, Kim, and Mom*

In high school, we were exposed to the Black Panther Party. Their message was radical and not supportive of Dr. King's nonviolent approach to the ills that plagued us because of racism. I was introduced to the radical ideas of H. Rap Brown, Stokely Carmichael, and Angela Davis. They were great Black individuals who chose to speak out about our troubles and to let the world know we were injured and not happy in the world created for us by whites in America. My family chose Dr. King's philosophy.

My high school years were the best years of my life. This was a time when I had some idea of what I wanted to do with my life. Peabody was our pathway to adulthood and being on our own. I loved meeting others from the other side of town. I had attended Jones Street, and I did not know students from Lincoln Road. We all met up at Peabody as sophomores. Peabody High was a great school and provided many programs.

During high school, in addition to following political figures, I was part of the choir, a fun and rewarding experience. Mrs. Morrison, our choir instructor, demanded excellence, and we rose to her high expectations. She put in numerous hours with us individually and as a group to perform at the highest levels. We sang songs performed by Black college choirs. My favorite were Negro spirituals. Music was the only class I made straight A's in. Mrs. Morrison was so deep and intense; she made me learn music from its origin. To this day, I love music. That love and appreciation for music started at Peabody.

Peabody had the best teachers. We benefitted from their wisdom and experience. This caused us to grow up and get involved. They cared about us. I loved Peabody so much because it gave me the opportunity to increase my knowledge and to do something meaningful every day. It never deviated from its purpose of educating us no matter what — even when there were more than 30 students in a class. Its fabulous auditorium was built to hold graduations, drama productions, and other special ceremonies and activities. The building was airconditioned and had plenty of room for all the students and their family members. The food in our cafeteria was delicious, balanced, and prepared by women who lived in our community. As you can see, there are so many reasons to love and respect Peabody. It will forever hold a special place in my heart.

After completing high school, I attended Southern University, and that was an incredible experience. I was part of the campus protest for racial equality. Because I was so caught up in the political protests at school, my grades suffered, and the university suggested that I take a semester off to reset. Unfortunately, I never returned, and that was a decision I regret to this day. I never went back. What a mistake!

In 1971, with no degree in hand, but plenty of world experience, I headed for the job market in Alexandria. I applied to take the Civil Service test, but the supervisor, a white woman, told me for some strange reason that I needed to bring my very own typewriter. When I questioned this odd request, she simply ignored me. It was difficult searching for a job, so I became depressed. At least I didn't have to guess the number of jelly beans in a jar, as our people were asked to do in order to be eligible to vote, but, to me, the typewriter was as ridiculous a request.

At this point my sister, Patricia, who had previously moved to New York, invited me there. All I can say is New York was just "Wow"! There, I learned pretty quickly that you have to always be on high alert because the racists wore the sheets under their clothes. For the first time, I understood why my mom worked so hard to have us exposed to as much as possible. She was aware of hatred against Blacks and wanted us to be prepared.

In the big city, there were quite a few opportunities, and I found employment at a major bank the first week. Although I was in an entry-level position, I had a job making my own money. I later found an apartment and was enjoying my newly gained independence. After working a couple of years, I decided it was time to move up within the bank. I was hired for a position in the Commercial Loan Division, which was my first exposure to being the only Black in a workplace. As I moved and upgraded several more times, I got used to being the only Black person at the table. And, it was at this time, that I regretted not getting my degree. It became obvious that I needed my bachelor's degree to move up in the company. I resigned and was hired by American Express, and at that time, the company had a customer base of 35 million. I knew at that point there would be lots of jobs and training programs such as Dale Carnegie and others, and I took advantage of all of these programs. I can say that there were some ugly experiences with Bank & Trust that I did not experience at AMEX. All in all, I had a wonderful time in New York and later retired as a part of management.

New York was not all work. I took advantage of all that the city had to offer, especially events with an emphasis on Black performance: Broadway plays, ballets, various concert performances, not to mention attending large black churches and frequenting Black-owned restaurants. And most importantly, while in New York, I met my husband Rudolph Venable in 1971. He was a kind and gentle brother and knew so much about Black people and what was going on in the world. I had never met anyone quite like him. All I ever knew was to work and take care of myself. Living with a husband who was so "anti-system" exposed me to a different way of thinking and living. I never thought about my life and not having a job. I was impressed, and we married in 1985, and now we are going on 35-plus years together. Over 35 years of commitment and love is as grand as it gets.

In the early '90s, my husband and I made the journey back South, and our first stop was Richmond, Virginia. In Richmond, I had several jobs that did not pay what I was used to, and my husband, who was part of Local #1 Plumber's Union of New York, did not want to work. We moved from Richmond to Dallas where I reunited with my dad after 30 years. I found employment with the Army & Air Force Exchange Service. The work was interesting and gave me a peek into military operations. We supplied goods to the PX or BX, and we helped military men spend their money on good decisions. I'm happy to say that during this time, the treatment of Blacks was a little better, and the pay was decent. But all of management was white. And they had no shame in letting us know it would stay that way. The sting of racism has never left me.

My father had two shoe repair shops and gave my husband a job in his business. He finally found his perfect job after 30 years. This job allowed him not to be so *restricted* in the working world. The first part of my life in Dallas was very frustrating, however, I was determined to make my marriage work and make sense.

I thought we were getting better since we were both employed at the same time. Well, here we go again. My dad, for health reasons, closed his business, and my husband was a free spirit, again. I was taking care of us, but my salary was not enough. I was so upset, I decided not to work and to *experience* his world. We were not able to take care of ourselves and became homeless. I thought it couldn't get worse. Well, it did. We roamed the streets of Dallas and slept in a shelter. Life had no purpose but to stay alive.

In 2004, we got the news, that my mother was sick, so we packed our belongings and headed to Alexandria, the place of my birth. She suffered from the first stage of Alzheimer's. Wow, I was really being tested. Being homeless made it an easy decision to move back home to take care of my mother. I loved *her* so. It was hard to see the woman I know slowly withdraw. Some days she knew me, and some days she did not.

It's hard to write about this.

My husband played a great part in taking care of my mother. He'd cook her three meals a day and did all the grocery shopping and helped to take care of my mom when I had a moment. I finally found a new love for my husband. It was a pleasure for him to take care of my mom.

I had a purpose, and God's help guided me through the pain. Being with my mother also brought me a bit closer to my sister and her daughter, Kim. I am proud of them. My sister, Dr. Patricia Hamilton Martin, who entered Southern University as a freshman at the age of 15, graduated at 19 and moved to New York and earned a doctorate from New York University. She and Kim, a highly successful real estate agent, faced some of the same workforce issues as I did as a Black female but prevailed. Kim works tirelessly on behalf of Black people. Although she is a generation after me, her workplace experiences parallel mine in many ways, but good Southern Black girls learn from the generations that precede them. I am doubly grateful for how caring for my mother strengthened my relationship with my sister. I had a good mother. She was smart and deeply religious. She died peacefully in 2010.

Upon my return to Alexandria, I noticed a lot of neighborhoods had changed, and I didn't recognize any of the residents, so I decided to reintroduce myself. As I think about Lower Third and Main Street, I can honestly say "back in day," we had a good time. Even though it was segregated, we all knew each other and supported one another. When I looked at my old neighborhood, I saw our young men and some young girls whistling on the corners using drugs. This just broke my heart. Back in our day, we were biking, skating, playing dodge ball and stickball. We had a great time. We did not need drugs to have fun. I can only think, "My, how times have changed."

I guess when I look at my generation, we were determined to change our way of life. So today, I am amazed that many of the Lower Third youngsters have no hope and rely on the "crazy check" to get over each month. But I will not give up hope, and I will continue to talk to them and tell them about our struggles in hopes that they will one day SNAP out of it. We now have a Black mayor, a Peabody alum, so new programs may become available for our kids.

After my mother's death, I participated in planning the last two Peabody Class of 1968 reunions. That has given me great joy because I reunited with friends. I have fond memories of my time with my classmates and our times at Peabody High. We have all done good things, which explains why at 70 years of age we are still "kicking it."

The last five years have not been easy for me, as I have had several health scares. I had a TIA (transient ischemic attack, ministroke) and throat cancer. I came through both, and I'm doing great now. I know this was not all done by me but by the work of my God through Jesus Christ. He delivered me. I was nurtured by my longtime friends (Elaine, Helen, Kathryn, JoAnn, and others) with whom I have reconnected since returning home. The experiences we shared those many years ago in the segregated environment of Alexandria bind us to one another in a way in that many will not understand. Thank you for allowing me to participate in this book project. My life has been challenging. I share the details of my life in this narrative with the hope of helping others. Despite the challenges, I would not change one moment. Love to all people, especially my classmates.

# AN ANSWERED PRAYER

*"If you remain in me and my words remain in you, ask whatever you wish, and it will be done for you. You did not choose me, but I chose you and appointed you so that you might go and bear fruit — fruit that will last — and so that whatever you ask in my name the Father will give you."*

JOHN 15: 7,16

## Joseph R. Jett

*I had a checking account at Rapides Bank when I was in high school; stores would not take a check from me. I guess they thought that a young Black could not have a legal checking account.*

WELL, MY LIFE, as I know it, started in Bunkie, Louisiana, a small town little more than 30 miles south of Alexandria, with my maternal grandparents, Robert and Mary Ellen Williams. I did not get to know my grandfather because my grandparents divorced before I was born. Two children were born from that union, my mother and her sister. My grandmother later met a man, married, and moved to Woodworth, LA.

My father served in the U. S. Marine Corp from 1942 to 1946. He told us stories about being arrested every time he came home because there were so few Blacks in the marines. While growing up in Woodworth, my mother, Lucille, met him. They married after his military service ended.

*Grandmother Mary Ellen Williams*

*Parents: Joseph and Lucille Jett*

In addition to me, they had three girls and one boy. I did not know my grandmother on my father's side, but my grandfather was named Elijah Jett. He and his family were landowners in Woodworth. His family owned over 100 acres of land, a portion of which we maintain and manage to this day.

*Great grandparents: Elijah and Lerleah Jett*

My father worked for the railroad when I was small, and later in his life, he worked a number of jobs. He always worked. I cannot ever remember him not having a job. We moved to Alexandria where I was born. We lived on Wells Boulevard in an area called Willow Glen, referred to as the Pecan Grove by some. The street was dirt and gravel with pecan trees lining the center, giving it the name boulevard. Our community consisted of five streets. We had the usual neighborhood with a church and small grocery store. We literally knew everyone in the neighborhood. The area we lived in was located one block off Highway 71 South. Across that highway, was a white populated subdivision named Airview Terrace that Blacks could enter only if they were working in that neighborhood. Oh, we had a railroad track behind the community. As you know, in the South railroad tracks are wherever Black people live. It was a great neighborhood because everyone looked after each other. Sharing was a major feature of the area.

Riding the city bus was part of my life as a teenager. It was the thing that I hated most about living in the South. I can remember getting on the bus a block from our house. You would see only Black people seated at the back of the bus or standing behind this white line painted on the floor that indicated no Blacks can sit in front of this line. You could come through the front door and pay the same to ride the bus as the white person but had to stand if the Black area was full even when there were open seats available in the white section. The only reason the buses went into white neighborhoods was because Blacks worked in the homes and yards of whites. When you made it to downtown Alexandria, you would find places like W.T. Grant, S & H Kress, the Paramount Theater, Schnack Jewelry, Walgreen's, J.C. Penney, Stein's, and the Baptist Hospital. I could go on. What I remember most of all was that many of these stores had lunch and candy counters. Blacks could purchase items in these stores, but we could not sit at the lunch counters to eat or drink.

I cannot begin to tell you how I hated going to the Charity Hospital located in Pineville across Red River from Alexandria. You would sit in a little building outside the entrance gate with a divider between Blacks and whites. You would have to sit for hours before receiving service. I will never forget sitting in that small area when a Black man came in bleeding from his head. Whites that came in after this man were seen before him. The worst part of the situation was there was not a thing we could do or say about what was happening. Experience had taught us that we were second rate citizens who received nothing before the white man. Unfortunately, that is still happening today, especially in hospitals. Situations like that were irritating. When we would get our textbooks at the beginning of the school year, the teacher would issue you a book along with a sticker for your name to put over the original name page because the book was used. The names we pasted over were the names of white children. The books had come from the white schools; they got the new books.

The formative years of my education started at J. B. Lafargue Elementary School, first through sixth grades, followed by Lincoln Road Junior High, seventh through ninth grades, and Peabody High for 10<sup>th</sup> through 12<sup>th</sup>. Looking back on those years, I can say they were the best years of my life. I made new friends and explored new areas of the city. As far as work history during school, I had my share of jobs. I picked pecans for three cents a pound, cleaned flower beds, washed dishes at a hotel, and some days cleaned up at a carwash. This was before entering high school. When I got to Peabody, every day after school, I would catch a bus to England Air Force Base and sack groceries at the commissary until 7 p.m., then catch a bus home. What made me feel I needed an income at a young age was asking my father for $5 when I was in sixth grade to take an end of the year trip with my class to Chicot State Park. He lectured me about an hour on how long it took him to earn $5. After that lecture, I promised myself to always have my own. Oh, yes, I had a checking account at Rapides Bank when I was in high school; stores would not take a check from me. I guess they thought that a young Black could not have a legal checking account. I also had charge accounts at the Fair Store and Gem Jewelry. I bought my first car, a 1957 Chevy, for $45.00. I guess I can thank my grandfather Elijah Jett who lived to be 104 years old. He always quoted these words of the Billy Holiday song, "Mama may have, papa may have, but God bless the child that's got his own."

My mother worked at Bolton High School in the cafeteria. On weekends, she and some of her co-workers would work parties for the school board members. She would also work at the Greenbrier Motel. During those times, we had the advantage of having the extended family with us. Our great grandmother lived with us and allowed my mother to work other jobs. I can remember my great grandmother very well. She provided the childcare when my mother was working. Looking back, I can still see her smoking her pipe and always wearing an apron. She took care of us whenever we had an injury using her homemade cures.

*Great Grandmother Jenetta Scott*

She was the doctor at our house. If you stuck a nail in your foot, she would place a piece of fat salt pork tied in a rag on the injured area, in her words, "to draw out the soreness". For mumps, she would spread sardine oil over your face and tie a rag from the top of your head around the bottom of your chin to prevent the mumps from falling on a boy. (Form your own picture of falling.) For wasp or bee stings, she would slather the stung skin with tobacco juice. Thank God for Momma. She saved us from inhospitable hospital visits. Because of the way we were treated at the hospital, you did not go unless you were close to death.

I can remember every Friday night was family night. My mother would get home from work and start cooking that buffalo and goo fish. Our grandparents would come to our house for fish and to catch up on what went on during the past week. The men would watch "Gillette Cavalcade of Sports" boxing on our black and white television, as the children played. This tradition had gone on so long that people from the neighborhood would stop in for dinner. My family still carries on that tradition whenever we can get together. My wife and I eat fish on Fridays when I feel like cooking.

I remember my first time traveling out of the state. It was the summer between junior and senior year of high school. My uncle was in the U.S. Air Force, stationed at Mather Air Force Base, Sacramento, CA. I had worked and saved money to take my first vacation. I bought a bus ticket on the Continental Trailways Bus Line, and it cost me a whopping $61. In 1967, that was lot of money for a 17-year-old. I caught the bus from the station on Jackson Street on Monday evening at 4, heading for California. I was on that bus from Monday at 4 p.m. until Thursday at 10:30 p.m. My mistake was not buying an express ticket. I stopped in places I could not pronounce the names of. On my return trip, I paid extra and got home fast. While on vacation, I saw the mixing of Blacks and whites, which was not normal for me. It was like another world out there, the tall buildings, traffic on the streets, the way people dressed and talked. They even made fun of the way I talked. When I returned home from my summer vacation for my senior year, I did not say anything about college because I had a sister at Grambling, and I did not think my parents could afford also to send me to college.

After finishing high school, I continued to work along with enrolling at Louisiana State University Alexandria (LSUA) as a Business Administration major. It was clear that we were not wanted at LSUA. They enrolled most of us in remedial courses. Some of the jobs I held were at Blackman's Laundry, Baker Manufacturing, and Vanderhoeven Drugs. I have no idea how I worked those jobs in a two-year period, but somehow, I did. I was a student at LSUA for one and a half semesters, when some of the Black male students began receiving draft notices for the army for some unknown

reason. As a result, some of us decided to take the test for the air force so that if you got drafted you could go into the air force instead of the army. Well, I took the test on a Monday. When I got home from school the following Friday, I had a bus ticket and a map saying I needed to be in New Orleans on Sunday to be sworn into the U. S. Air Force. After entering the air force, they sent me to school to be an aircraft mechanic. After finishing that school, I was stationed at Barksdale Air Force Base in Bossier City as a mechanic and crew chief on the KC 135 Tanker. I also worked on B-52 Bombers. The aircraft mechanic position was highly technical and required considerable skill. Most of the aircraft mechanics and crew chiefs were Black. I was not offered an increase in rank until I decided to separate from the military. If I would reenlist, they would give me a promotion. I turned it down. I had a four-year stay in the military. I got a chance to see Okinawa, Guam, and Taiwan.

My plan was to make a career in the military, but after getting married and being away from my wife on temporary duty in other countries, I separated from the military and returned to Alexandria because I had a wife waiting for me. I got married in1971 to a girlfriend I met in junior high school. I started working at the VA Hospital about a month after returning home. Upon applying for employment at the hospital with no experience in the medical field, there were good paying positions, but I was only offered positions in nursing service, housekeeping, and food service.

I needed a job. We had a child on the way, so I worked in nursing service for the first six years of my employment. I worked evening and night shifts, while taking classes at Northwestern State University on England Air Force Base. This allowed me an opportunity to apply and become a Physical Therapy Technician. When I began working in the rehabilitation department, I was the first Black to work in that department, and this was in 1980. I was the only Black in the department for the next 12 years. Being in those positions, you still had to perform above the average white co-worker, which was not a problem for me because I was familiar with how the workforce operated. Don't fool yourself; it does not matter what job or position you have, racism exists. When I started work at the VA Hospital, I went to the library on my lunch break and read history about the facility. I found out that during the time when the tuberculosis epidemic was strong, the VA had most of the Black employees work those floors, placing them in direct contact with the disease. The hospital also had separate dining halls for Blacks and whites. I finally was given a promotion the year before I retired. During my time on the job, they held back promotional and other opportunities. Because I had been in the military, this treatment was no surprise to me.

I guess to sum all of this up about Alexandria, it still has a way to go as far as being an ideal place for Black people to live. We have let old money families hold us back, but I came back to live knowing what was here. I say all the time we have the same things larger cities have — they just have more of it. I can remember when I was about 13, working in a flower bed and looking around at all the large brick homes in the all-white neighborhood of Airview Terrace. I asked God to give me the strength and knowledge to afford and own a brick home while being financially comfortable. I can truly say that God has answered a small 13-year-old boy's prayer. Only God has made it possible for me to tolerate and endure all the things that I have personally gone up against to get to where I am today. He gave me the knowledge to know when to hold my tongue, and he gave the knowledge to speak out. He gave me the strength to get up in the morning and go to that job and deal with those people and things that were against me. I would say to myself all the time that I cannot give up because God did not give up on me. He has a reward for me. I'll end by saying, Only God.

# MAKING DO, MASTERING PERSEVERANCE

*"The death of Dr. Martin Luther King Jr. has raised fear for the nation's future. His death also has raided the hope that Americans might at least embrace the brotherhood for which he died."*

MICHAEL R. JOHNSON,
*Valedictory Address, May 16, 1968*

## Michael R. Johnson

Wᴴᴬᵀ ᴬ ᴅɪꜰꜰᴇʀᴇɴᴄᴇ one day made. I remember sitting in Miss Baker's English class on April 5, 1968, still saddened and shocked over the horrible news bulletin the night before of the assassination of Dr. Martin Luther King Jr. It was all over the evening TV stations, and my parents and I could only stare in disbelief. Only 24 hours prior, I had been sitting carefree in class at the same school desk, most likely daydreaming about senior class activities, prom, house parties and next month's graduation. I would be heading to college in the fall, the first in my family of seven kids to do so. The country was at war in Vietnam, and my two older brothers already had been drafted, the oldest, Bill, by the U.S. Army, the second oldest, Jerry, by volunteer service in the U.S. Navy. As the thirdborn son with a deferred classification, my parents assumed I would lead the way to higher education for my four younger brothers and sisters.

*"In this 21ˢᵗ century, if I've learned anything from growing up in a segregated world where "the struggle continues" was and continues to be the catchphrase of every season, it's that there are no people on earth sturdier and more durable than the beautiful African Americans that helped shape who I am."*

From the moment in early spring that I'd been named valedictorian of my class, I had been meeting once a week after school with Miss Marguerite Baker to work on and practice my valedictory address. When she approached me that day after Dr. King's death to explain that I would need to rewrite my speech to reflect the horrible current event, I wasn't surprised, but the thought of a revision made the nightmare more real.

Dr. King had been an inspiration to all Black Americans, but my generation, the Baby Boomers, would be the first to fully reap benefits from the Civil Rights Act of 1965 that he had courageously and tirelessly fought for. Unlike our parents and their parents before, we would have opportunities they were allowed only to dream about.

My parents were humble people, hardworking, deeply religious, and always giving. I know a lot of people say this about a parent, but my dad, William Douglas Johnson Sr., was and is the smartest man I know. (I credit him for my math genes.) My mother, Helen Marie Jones Johnson, was and is the most generous person I know. There are no better role models, and as of this writing, I am blessed to still have them on this earth.

*Mom at 16, Dad at 18*

*William and Helen Johnson with first great granddaughter, October 23, 2019*

My dad's Nelson family tree on his mother Mary's (our ma-ma) side is rooted in Colfax, about an hour's drive, northwest of Alexandria. His father, William Johnson (our pa-pa), was a native of Alexandria where Dad also was born. My grandfather built the family home from the ground up with very little help in the historic all-Black Sonia Quarters that Dad grew up in. Pa-pa would years later purchase a nearby house for my parents as a wedding gift. It was their first and only home, a modest three-room shotgun structure that Dad would almost singlehandedly remodel, improve, and add to as the family expanded. He had a natural gift for architecture and geometric space and numbers. As the family home improved from midcentury all the way up to the mid-1990s, with add-ons to accommodate the grandchildren's summer visits, I continued to marvel at his talent. I still think about the possibilities and potential this great man could've realized had Black Americans of his and previous generations been born with the same privilege as white Americans.

Like most of his kids after, Dad had attended Peabody High School. While he excelled academically, he also was a gifted triathlete, lettering in basketball, football, and track.

*Dad, right, in 1945 with track team member and coach*

*Family Portrait of first five siblings*

It was at Peabody where he met and fell in love with the beautiful and charismatic Helen Marie Jones, one of the school's varsity cheerleaders. Her family on her mother's ("Mama Edith" Jones') side originated in Natchitoches, her dad's (Papa Andrew Jones') people come from Taylor Hill, a small community outside of Alexandria. My mother was born in Alexandria.

Before his senior year, summer 1944, my father had visited Grambling College out of interest in academics and its basketball program. With World War II in play and a draft vulnerability, Professor David Iles, his principal, and a member of the Alexandria draft board, advised my father to seek a college deferment, and by the following April he would have one in hand. It would become a moot point because by summer the war was near ending, and after graduation, my father decided to pass on college and instead ask my mother to marry him. On June 20, 1945, off they were as a newly married couple.

In the beginning, my parents struggled like most young Black couples starting family life in the middle of the Jim Crow South. By 1951, they had four boys. To provide for us, my father worked several jobs, the most substantial and steady was as store manager and head butcher for my great aunt and great uncle's grocery store in the Sonia Quarters. Clayton's Grocery Store was one of the few Black-owned businesses in the area. After my first of two sisters, Beverly Ann, came along in 1956, and with more mouths to feed, out of necessity, his salary eventually would be supplemented with my mother's salary from her first job where she was hired as a domestic worker for the family of a local doctor. Because she was one of the few ladies in her church and neighborhood circle with a driver's license, she often would offer rides in the family's Ford station wagon to friends heading to jobs in the same all-white community.

The doctor, who was a graduate of LSU School of Medicine, we discovered, was a unique white employer at that time. He wanted to know more about Black life in ways that transcended your typical white boss/Black maid tradition. He took genuine interest in our lifestyle and appreciated our core values. Of course, this initially was met with skepticism by all of us, but our curiosity for this man would eventually be quieted by his authenticity. His children would sometimes come over to play in our backyard, and we would sometimes in summer tag along with my mother on her workdays and hang out with the doctor's children as playmates.

My mother later resigned from her work at the doctor's home after getting her credentials and a salaried position in the Rapides Parish School District as a nutrition lunchroom manager at a neighborhood elementary school, a job she kept until retiring in the 1990s. Upon her leaving domestic work, as "a perk," her employer, the doctor, provided no-cost healthcare through his private practice for my parents and all of us kids. The healthcare benefit would continue to his retirement in 1989.

As she began her new career in the mid-1960s, my mother, whom we Johnson children lovingly call "MaDear," made time as a busy working mom for involvement in her church ministries, particularly those relating to community outreach. After retiring, she spent most of her time in the 1990s through the aughts as secretary of her community's watch organization, fighting for the betterment of her beloved Sonia Quarters. Because they knew she had their voices, everyday citizens and neighbors would call on her when city services failed them, or their civic concerns needed to be heard. MaDear would diligently attend city council meetings, taking notes on agenda items regarding Sonia Quarters issues and after give necessary feedback to those impacted. Her city councilperson and other elected local leaders knew her name, and more special to her, the cops on the beat knew her and never hesitated to stop in for a cup of Community Coffee and listen to her worries about neighborhood safety matters.

From MaDear's push for afterschool programs for the younger latchkey students, advocating neighborhood street cleanups and other improvements, anticrime-antidrug and regular safety drives, her community campaign efforts were not ignored. Her hard

*MaDear standing in front
of the meeting room named
for her by the city*

work and passion earned her the honorary title of "Mayor of Sonia Quarters." In 2004, to her greatest delight, shortly after the opening of the brand-new Roy O. Martin Community Center, the city paid tribute to her at the unveiling of the The Helen M. Johnson Conference Rooms named for her.

MaDear also after retiring, spent 18 years as a volunteer at the Huey P. Long Charity Hospital surgery waiting room, offering services and support to patients' family members and friends.

My mother's strong faith and charitable nature had a big influence on her former employer's philanthropy. She and Dad remained connected to the doctor through more means than his generous caring for their health. The doctor had insisted on keeping our two families' relationship close. He occasionally would invite my parents to social events he and his wife hosted, and they often would be the only Blacks attending. As Dad puts it, the doctor would look "clear past the shocked facial expressions" from his white guests. "He always told us how much he admired our work in the community," my dad mentioned in a conversation retelling the story of their friendship.

Even more significantly than keeping our family's friendship, in addition to serving as a volunteer doctor in Vietnam in the late 1960s and working on other medical missions around the globe, the doctor made good on a pledge he made to support the less fortunate in our Black community. He became known in the Alexandria-Pineville area for helping the needy, donating money and often showing up alongside my parents and other black leaders to help in causes benefitting the disadvantaged. My mother always said that he insisted that his good deeds be accepted with no questions asked. For those skeptics who learned of him and wondered why he wanted to help, she and Dad would share the moment they, too, as skeptics, first asked him was he sure he wanted to write such a big check? His reply, "W.D., Helen, it's only money."

One of his signature acts of benevolence came each year on Thanksgiving Day. In the early 1960s, when the doctor learned of the community's annual Lee Street Garage Thanksgiving Dinner for the Needy that had been in place for two years, he wanted to help. He called the original sponsors, two well-known local Black ministers, The Reverend Euell Williams, a Rapides Parish School Board member at the time, and The Reverend Willie Lee, owner of Lee's Garage, and asked if he could help. Help he did, donating money and food and standing in line with his wife next to my parents, together with his cosponsors, the two ministers, and countless other volunteers, serving holiday dinners to those without. Rev. Williams in the doctor's obituary praised him for his philanthropy. "For the past 27 years, he and [his wife] have been a part of feeding the hungry. He always wanted to do something for the poor." Rev. Williams and the doctor also set up and ran a free health clinic for the uninsured and seniors at the St. Lawrence Missionary Baptist Church in Alexandria.

It always would amaze me that this white man who kept a low profile was choosing openly to do good with no motive, no quid pro quo. There was absolutely nothing in it for him. Which is why I include his rare story of humanity and humility in my story. In the late 1960s when I became more aware, before any of those family discussions about news reports of racist acts of violence and discrimination in general against Black people, my parents would point to the doctor, the one exception to hold on to. He gave them hope. Early on in middle school, he nicknamed me "The Professor," which gave my parents a big kick. He also gave me a generous savings bond for graduation that I of course held on to beyond its full maturity, as he had predicted I would do. He also told them that I would be a success. When he passed away fittingly Thanksgiving Week 1999, per his and his family's request, my mother eulogized him at his funeral and my father served as one of his pallbearers. And to this day, his grown children stay in contact with my parents and younger siblings.

Before my mother started working a steady job, the spring before kindergarten after I turned 5, my paternal grandparents who by then lived in Washington, D.C., were visiting us. My grandmother wanted me to go back with them for a stay through summer. This was the earliest time I recall having an interest in mathematics. During my stay with them, my two grands would teach me numbers by playing money games with me. They would give me the loose change from their pockets and Ma-Ma's pocketbook. Each time they emptied them they would ask me to count the coins and add it to my already growing stash. I never got it wrong. I was so good at money by the time I returned home, my mother would insist that I accompany her to the grocery store to help her tally at checkout. I became her human calculator.

The trip to D.C. was an adventure in many ways. At least as a child that's what I thought until I learned the cold hard reality of racism in the segregated South. On the trip there from Alexandria, my grandfather drove their car, and on the return, my grandmother accompanied me by train. Both events were firsts for me. During the road trip, we made a number of stops on the way, mostly bathroom stops, but, as I recall, the bathrooms were outdoor nature spots off the road, sometimes into wooded areas. I figured out as I grew older why my grandparents had packed toilet paper, as well as food for meals. Places to eat and lodging for Black travelers on roundtrips were nonexistent. On the return journey by train, the passenger cars most likely were segregated, but that didn't stick

*Maternal grandparents Andrew and Edith Jones (left), October 7, 1978, and Paternal grandparents William and Mary Johnson, 1950*

with me as much as the road trip stops. In my 5-year-old mind, who cared about who was on the train? My grandparents had given me a trainset that summer, and all I remember was playing with my toy trains and the thrill of being on an actual train ride.

One self-inflicted scary story did come out of my D.C. adventure. It was more of a horror for the adults than for me. A family outing on the Washington Mall with my grands to enjoy the Fourth of July celebrations turned into a nightmare when I got separated from them. After hours of exasperation on their part, we finally were reunited in a D.C. police station where I had been entertained by friendly cops who had given me a chocolate covered ice cream bar on a stick. My grands would tell the story and repeat the first words I said to them when after hours of their searching, they found me. "Policemen are your friends," I told them.

*Fourth grade at South Alexandria*

The only memory I retained from what had to have been a traumatizing experience was the crying until the police found me and sitting in the police station smiling when they gave me the ice cream. Turned out that two officers, one white, one Black, had found me wandering alone on the grounds after losing my grandparents. My grands would later explain that they had been viewing President Dwight Eisenhower's traditional military style parade, watching me get excited seeing the huge tanks and artillery, and in an instant, I had disappeared out of their eyesight. There fortunately was one good thing for Black children that came out of the 1950s. All children, no matter the race, were required to wear civilian dog tags, and my grandparents had gotten one for me that contained their contact information. After they returned home feeling helpless and hopeless, they received the police notification that I had been found.

It took years before MaDear could recover from this event and laugh with others recapping the story. For the sake of repeating family history, my adventurous daughter at only a slightly older age than 5, decades later in a huge downtown D.C. hotel while at a Nelson Family Reunion, would separate from her older cousins in charge of keeping an eye on her. It would take 30 minutes of total panic before she was found "moseying," as MaDear and Dad teasingly describe it, on an upper floor in search of the hotel's indoor swimming pool that she had overheard the cousins discussing.

After the trip, by that fall, I was ready for kindergarten. In the Sonia Quarters, there were several kindergarten choices. I went to Miss Simon's Kindergarten. There, I learned the ABCs that set the stage for the beginnings of my education. I later moved up to South Alexandria Elementary for grades first through sixth. My first teacher, Mrs. Lofton, was very special to me. I remember how much patience she showed to me and my classmates. Even if we had failures on our lessons, she would encourage us to try again until there was success. You never forget your very first schoolteacher.

I never forgot any of the caring Black teachers who kept me grounded and focused on learning. They made me hungry for knowledge, and they were the reason I loved school. Second and third grades were easiest because I had no fears of what was to come. When I started fourth grade, I began to find even more interests in mathematics. My teacher, Mrs. Hayes, was unforgettable. Through her, I was able to build on my foundation with more math fundamentals.

I moved on to Lincoln Road Junior High School, and at this juncture my interest in math was sky high. In junior, high I played on the junior varsity and varsity basketball teams. Right off the bat, I lettered in academics, and lucky me, I had in my opinion a brilliant math teacher in Miss Davis. She became my first math mentor and inspired me to pursue my passion for numbers. Those years at Lincoln Road were some of my most memorable.

As I remembered, my childhood upbringing before and during high school years, my siblings and I were pretty much contained to the Sonia Quarters. My parents held the reins somewhat tight on me and my siblings, and our friends knew this and respected their rules. Both were extra cautious about taking us outside of our neighborhood boundaries. All our activities were within the borders.

Our family's two churches, one for Dad, one for MaDear, were in walking distances. Our churchgoing dynamic was a bit unique, but it worked for us. Dad had grown up and was baptized in his family church, Nazarene Missionary Baptist, and MaDear's mother, whom we called Mama Edith, had been one of the founders of MaDear's, Second Evergreen Baptist Church. As devoted lifelong members, each held on to their affiliations, and agreed that the first five of us would join Dad's church. On occasion, we would visit my mother's church, and she, my dad's. When my baby sister, Cynthia, the last child, came along, my mother insisted that she join her church.

As young children, especially when MaDear started working, my three brothers and I as the four oldest children were given chores and taught how to keep things at home orderly. I did my share of dishes, though I was primarily the one conveniently trying to get out of work and stealing time to read my comic books or watch *Star Trek* and *My Favorite Martian* on TV. When I would be busted, I paid for it double time.

In the deep days of segregation when we were little, our protective mother occasionally would take us with her to shop downtown. She would drive, or occasionally we'd go by city bus. On the rare times we rode the bus, before heading out, MaDear would remind us, like always, to be on our best behavior. She also would instruct us to follow her once we got on the bus. It never occurred to me until I got older and learned about segregated buses that we were doing anything other than finding seats on the bus to be close to our mother. When we were old enough to ride on our own, as Black teenagers, my brothers and friends would take full advantage of a privilege we had been robbed of.

Looking back, the neighborhoods in Sonia Quarters didn't have planned parks or playgrounds for recreation. Certainly, there were none close to our neighborhood home on Houston Street, so we created our own. Creating our own meant that the concrete streets we all lived on became a place to play ball, ride our stick horses and even run races. When it came time for learning how to swim, the one public swimming pool for Blacks near Peabody High School was the only option. For clueless 7-year-olds raring to learn, it did the job. We had no clue at the time of what facilities were like on the other side of town, but as we grew older and learned about race inequities it was easy to imagine it was superior to ours. And, it was. We pretty much taught one another how to swim. My two older brothers learned on their own and became expert swimmers. When it came time for me and my brother, Lee Anthony, (who's less than two years younger), we jumped in and relied on their knowhow. That worked. To this day, all of us Johnsons are much more than sufficient swimmers.

It became increasingly clear to all, though, that the street was not the ideal recreation spot, and something would have to be done for safety's sake. In my immediate neighborhood, my parents stepped in and provided a resolution. Dad bought and installed a basketball court behind our home, which thankfully sat on a very generous size lot with plenty of green space for play. Not only did Dad provide a basketball court, but he also came up with ways to carve out a table tennis area, a volleyball and badminton court and a spot for throwing horseshoes.

It became such a welcomed space, friends named it "The Johnson Boys Playground". We hosted games with the best basketball talent in the Sonia Quarters. Classmates, playmates and other visitors played ball until the sun went down, or on some occasions, when Dad would call end of play for the day. My mother also chimed in on many days with refreshments. For most friends, they came not only to play basketball, but for her snacks. Some still recall her signature tuna fish sandwiches. I didn't quite appreciate it at the time, but those days were great times that made our already close neighborhood even closer.

High school came all too soon. By 10th grade, my course of direction was full steam ahead for mathematics. Under the tutelage of two of Peabody's best and brightest, Mr. Ernest Bowman and Mr. Henry Booze, I mastered Advanced Mathematics, Algebra II, Geometry, Trigonometry, and Calculus. The two teachers were my most avid mentors.

Peabody's teachers overall shaped and instilled a hunger for learning. American Civics, Biology, and American History, I grabbed hold and kept all of it. (I'm often accused of or credited for knowing too much history and science trivia.) Miss Marguerite Baker, my senior year English teacher, helped me take my use of language and writing to levels that would enhance my success in college and throughout my professional life. And, my personal life. My college sweetheart and eventual life partner credits my love letters for snagging her years later. I was disappointed to learn that after our class graduated, Miss Baker had left the esteemed Peabody faculty for a new position at the cross-town predominantly white Bolton High School. Such loss was one of many of the pitfalls during school desegregation in countless Black communities across the state.

Looking back at my uniquely special time in high school, I think about Beverly Ann and Daniel Wayne, my two younger siblings whom, by school desegregation law, were assigned to attend predominantly white Bolton. Though they went on to have successful professional careers, their high school experiences, breaking with the Johnson Family tradition that began with my father, was a far cry from the exceptionally caring Peabody world their older siblings had relished. Their extraordinary stories of bravery and persistence, however, made me a proud big brother. As Dad reminded me recently, things have a way of coming full circle. By the time my hoopster Baby Sister, Cynthia Marie, came of age, Peabody High School had become Peabody Magnet High School, and she had a choice. She rounded the corner to Peabody without hesitation and played forward for the Lady Warhorse Basketball team. Like her dad and her four older siblings, the family's registered nurse would say she did "alright," too.

Second semester, as my high school days were coming to an end, 1 turned my attention to my college decision. I was blessed to have three universities offer full academic scholarships. Purdue was first to offer, followed by Grambling College and the University of Southwest Louisiana. I had had the opportunity to see USL's campus in Lafayette. I thought the visit went well, and the campus was impressive. It was then a predominantly white university, and, at the time, my decision had to be made. The assassination of Dr. Martin Luther King Jr. was still fresh on my mind. Having grown up in the Jim Crow South, the sudden killing of the great Black leader gave me reason for pause. It also didn't take me long to eliminate Purdue University, even though it would have pleased our family friend, the doctor my mother had worked for. The Purdue scholarship specifically was for pre-medicine study toward a degree in medicine. I wasn't certain that was the path for me, and I wasn't sure about the cold winters.

My decision was clear and rational. Grambling College, along with Southern University, two reputable state historical Black colleges, had been the choice of so

many educators I admired, and the majority of them had been my junior and high
school teachers and guides. During junior high, Mr. George Thompson, our basketball coach, had rewarded our winning basketball team with a trip to Grambling to
see the team play. I got to see the campus, and as it turned out, it was the final year
for Grambling legend and future NBA All-Star Willis Reed. We got to see him play
and afterward visit the team and Head Basketball Coach Fred Hobdy in the team
locker room.

In the fall of 1968, I headed to Grambling to pursue a degree in Applied
Mathematics. Right off the bat, I enjoyed my college experience. The freedom to
exist in this quasi-adult environment was eye opening. I would be totally responsible for me. I no longer would have my parents around, and no longer could rely
on them for my daily existence. Through it all, I must say my college experience
was undoubtedly the most significant of my life. It was the rehearsal for real life.
One notable first came my junior year when for the first time I took two classes
under a white educator. Dr. William Cummings, head of Grambling's Physics
Department and a former Rice University prof, taught General Physics 101and
102, required courses under my math major. He was an excellent teacher. After
receiving my undergraduate degree in May 1972, I was awarded a master's fellowship in mathematics as a graduate teaching assistant from Oklahoma State
University (OSU), and the following August, off to Stillwater, OK I headed.
From Grambling to OSU, I would experience a complete culture reversal. For the
first time in my life, I was in an environment totally dominated by white people. My
graduate advisor was white, my graduate peers were white, my classes were predominantly white, and the classes I taught were predominantly white. This was a period
of true soul-searching. I gave a lot of thought to conversations I would have back
in the day with the good doctor, my mother's former employer and good friend of
our family. He was a realist, and he knew in the age of desegregation that I would
face such experiences. I remembered our frank talks on racial matters and race relations and interactions with whites. He told me to never lose sight of whom I am
and what equality means. "Look them (whites) in the eye, and if appropriate, extend

a hand with a firm handshake." Dad and he added that the same advice would apply to all humans regardless of skin color. It was not complicated, and during grad school and beyond, it worked.

While finishing my master's work at OSU, I attended a job recruitment workshop hosted by the IBM Corporation, a company looking for graduates in mathematics. I interviewed with the recruiter, and he asked me to submit my resume. Those were the 1970s when corporations showed up in person, looking for talent. For corporate America and qualified African American job seekers, it was a win-win because companies in those times sincerely wanted to give people of color a chance in the workplace. Before long, IBM had offered me a job as a programmer with the Federal System Division in Gaithersburg, MD, a then-exurb, a little north of Washington, D.C. I accepted the offer and began my career in the world of computer technology.

My association with white people would become commonplace in the Big Blue world. My first officemate was a white woman who became a very dear friend and colleague. To my welcome surprise, my very first IBM manager was African American. She was smart and kind, and with her encouragement and leadership, transition into the IBM corporate life was made a lot easier. I found IBM's Federal Systems Division to be somewhat unique. It was the division that dealt with federal government contracts. Again, like college and grad school, this was the '70s enlightenment era, post 1960s Civil Rights laws. All U.S. Government contracts involved provisions for inclusion and racial equality in all aspects of the work.

I would remain at IBM through four decades, retiring as, what many of the company old-timers there in my youth were called, "a gray beard". I was fortunate throughout my career to work on a diversity of projects and assignments and travel to other corporate sites across the country, using my skills as a program developer and systems engineer. I was also fortunate to join the company at a time when employees of color for IBM were becoming less of a novelty, and I could have the luxury of finding mentors who looked like me. Looking back over the decades, one of the most fulfilling experiences throughout my career was seeing, getting to work with, and, in some cases, mentoring young Black professionals coming in behind me. That, I can gladly say, included my youngest brother, Daniel, who joined the company nine years after I became an IBMer.

In this 21$^{st}$ century, if I've learned anything from growing up in a segregated world where "the struggle continues" was and continues to be the catchphrase of every season, it's that there are no people on earth sturdier and more durable than the beautiful African Americans that helped shape who I am. Dr. King knew the struggle would continue. He knew that everything old is new again. This story opened with the somber words of the hopeful though somewhat concerned 18-year-old I was and ends with the following excerpt from the same May 16, 1968, graduation address. The expressions then may not feel now like more than a half-century old:

> "The struggle, which surely will continue, must be conducted with dignity and courage, as shown by Dr. King.…This is not the time for apathy or complacency. This is a time for all Americans to (take) stride vigorously and positively — It is a time for all Americans to (take) stride toward social change and freedom."

# PART THREE

# PEABODY: OUR COMMUNITY'S HIGH SCHOOL

*"The function of education is to teach one to think
intensively and to think critically. Intelligence plus
character — that is the goal of true education."*

MARTIN LUTHER KING JR.

*Peabody Industrial Institute—1913*

EVERY CONTRIBUTOR TO this volume has in common a love for and dedication to Peabody High School. It holds a significant place in the life of each writer and for good reason. The essential strength of a community is measured by the quality of its schools. Since Reconstruction, education has been an integral part of Alexandria's Black community. As this book's contributors and their almost 300 classmates were being born, the birth of a new era, targeting equal education rights, was on the horizon. The new era began with the 1954 U.S. Supreme Court *Brown v. Board of Education of Topeka* decision, some 58 years after New Orleans native Homer A. Plessy was tossed from his first-class train seat, after deliberately violating the state's Separate Car Act of 1890. In May1896, the Supreme Court issued a 7-1 decision against Plessy, establishing the "separate but equal" ruling as the law of the land for decades to come.

*Peabody Negro School, constructed in 1919 on Third Street*

A year earlier, in 1895, J. B. Lafargue had opened the doors of Peabody State Normal Industrial and Agricultural School (later to become Peabody High School) on Third Street in Alexandria. Post-Civil War, formal education for freed slaves in Central Louisiana was scarce. After the war and up to the late 1800s, there are a indicators that point to the Rapides Parish Black churches as hubs and shelters for educating children. The history of Peabody provided herein and the narratives that follow shine a light on Black education in general and the school's enduring legacy and place in the hearts of its alums.

## A Tribute to Professors J.B. Lafargue and D.F. Iles

When Louisiana was restored to the Union in 1868, the state was required to make changes to its constitution. In addition to abolishing slavery, granting citizenship and voting rights to former slaves, integrating schools became a priority. From 1865 to 1868, staunch segregationist Robert M. Lusher served as the state superintendent of schools and declined to run for office because he refused to preside over mixing races in the schools. During the period, in 1867, Philadelphia philanthropist and banker George Peabody established the Peabody Fund to help with general education and teacher training for both whites and Blacks in the Deep South and West Virginia, areas he deemed to be in greatest need post-Civil War. As superintendent at the time the Peabody allotment for Louisiana was being released, Lusher was named agent of funds and designated the funds for white schools.

Despite Lusher's attempts before the war and post Reconstruction to help only schools for whites, there are documented exceptions countering his misapplication of the Peabody funds in those early years of the program. As noted by the Southern Education Foundation, Inc., the Peabody Fund, Inc. distributed $16,600 in 1870 to support African American schools, enrolling more than 100,000 African American students across the country. From 1872 to 1876, an African American, William G. Brown, was elected and served as the state superintendent of education. His tenure is well-documented and his many accomplishments as well as his challenges as a Black in the position noted. Lusher assumed the position when Brown's tenure along with Reconstruction was ending in 1876.

As Blacks in the community continued the journey to achieving education access and advantages in a new system of freedom, Black churches and associations as early as the late 1800s were providing schools for Black children in Rapides Parish.

Announcements inviting the public to attend commencement exercises and to enroll next term in the Shiloh Baptist Church Central Louisiana Academy for Colored appeared regularly in the *Alexandria Daily Town Talk* from the late 1800s well into the 20th century. Two 1908 newspaper notices reveal the academy's founding year, 1889, and its mission, "for the education of colored youth under the direction of the Eighth District Baptist Association."

This was the backdrop upon which J. B. Lafargue began his work in Alexandria. Thirty years after the Emancipation Proclamation and a botched

**PROF. J. B. LAFARGUE**
Principal City Public School and Peabody Industrial Institute

Reconstruction period, central Louisiana's Rapides Parish was slow to move on equal education, as political and business leaders throughout the Deep South fought vigorously against new rights for Black people. J. B. Lafargue's timing and practical approach to change was in demand in a segregated system rife with inequality. He was the right man at the right time. Born June 5, 1865, in Avoyelles Parish, he came from a family of teachers and had a broad vision of education. Based on the multiple papers and letters attributed to Lafargue and his ensuing actions, he kept his focus on the state's funding of public schools, a then-budding learning system if sufficiently supported, would be more viable and sustainable for newly emancipated families. He ultimately left Avoyelles Parish during the latter part of the century and moved to Rapides Parish armed with possibilities.

In 1889, the Alexandria School Board handed over the two-story building on Third Street that became known as Peabody Industrial Institute to prepare young black students in industrial work. Rapides Parish schools, like so many others in Louisiana, needed skilled teachers. After the building had been acquired, Lafargue began writing to his U.S. senators and congressman, the governor, and state superintendent of education, seeking funding for Alexandria's own normal school. (The purpose of a normal school is to train high school graduates to become teachers.)

Lafargue's goal was to institute a teacher training program to help the select few with high school diplomas in Rapides Parish become public elementary school teachers.

Documented handwritten replies to his letters were encouraging. Lafargue's strategy of using his cooperative disposition with his commanding nature perhaps influenced his petitioning success. "Typical of the Avoyelles Negro, he always worked for and with the white man, always hoping that his day would come, and it did," an unnamed observer at the time wrote of Lafargue. Putting it plainly, as Peabody High 1959 alum Charles Smith did, J.B. Lafargue "was ahead of his time." While Smith was born in a different era, as keeper and eventual preserver of the Lafargue family documents, the former Alexandria City Councilman claims a spiritual emotional bond to Lafargue, The Man. "I feel like I know him."[5]

In 1895, in a building that once served as a hospital, Professor J.B. Lafargue, at the age of 30, opened the doors to Peabody State Normal Industrial and Agricultural School for grades 1 through 7 on Third Street. Mr. Lafargue's wife, Sarah C.B. Mayo Lafargue, college educated and an experienced teacher, was the first to be hired. She equaled her husband in commitment to educating Black children, according to multiple testimonials found in the Lafargue family documents.

By the 1913-14 school session, success was evident. In the published annual report, *A Summary of the Colored Public-School Teachers of Rapides Parish*," Rapides Parish Superintendent D.B. Showalter wrote, "The colored public schools of Rapides Parish have made commendable progress during the past few years. Every teacher is now holding a certificate." Mr. Showalter's written message continued to laud successes: "Through his energy and superior leadership, Prof J.B. Lafargue has managed

---

[5]       Mr. Charles Fredrick Smith, former Alexandria City Councilman, collaborated with the late Alice Faye McClinton Belmon of Alexandria, a "real go-getter" and a history and genealogy enthusiast, on an unpublished book, *Peabody Normal and Industrial School*. The book is a compilation of original documents related to the Lafargue family. Mr. Smith inherited the documents from his godmother (whose parents were close to the Lafargue family). Their joint work, now housed in the Alexandria Historical and Genealogical Library, includes an assortment of personal papers and correspondences, typewritten and handwritten, U.S. Census and genealogy reports, marriage licenses, citizenship applications, obituaries, family portraits and other relative photographs, tributes and generational accounts of family history and testimonials. The book serves as a source for information contained herein.

successfully the colored teachers' institutes from year to year and has succeeded in arousing interest in the agriculture and industrial work in schools in the parish."

Helen
Augustine Sally Johnson -
C.A Chatman
Sarah Lafargue, J.B. Lafargue, Maria Lawson, Lex Berry - David Iles

In his history of the *Town Talk*, Spletstoser makes the following important point: In 1912, "the Rapides Parish school board maintained Alexandria Central High School on Seventh Street, West End Grammar School on Bolton Avenue and a small ungraded learning center on Pineville's Lakeview Street." He states that these schools served about 1,200 white students and that the cities also had "a meager all-purpose facility for the instruction of black children". As a result of a *Town Talk* editorial on overcrowded schools at the time, the president of Rapides Bank and his wife donated land with a challenge to the community to approve a bond to build a white high school. The action started a movement that resulted in the construction of other white schools, as well as Peabody High School on Third Street in 1919 and South Alexandria Elementary School in the Sonia Quarters in 1925, according to Spletstoser.

In the decades after the Peabody Normal and Industrial School opened, enrollment extended to 12th grade, and, in 1938, the school officially became Peabody High

## FOR COLORED TEACHERS

**ALEXANDRIA SUMMER NORMAL SCHOOL WILL BE HELD FROM JUNE 5TH TO JULY 15TH.**

The Alexandria Summer Normal School for Colored Teachers will be held in this city from June 5th to July 15th—a term of six weeks.

The session of the summer normal will be held in the buildings of the Peabody, Normal and Industrial Institute, of which Prof. J. B. Lafargue is principal. This school is admirably situated for effective school work, being removed, as it is, from the congested business centers, and yet easily accessible to all parts of the city.

The faculty of the Colored Summer Normal will be as follows:

J. M. Frazier, conductor; J. B. Lafargue, secretary and local manager; J. M. Frazier, pedagogy; M. J. Foster, history; Maggie A. Nance, model school; W. A. McMahan, geography and agriculture; F. M. Boley, mathematics; J. W. Hunter, penmanship and English; Angele Charbonet, domestic science; C. A. Martin, shopwork.

*One of numerous "ads" appearing in the Weekly Town Talk over the years sharing details about programs offered for teachers and students at Peabody. This one from May 20, 1916*

School and for the first time was authorized to award high school diplomas to Black students.

In addition to his other accomplishments, Lafargue is credited as founder of the Colored State Teacher's Association, an organization similar to the National Parent Teachers Association. He also organized the Negro Civic League in Alexandria to push for the best training for classroom leaders. "We don't need to hide history, we need to pass it on," Charles Fredrick Smith said. "Peabody made me who I am. Mr. Lafargue made it all possible."

As the Lafargue reign was coming to an end, a logical changing of the guard took place. David Faxton Iles (Professor Iles) had enrolled as a student at Peabody Training School in 1918. Because there was no high school for African Americans in Rapides Parish in 1925, Iles was forced to attend high school at Leland College, the nearest historically Black college to Alexandria. There, he also received both a high school diploma and college degree. Iles returned to Rapides Parish, and, in 1934, accepted a position as a Peabody Social Studies teacher. He became Peabody High School's second principal in 1937 upon the retirement of Prof J.B. Lafargue.

*Peabody High School constructed in 1953, facing Broadway*

Prof Iles remained principal for 35 years, expanding the curriculum, introducing new 20th century learning concepts, and keeping the Lafargue legacy. He also oversaw the construction of the new and separate Peabody High School facing Broadway Avenue. The Third Street facility became Peabody elementary and served grades 1 through 8 while Professor Iles moved with the 9th through 12th graders to the new site in 1952. In fall 1965, 16 years later, the contributors to this volume and the rest of the class of 1968 began filling the hall-

ways for their journey. During his tenure, Principal Iles transformed Peabody from an industrial and agricultural school to an institution offering curriculum in industrial shop and home economics, programs Lafargue had fought hard to acquire. In addition, he ensured that the comprehensive high school core courses and fine arts programs continued to grow and flourish.

A school begun during Reconstruction for a people who had no idea what the future held for them has endured for more than a century and a quarter against, in some cases, impossible odds. Now, 126 years later, the wooden two-story building and later the three-story building at Third and Bogan Streets are gone. One facility became two in 1952. In its place today is Peabody Montessori Elementary School, a 21st century reminder of how the story began and the extent to which times have changed. Black and white students now learn and play together on that hallowed ground where an iron marker notes its origin as "Peabody Negro School" and its progenitors, the leaders and teachers who started it all. In 1998, Peggie Griffin Davis, a member of the Class of 1968, was appointed principal and charged with overseeing the building and development of the state-of-the-art facility, replacing the 1952 structure. For foot printers Profs Lafargue and Iles, it was a winning bet. Peabody is now a magnet high school.

Before there was a *Brown v. Board* ruling, though, Alexandria was gifted with J.B. Lafargue and D.F. Iles. The two education leaders are central in Peabody High

School's storied history and responsible for the outstanding institution it became and the influence it continues to have on the lives of all who matriculated there. For 77 years consecutively, the two men lit the way, educating and inspiring Alexandria's young African Americans from the dim late 19th century segregation days to the bullish 20th century civil rights era and beyond. They are the stalwarts who were committed to preparing Black students for a world that was not welcoming to former slaves and their children and grandchildren. Both knew that education was key to strengthening Black people and Black communities and devoted their lives to that purpose.

## THE TEACHING EXPERIENCE UNDER PROFESSOR D.F. ILES

Earnest Bowman
Math Instructor and Boys Basketball Coach
Peabody High School
1963-1985

I met Professor Iles in May 1961. Mr. Iles and then school administrator for Black schools, Sidney Townsend, came to Grambling and recruited me as a math teacher for Peabody. During that time, many of the metropolitan schools only hired teachers who had scored over 400 on the National Teachers Exam. My score was well above the 400, and I was offered a job at Peabody. After graduation, I was classified as "1A" by the military. I worked at Peabody for about a month and was drafted.

I returned to teach at Peabody in August 1963 and taught geometry and Algebra II. I will never forget Mr. Iles calling me into his office after the first six weeks when we had to turn in a progress report on our classes. In my report on my geometry students, I indicated that over half my students were failing. I was skilled in geometry, and I assumed that the things that were taught were easy. Prof Iles (a designated name for Principal Iles) gave me one of the greatest lessons I received as a teacher during my entire career. Prof told me, "Mr. Bowman, we hired you because you knew math, and that's good, but your job as a teacher is not to show how much you know but to bring out what the students need to know." That changed my philosophy of teaching.

On another occasion, Mr. Iles called me into his office and shared that the white high schools, Bolton, Pineville, and others in the parish, were teaching calculus and other advanced math courses to their students. He told me to initiate a class to teach advanced mathematics at Peabody, and we can call it what we want. That's what we did, and the results produced some of the greatest students in this country. Prof assigned only the most qualified and advanced teachers to teach the higher-level classes.

Behind his back, the male teachers called Professor Iles "the bullet" because he would "pop up" in your class at any time to evaluate your teaching and the students' behavior. "The bullet is coming!"

I was told by some of the former Black principals of Rapides Parish that Mr. Iles was the only Black principal in the parish who would speak up for the Black schools at principals and school board meetings. He loved Peabody and did his best to look out for the interest of the school and the Black community in Alexandria. At that time Black educators knew they were preparing Black students to compete with all races, particularly whites, for private sector jobs and opportunities in politics and other areas. For this cause, there were concerted efforts to prepare young people for such a future.

*Peabody Magnet High School 2021*

# THIS IS MY JOURNEY, NOT MY DESTINATION

*"In all of us, there is a hunger, marrow-deep, to know our heritage — to know who we are where we come from. Without this enriching knowledge, there is a hollow yearning. No matter what our attainments in life, there is still a vacuum. An emptiness, and the most disquieting loneliness."*
— ALEX HALEY

## Dr. Willie James Johnson

I WAS BORN ON August 22, 1950, in Huey P. Long Charity Hospital in Pineville, Louisiana. I got my first name, Willie, from my favorite aunt's husband, Uncle Willie. He was a country preacher and a very snazzy dresser with a starched shirt and black suit. My middle name comes from my mother's oldest brother, Jim, whose given name was James. So, that is how I became Willie James. My mother did not like calling me Willie, so she nicknamed me "Billy," and that has remained with me all my life.

*The young men in our class were very aware of the Vietnam War, and we recognized we would have to serve and fight in that war. But, our main focus was on the area of racial inequality and racial change in America.*

I'm the fourth child of Martha and Cornelius Johnson. My paternal grandparents were Dave and Mary Robinson Johnson. My father was born in Red Cross, Louisiana, and my mother was born in Bayou Rapides, Louisiana. My grandfather was Dave Johnson, born in Red Cross, Pointe Coupee Parish, Louisiana in 1867 during the post-slavery era. There was limited recorded information about my great-great-grandfather Tom (Thomas) Johnson, who was born in Texas. Dave Johnson was not reared as a slave. Census records state that he was a farmworker. From stories passed down, Grandpa Dave had seven brothers, and, of course, like most Black families in the South during that time, little is known about his siblings. During the early years of his life, his family migrated from Pointe Coupee Parish to Bayou Rapides. He met and married Mary Robinson on February 27, 1900. This marriage was blessed with five children: Freddie, Annie, Carrie, Janie, and Cornelius (my father).

Mary Robinson was my grandmother. She was born in 1872 in Louisiana. Her mother and father were Brisscoe and Sharlot Robinson. Her mother's maiden name was Sharlot Lard. The ancestry documents revealed that Sharlot Lard's mother was Della Lard Warner, my great-great grandmother. According to the 1860 United States Federal Census, she resided in Moreland Township, Missouri, and unfortunately, no other records were found after that date. I hope to find out more about my mother's side of the family soon.

I have six other siblings, my oldest sister, Susie Marie, followed by Cornelius, Jr., then my brother above me, Louis. I am next in line, then there is Novalee, and Donald

Ray. My baby sister, Denise Ann, is the last born. Growing up, the boys shared a room and beds. I had the "privilege" of sleeping with my baby brother.

One thing that was instilled in me from childhood to adulthood was to never tell lies. My dad always taught me that your word is your bond. Don't tell a person what you will do when you have no intention of keeping a promise. As a child, I was raised in the Baptist faith. I was baptized in the Methodist faith. My first wife was from the Church of England and my second wife was Catholic. I now worship in a non-denominational church. First thing, I believe in God. My main belief is that we are all sinners saved by God's grace. "I look to the hills from whence cometh my help, my help cometh from the Lord." (Psalm 121:1-2, KJV) During my childhood, I lived in the segregated Louisiana city of Alexandria. From the third grade until high school, I was a Sonia Quarters boy, 1429 Vance Avenue. When I was growing up, I had a hound dog named Duke, who loved soul food, which meant he ate what we ate. Like me, Duke loved the fried chicken served at the Sunday dinner meal.

When I was five, I was acutely aware that things were different for me as a young Black boy living in segregated Alexandria. There were things that made me understand that there were two Americas, one for whites and another for Blacks. In the 1950s, we were considered "colored." I vividly remember using separate water fountains and bathrooms, with the "Colored" sign prominently displayed. I remember when we wanted meals at the local white restaurants, we had to order our food and pick it up at the side or the back entrance. There was no dining-in. I also could not ride in the front of the public city buses. I recall hearing about the Ku Klux Klan and the fear and terror they brought with them.

In1963, when I was a student at Lincoln Road Junior High School, the KKK set a cross on fire in front of our art building. I still can remember the fear that it brought into my life. Jim Crow laws affected ordinary things in our everyday lives. As kids, we would go downtown to Kress, our five and dime store, and at the rear of the building were the "White" and "Colored" water fountains and restrooms. When we wanted a drink of water, we would form a semicircle and drink from the white fountain one at a time. The Colored fountain was nasty, and we would not drink from it.

Social and entertainment areas were segregated, too. I always loved going to the movie theater. The "colored" theater was the Ritz Theater on Lee Street. The movies played continuously, so you could spend the day at the Ritz. On Saturday mornings, we would go to the Paramount Theater where the white people sat downstairs, and the Colored people sat upstairs. The owner of the other theater, The Don, located on Bolton Avenue, did not want to integrate after the Civil Rights laws were passed, so the owner closed it down.

I also realized at a young age that religion was segregated, and I could not understand how Sunday mornings could be the most segregated day in the United States. All those religious white people telling God how much they loved Him, but at the same time, they had so much hatred in their hearts for Black people. I have to leave that in the hands of God. First John 4:16 and 20 say it better: "Whoever lives in love, lives in God, and God in him. We love him because he first loved us. If anyone says, I love God, yet hates his brother, he is a liar, for anyone who does not love his brother, which he has seen, cannot love God, whom he has not seen."

My mother taught me a valuable lesson about racism. Growing up, my parents talked to me about how to act around white people. My mother worked as a domestic for a white family across town. From time to time, she would take me to help her. My mother would remind me not to take anything that was not mine. I do remember one day while I was cleaning under the bed, I found a $5 bill on the floor. When I showed it to my mother, she explained that white people would intentionally leave money around to see if you would steal it because they felt we all were thieves. That lesson has stayed with me all these years.

As I got older, I came to understand that "Jim Crow" was a collection of state and local statutes that legalized racial segregation. The Black Codes were the roots of Jim Crow laws that began as early as 1865, immediately after the abolition of slavery in the United States. The most dangerous organization of the Jim Crow era when I was growing up was the Ku Klux Klan. They grew into a secret society whose purpose was to terrorize Black communities. The group exists today.

I now live three blocks from Bolton High, the school in my neighborhood, that before desegregation was for whites only. I got a chance to go inside Bolton High

School in 1968 to take the ACT/SAT. During that time, I noticed the school had new science lab equipment and new textbooks. I had never in my school life had a new textbook.

My high school experience has remained powerful throughout my life. I often think about those days at Ole Peabody. Principal D.F. Iles, said to us, "It is my wish that each of you of the 1968 graduating class will be a better person when you leave than you were when you came."

That was certainly true for me. I attended the all-Black Peabody Senior High School from 10th through 12th grades. We had a well-known mascot: The Warhorse. Our school colors were green and white. On nice days, I would walk to school. I would go through the mill and hit the railroad tracks. If it rained, I would ride the school bus. The teachers at Peabody were great, and I clearly remember Mr. Arthur Allen, Coach Davis, Mrs. Baker, and Mrs. Robinson. My favorite teacher was Mrs. Stemley (American History). I have many fond memories as a member of the LIALO (Louisiana Interscholastic Athletic and Literary Association) recognized Debate Team, and a member of the Bi-Phy-Chem Club and Troop 1009 of the National Thespian Society.

One of my biggest memories is our senior play: *The Storm*. William Shakespeare best summarized our activities at the Peabody Senior High School when he wrote: "The whole world is a stage, and all the men and women merely actors. They have their exits and their entrances, and in his lifetime a man will play many parts, his life separated into seven acts." Going to the prom with Shirley Goodman is a fun memory, and, oh, the class rings. If you were going "steady," you gave the ring to your girl so that she could wear it on a chain around her neck. I never knew what happened to that ring, and after all these years, I guess I'll never find out.

Peabody was a great school — it provided me with a quality education that was comparable to many other high schools given the many disadvantages we had to endure. Peabody added so much to my understanding of the world, that quality comes from many different sources — mainly the teachers, our school administration, and the student body.

Peabody was the center of our universe. It provided us with not only quality education but also with the ability to exceed, examine and evaluate many different situations and come up with an effective plan of action. We were prepared for our future in an everchanging world. Our Class of 1968, in my opinion, was one of the greatest classes to enter the halls of our historic high school. We were trailblazers. Our classmates represent professions across the spectrum: lawyers, nurses, doctors, educators, administrators, in the public and private sectors, as well as finance, business and technology experts.

Two factors account for this success — teachers and students. Many of the teachers were young visionaries, while others were seasoned professionals, all committed to our success. The second factor, students responsibly questioned the status quo in preparing for the future. At Peabody, we were ready, willing, and able to tackle the world and help make world-changing decisions.

The young men in our class were very aware of the Vietnam War, and we recognized we would have to serve and fight in that war. But our main focus was on the area of racial inequality and racial change in America.

The Rev. Dr. Martin Luther King Jr. was assassinated the month before we graduated. Many on the other side felt that by killing Dr. King, The Dreamer, that they could kill The Dream. The other side further thought that the death of Robert Kennedy would be a double blow to the advancement of Blacks in our society. It's 2021, and the fight continues. The United States of America is a divided nation. Advancement may have slowed in these divided times, but the slowdown is not expected to dim the fire that could not be extinguished.

As we prepared to leave the safety of Peabody, the music at the time reflected what was happening in the world around us in 1968, and the songs played a key role in our lives. The lyrics were uplifting and motivating messages, from James Brown's encouraging us to "Say it Loud — I'm Black and I'm Proud," to powerful song titles by The Impressions telling the stories of the day, "We're a Winner," "People Get Ready," and "Keep on Pushing."

When I left Peabody, I was one of many students who had fulfilled Professor Iles' wish that we would be better when we left Peabody than when we came. After high school, I attended Louisiana Polytechnic Institute (now Louisiana Tech University) in Ruston. Tech had been recently integrated, and it was a new experience for me to go to school with whites. My classes were predominantly white. I relied heavily on what I had been taught and on my good study habits, which helped me tremendously. If I found a professor that I felt was honest and fair in his grading, I would try to get that professor for future classes. I also relied on our social organization, Soul Tech, for help. Soul Tech was an organization founded by Black students for Black students to encourage friendship through campus outings and community events and spark open discussions and interactions with Black students from around the world.

At the university, most of the male freshmen lived in Hutchinson Hall. My roommate was AC Hollis. One day we came out of the room to find "nigger" notes left on our door, and the next week a trash can was placed outside our door and set on fire. My roommate and I put out the fire. We never reported it to the housemother, and we never had that problem or the notes again. In 1968, there was very little social interaction between white and Black students. Back then, it was widely believed by Black students that white students at Louisiana Tech followed the old racist belief, "You should go back to Africa." At the time, it was an insult used across the country against Black Americans. Today, it is used against other nonwhites and foreigners. I read in the *Urban Dictionary* that most racist communities also happen to be the least educated among whites. The explanation helps me to understand in some small measure why Blacks are hated so much by white people. I came to this understanding about white people at an early age. The belief is that if it is right, it is white, or the best way.

Stories of what I believe to be racist behavior are real. In late 1969 after my first year at Louisiana Tech, I had begun receiving Social Security payments from my father's death. That meant I would have the money every month to pay back a student loan. My mother and I went to Rapides Bank where my mother had had an account for decades. All the necessary loan paperwork was completed. He asked several questions, and I noticed the change in his attitude when he asked about the college I was attending. My mother proudly told him that I was attending Tech and that I was on the Dean's List. He told us that it would be a few days, and he would have someone call. A person from the bank called to inform me that they could not grant me the loan. I was disappointed, but I have come to accept systematic racism from white people.

To tell the whole truth, I was very angry. I had a conversation with my mother about the situation and reminded her that I would lose my Social Security payment if I was not in school and that my draft status for not being in school would change from deferment to 1F. My draft lottery number was 21, so I would be drafted in 1970. I made the decision to enlist rather than be drafted. I went down to the Navy recruiter's office, took the test, and three weeks later I was told

to come to the office. When I arrived, the sailor in charge told me that everything was approved, and I was selected to train in nuclear systems. I was excited until I asked what that was. He said after my training I would be assigned to submarine duty. That hit me like a rock. I didn't want anything under the water.

I stood outside with tears in my eyes, then a miracle came. The Air Force recruiter standing nearby asked me had I considered the United States Air Force. He said he could get me in if I was interested, and I agreed immediately. I completed the required paperwork, and the recruiter instructed me to return the following Thursday, and off I went on a Trailways bus to New Orleans for my physical that same day. On March 17, 1970, I was officially inducted into the United States Air Force. In May 1970, I graduated from Basic Training and proceeded to the 4600th Security Police

Squadron for direct duty assignment. My training at Ent AFB, named for Major General Uzal Girard Ent, in Colorado Springs, Colorado, lasted until October 1970. By late October, I had been assigned to the 7551st Security Police Section at Royal Air Force Greenham Common, in Newbury, England.

When I arrived at the base, I had grown in my understanding of the world. I understood that as a Black man I had to stand up and not take stuff from white people, and I quickly found out that the military climate would be no different. I became a radical, and I believed in the Black Power Movement. Bobby Seale, Angela Davis, H. Hap Brown, Stokely Carmichael, Huey P. Newton, and Eldridge Cleaver, I believed in all of them. Newton and Seale were the founders of the Black Panther Party. In my room on the base in England, I displayed a picture of Huey P. Newton, sitting in a bamboo chair holding a rifle in his right hand and a spear in his left. During weekly dorm inspections, my room always got an excellent rating, and the unit decided that all posters on the wall should be in a frame. It did not apply to the rebel flags. I had a woodworker in Newbury make me a beautiful picture frame and mounted my poster into that frame. During my first four years in the air force, I recognized many instances of racial injustice. No matter how badly white people behaved, military leadership would always place that circle of protection around them. I thought that was an isolated incident, but during my 26 years in the air force, I witnessed preferential treatment to whites so many times that I lost count. I know firsthand the toll that racism takes on so many Black Americans, and just like in civilian life, Jim Crow was alive and well in the US Air Force.

Through it all, being in the air force was an exceptional experience for me. In my assignments, I saw the benefits of my education, upbringing, and values. My air force record was exceptional. I won many awards for my job performance. On April 1, 1996, after 26 years of dedicated work, I retired from the United States Air Force where, at the time, I was serving in the Grade/Rank of E-8 (Senior Master Sergeant and worked as a Law Enforcement Superintendent and a First Sergeant. That day I was awarded my sixth Meritorious Service Medal. From there, I had one goal, the continuation of my education.

With my two-year tenure at Louisiana Tech University behind me, after retirement, I took courses at Capitol Radio Engineering Institute, Community College of the Air Force, and City Colleges of Chicago and received B.S. and B.A. degrees at Americus and Ashwood Universities, respectively. I earned my master's and doctoral degrees from Madison University.

I was married to the late Frances Romar Johnson on July 30, 2005. She went home to be with the Lord on April 16, 2019. We met at a family reunion picnic, and I invited her to a movie. I always knew that there was something special between us. After some time and conversations, we began dating. On Christmas Day 2004, I asked her the Big Question, and she said, "Yes". Six months later, we were married in Alexandria by my childhood friend and classmate — The Right Honorable Rev. Larry D. Smith. We honeymooned in San Antonio, Texas. I have three children, Willie James (Will), from my prior marriage. Mildred (Millie), and Henry (Big Hen) are my second and third children respectively. We have five grandchildren, Aidan (AI), Akiya (KiKi), Franjone' (Franny), Quentin, Jr. (Tigger), and Henry III (Trey).

I am an avid traveler in the area of cruising. I have been a travel agent for over eight years, and I have been on 22 cruises. My favorite trip was a 1972 Mediterranean cruise. The best part of this trip was seeing things that I had only read about or seen on television. As a travel agent who specializes in the cruise sector, I have been enormously blessed. There is nothing in the world like being on the open sea or ocean, relaxing and enjoying life.

On the other side of pleasurable travel experiences and military service abroad, I have found that the serious side of life includes being active in the community and understanding the power of getting people who look like me in political positions. And, yes, that sometimes means voting for a person just because they are Black. White people will try to guilt-trip us about this, but they have done this for years. I have experienced many forms of racism and discrimination in many areas of my life. I can personally say that I see how racism affects Black people especially in the areas of housing, education and criminal justice.

On reflecting on my life and where I started and what I've accomplished, I've come to the understanding that God has an assignment for us all. So, I have learned to forgive whites for all the wrongs, but it is equally important to never forget those wrongs because not everyone shares the same beliefs. I have learned to simply pray and turn it over to God. Never forget from whence we came because that failure can make the past become our future. Dr. King said it this way: "We must develop and maintain the capacity to forgive. He who is devoid of the power to forgive is devoid of the power to love. There is some good in the worst of us and some evil in the best of us. When we discover this, we are less prone to hate our enemies."

I was born in Louisiana, and I've lived here much of my life. I have been around the world — not bad for a "little country boy" raised in Alexandria, Louisiana. I will leave my story with the following: Try to get as much out of life as you can. Here's a little tip for you to live by, it has always worked for me — If you think about it, it can be done.

God bless and live life.

# SEEING LIFE "THROUGH A GLASS WHITELY"

*"A time to plant and a time to pluck up…"*

ECCLESIASTES 3:2

## Rev. Ameal Jones

*I was pulled from the primordial grounds where the soil was hard, rocky, and cracked and somewhat deficient in necessary nutrients. Despite what that life gave us, my family drew heavily from their determination to overcome in the face of opposition and brutal forces. Raising Black children in a world that was designed for them NOT to succeed was a hell of a challenge.*

*Churchgoers were highly fascinated by a child preacher. I was a Boy Wonder. I had to stand on a box behind the pulpit to see and be seen.*

WHEN I DECIDED to join my high school classmates in this effort to reflect on my childhood and life in general under Jim Crow rule, I could not stop thinking about the speech given by philosophy professor, Dr. Charles W. Mills in a 2017-18 Central Division Presidential Address for the American Philosophical Association. "Through a Glass Whitely," the inspirational title of Dr. Mills' talk, remains with me to this day. It resonates because it comes from the language of the Apostle Paul's "through a glass darkly" in Paul's reference to how we see things obscurely now, as opposed to how we shall see them at the end of time.

For me, growing up in a segregated society shaped my world view and negatively influenced my perceptions. I see my life, as I lived it in the captivity of European consciousness and colonialism, and I now interpret reality not through a "glass darkly" but through a "glass whitely". What follows is an abbreviated chronicling of my journey from the damaging clutches and psychological and spiritual blind spots of racism and colonialism to true self-knowledge and liberation and commencement of my exodus and release into my new self and destiny.

## LITTLE HOUSE ON THE PLANTATION

I was raised on the Moreland Plantation in Rapides Parish in Central Louisiana. The plantation was originally owned by the secessionist governor of Louisiana, Thomas Overton Moore, who was a slaveholder. The plantation was burned to the ground during the Civil War. It was rebuilt after the Civil War and not a building is left standing today, only a leaning historical marker and trees where the plantation home and shacks used to be.

*Former location of Mooreland Plantation*

My family lived on the plantation from my birth until 1962. Houses on the property were located about 40 feet from Highway 71 (Old Baton Rouge Highway). The plantation was situated between the Inglewood Plantation and the Chambers Dairy Farm and plantation near Bayou Robert.

Moreland was certainly not a desirable place to live if you were Black because you were still in bondage in the second half of the 20th century. The houses were wood framed with tin roofs. There were cracks in the walls and the floors. We used pages from *Look* magazine, Sears & Roebuck catalog, and newspapers to plaster the walls. The floors were wooden and had to be frequently mopped. Our house had three rooms: a front room, middle room, and a kitchen. None of the houses on the Moreland Plantation had electricity, indoor running water, or bathrooms. The toilet was outdoors in a small building called an outhouse. Baths were taken in a Number 3 tub.

That little brown house sat on brick pillars, had two doors (front and back), front porch, iron stoves (one for cooking meals, the other one for supplying heat for the front room). The middle room had no heat. There was an icebox with ice purchased in blocks of 25, 50 or 75 pounds to keep foods and beverages cool because there was no electricity. Light was provided by kerosene lamps. Water for cooking, bathing, and washing was drawn from a hydration near the church where we were members. The hydration was located on the Inglewood Plantation. We had to haul water in 10-gallon buckets, a tedious task for smaller children. Water was a precious commodity. Wasting water was a misdemeanor. Some families used water from a well. I did not like well water.

People had no system of refrigeration to keep their food cold; meats were often preserved with salt or smoked. Some folks had a smokehouse. Sweet and Irish potatoes were gathered and stored underground in what was called a *potatoes pump*. Vegetables and fruit were canned in jars to preserve for winter in lean times. Oh yes, the watermelon patch would be raided, and the search would be on to find the culprit. Our elders would counsel and warn us by saying, "If you lie, you'll steal, and if you steal, you'll kill." If your name was mentioned with the accused, even if you were not guilty, a good whipping would follow. In the eyes of my mother, stealing was a felony, and it was punishable by severe scolding, sometimes getting cussed out, and a real hard beating with hands and peach tree switches. She would often say during times for correction, "I brought you into this world, and I'll take you out."

Black people who lived in the 1940s up to the 1970s were considered "ground" people. Their food came from the earth (their gardens). They believed that meals should be prepared from scratch. In my home, we ate plenty of ground food and little meat with our meals. We ate beans, peas, okra, potatoes, cornbread, biscuits, greens, and other vegetables. Meats and sweets were eaten only on Sundays. Food left over from supper was saved and eaten for breakfast. One had to eat what was prepared and set before him or her. There weren't any choices. Everyone had to eat at the table at the same time. Mealtimes were special times for strengthening bonds and sharing stories. More than enough food was prepared because families thought about their neighbors. I ate many meals with strangers at our table. The stranger sometimes would be what people called a "hobo." The hobos would be Black, white, or Mexican. The kids were somewhat reluctant to sit and eat with strangers, but our parents made us sit at the table. Black people had a strong sense of communal values and often demonstrated responsibility for the neighborhood.

When our family's meal barrels ran low, neighbors would come to our aid. Sitting at a table and sharing a meal was an open invitation to receive and accept another as equal, and it was an acknowledgement of their humanity and dignity. My mother had to prepare for a family of eight seven days a week. She taught all of us how to cook, wash, sweep, keep house, wash clothes, and supervise our younger siblings. There was no such thing as a babysitter or daycare. Older siblings were assigned that responsibility. The job came with few instructions. It was an OJT (on the job training) experience. If your younger siblings got into some trouble, the other siblings would suffer a penalty, which included not only a fussing but even a whipping. Even after the abolishment of legal slavery, the use and sound of the whip could still be felt. I hear Black adults today say that they got whippings, and it did not kill them, and some even say it kept them out of jail and made them better people. Slavery left an indelible scar on the psyche of Black folk.

The house was surrounded by cotton, corn, beans, and hayfields. The cotton and corn would grow so tall, it sometimes would become difficult to see our neighbor's house. There wasn't much inspiration to glean from those fields. My hopes and aspirations went beyond the boundaries of that environmental void. Younger siblings wanted to follow in the footsteps of their older siblings and leave the plantation. Our parents would emphasize the importance of getting an education. I wished that more Black parents living on those plantations had pushed hard to educate their sons. Many parents believed that a boy could find a job anywhere. Their definition of a man was from shoulders down and not from shoulders up. To this day, many Black men seek jobs that require strenuous labor.

There was no shortage of strenuous jobs on the plantation where unemployment was not an issue. Everybody had to work. The job list included chopping and picking cotton, plowing with mules and tractors, chopping wood, pulling corn, feeding farm animals, stringing and fixing fences, cutting sugarcane and digging ditches and, of course, working as a yard boy, driving Miss Daisy and chauffeuring Mr. Charlie. My mother introduced me to the cottonfield at the age of 10. I was given a three-foot cotton sack to fill. I seldom picked enough cotton to fill it. I got tired and would fall asleep on my mother's 12-foot-long sack. My mother was a strong Black woman. She could work all day with a plug of Bull of the Woods chewing tobacco in her jaw or a pinch of Garrett snuff under her bottom lip. I tried both and my head would spin like a top, and that would be followed by a stomachache for days. I was driven by my mother's work ethic. Work made me feel good about myself for it boosted my self-esteem. I felt like I was helping my mother and my younger siblings. I came from the plantation where the only qualifications were muscle, backbone, and a desire and will to work.

The work was hard, the hours were long, and the pay was low. The pay for chopping cotton was $4 a day and $2 per hundred pounds of cotton. I'll never forget my little paycheck for chopping cotton at the end of five days. It was $17.50. My mother would take it every payday and use it to support our family. I even witnessed Black women collecting their husband's pay. They believed that a real man would take care of his family and/or his woman. Domestic work kept many Black mothers away from their children for most of the day. Fathers would return hours after mothers got home. Many days, weeks, and months we would go without seeing our parents until late hours in the evenings or nights. Older siblings would care for us until our parents would arrive. The house had to be cleaned, food cooked, younger siblings fed, bathed, and put to bed. As soon as we would hear the voices of our parents, we would get out of bed and run and greet them.

My mother worked many jobs from chopping and picking cotton, cutting sugarcane, doing domestic and laundry work, to undertaking tasks at Herbie K's, Noah's Potato Chip Co, and local nursing homes. She worked only a few weeks at the stinky chicken processing plant.

There were some sizeable families living on those plantations. Some households had 10 kids, some 12 to 15, and some had as many as 18 to 22, but I never heard of a child that went without. Parents knew how to beat the odds, rise, and courageously meet the challenges. This doesn't mean that every family maneuvered well. Our elders knew that "it takes a village to raise a child". We were claiming people as family who really weren't biologically kin to us. They strongly believed in and practiced the Negro spiritual, "I got shoes, you got shoes, all of God's children got shoes." From the very beginning, our ancestors, due to their deep roots in African spirituality, believed that real salvation has a sociological dimension.

Plantation families drew on that spirituality to deal with life's changes, challenges, strange phenomenon and the unknown. Black spirituality has many strands of beliefs, practices and expressions. African slaves did not arrive in America devoid of a strong spiritual center and connection. They were introduced to Western Euro-American white religiosity and church-anity and serious distortions, false representations and aberrations of Christianity. Oppressors have always used religion as the "handmaid" to enslavement. Black slaves were given the Jesus that their oppressors wanted them to have — the religious literature (Sunday School books, Bibles and pictures had white Jesus and white angels). Slaves attended white churches with their masters, but they had to sit in the balconies. Today, Blacks attend multiracial churches and sit next to whites. Making denominational shifts and changing churches does not change the conditions.

Our Sunday School teachers would tell us young people not to limit Jesus to that white picture of Him, for He's more than that. Slavery had a profound effect on the spirituality of many Black slaves, and it planted some seeds of distortion and unhealthy and incorrect views about God, the world, and the humanity of the slaves. Even the U. S. Constitution prior to the 14th and 15th Amendments defined the Negro as "three-fifths" of a man.

Our elders used to counsel us to learn to hold on to our money and save some for a rainy day. My mother would warn us about spending our money at the plantation store (Hard Times). She would say, "Do not let your money burn your hand and a hole in your pocket". I'm glad that I grew up in a time when living was not defined by money. There were times we did not see money in our home for months. We learned how to live without a paycheck. Our elders could take a little and make a lot. They knew how to work with scarcity and leftovers and make them sufficient.

Despite the challenges of living on the plantation, I enjoyed my home life. There were social glitches in the villages. We were trained to work and work long hard hours. Some days seemed at times to have no end. My older sister and I would join my mother and other adults on a long bus ride to the cottonfields. We had to rise early to catch the bus at 5 a.m. Sometimes we ran across snakes, dead animals, wasp nets, and signs of wild animals. It was in those fields that I heard and learned to sing the Negro spirituals. Occasionally, I would hear the blues. I enjoyed both because they told the story of my people's history and journey. Blues music is a part of Black history, and I claim that art. We would listen to the blues on Saturdays and sing gospel on Sundays. Blues highlighted the messy side to living. Old school music was and still is the real deal. Gospel music and Old School blues and rhythm and blues possess an element of immortality. We had an old phonograph attached to a battery that was a few inches longer that a car battery. There was also a long wire connected to it that ran up the wall and then outside the house to some type of antenna. We played records at the speed of 45, 33 1/3, and 78. We did our chores to those sounds. My mother would be washing a tub of clothes, and the iron wash pot would be resting on the fire filled with materials for the beds. A few minutes later, the clotheslines would be filled with clothes fluttering in the wind. In those days no one had the convenience of automatic washers and dryers.

My family worked the fields through the week, took care of other people's houses and children, and there was only Saturday to set their own houses in order. Working on Sundays was taboo. The state of Louisiana adhered to and obeyed the Blue Laws that had been imposed by the emperor Constantine and enforced by Napoleon Bonaparte.

Claude Anderson in *Black Wealth/White Labor: A New Perspective on Racial Inequality* wrote about how the American colonial system trained Blacks to invest in and build the empires of whites. In addition, the philosophy of the 18th century harsh slave master, Willie Lynch, had damaging and twisted effect on the minds, psyches and spirits of Blacks. It was a psychological tool and strategy used by whites to cause Blacks to compete, compare and even excoriate each other to the benefit of whites. I saw it play out in real life on the plantation. I witnessed a Black man beat another Black nearly to death before his wife. When Blacks fought each other, they went for the jugular vein. Black Lives Matter, BUT TO WHOM? The psychological chains of slavery are wrapped around the minds of Blacks even to this day. The philosophy of Willie Lynch taught Blacks not to support each other. We are still faced with some of the same issues today that I experienced on the plantation in the 1960s.

The plantation economics haunt me and our community to this day. Payday came after five days of chopping cotton in the amount of $17.50. Blacks stood in cotton-fields for hours in the hot sun. We were given a break for lunch. There was nowhere to sit. When the time came to use the bathroom, we had to walk off and find a place in tall weeds and grass. We stood in a long line waiting to get our pay. Pay was given in cash without any taxes taken. Many Black families worked those fields for 20 to 40 years and made many white plantation owners rich.

Blacks had to use wisely the little money and resources they had to sustain them through the winter months when work options were slim. Some winters would be cold and lean. My mother would take us back out into the fields when the harvest had ended to scrap cotton and pick pecans. We picked pecans on half. We had to pick one sack,100 pounds for ourselves, and one sack for the plantation owner. We got through those lean and harsh winters by scrapping cotton, picking pecans, and eating potatoes, salted meats, and food that had been preserved.

How often did we hear, "Do not let that little money burn a hole in your hand and pocket?" Our elders would advise us about learning how to hold on to our money. Young people often got warnings about hanging around the plantation store named Hard Times. One would seldom see a young person hanging around the store. The system that Blacks lived under was so calculated that after their long hours of strenuous labor, the earnings would end up back in the coffers of the white man. It was an unfair system of dependence. Blacks could not own and operate a business on plantations. The overseers owned and controlled everything. The overseers owned the land where we stood, walked, and worked. They owned the little shacks and houses where we had to sleep. They owned the water we drank. They owned the store and its contents. Imagine how those conditions shaped our view and perspective on life? It really was a white man's world. Blacks who grew up on plantations could hardly see any other reality. The presentation of God and Jesus that the slave masters had given led many Blacks to believe and accept the idea that that's the way it was supposed to be. Blacks were seen as slaves and entertainers for the white man. Unfortunately, many Blacks defended that philosophy and way of life.

It's difficult for some Blacks to say in one breath and sentence that they love Black people without including the words, "and you got to love everybody." Everybody means white people. Blacks have been trained to look outside and beyond themselves, their race and culture, and look to whites as their standard of excellence. Blacks who lived in plantation alley, plantations from Central Louisiana to Baton Rouge, often turned to whites for approval.

In 2020-2021, by my calculation, there's not a hamburger stand or a business of substantial status in Alexandria, Louisiana's Black community that can hire 10 Black people. In my opinion, the Black community in Rapides Parish hasn't seen anything major change in more than 50 years. There is a whole lot of going and coming to church and even changing from one church to another. But changing churches DOES NOT CHANGE conditions.

## LIFE OUTSIDE THE PLANTATION

From birth until we moved to Woodside in 1962, most of my time, including church attendance, was spent on the plantation. The church and the graveyard were on the plantation. Our lives were different from our counterparts who lived in town. Ours was an outpost, a rural lifestyle much closer to the existence of our enslaved forebears. We left the plantation to go into town, to school, and for medical attention.

## MY EDUCATIONAL JOURNEY

I attended public school in Alexandria. Evidence was everywhere to remind us that white society wanted us to stay in our place. All public buildings had signs for "Whites" and "Colored," and the courthouses had Confederate flags flying on the roof. Public transportation was segregated. I grew up in a time that was bent on preaching that Blacks were inferior and that they were to be treated differently. Segregation was social distancing based on false science, beliefs, and fears. There were two state superintendents of education, one for the white school system and one for the Black school system. They were separate and unequal in every way.

We were bussed from the plantation to Reed Avenue Elementary School, later renamed Julius Patrick, in the Oil Mill Quarters. I would enjoy the bus ride because it was a chance to get away from home and all the chores. I was embarrassed by the clothes that I wore because they often were torn. My shoes sometimes had holes in them. I would feel good about myself when I had new clothes and shoes to wear. Blacks had only a few places to purchase clothes, and so many students wore some of the same. Our teachers acted like a second parent. They were committed to our development. They got to know the students' parents and would often make home visits. When a teacher came to visit our home, my siblings and I would run and hide. Teachers also served like a truant officer who would monitor absenteeism. I was happy about the different kids that made up the student body. Some were from "the country", and some lived in the city. I enjoyed the food because it was prepared and cooked there. The cooks would see that all students had enough to eat. I ate everything on my plate.

There were as many Black male teachers as females. There was a good percentage of male teachers throughout my public education journey. The male teachers expressed an interest in our total wellbeing. Rarely would a male teacher be seen making home visits. Subjects such as Spelling, Writing and Arithmetic were done on a blackboard before the whole class. Teachers would discipline students who repeatedly failed to prepare for classwork. I'll never forget the title of a book we read, *Little Black Sambo*. We saw the book as something funny and had no *awareness* of the racist stereotypes. Some of the study materials were saturated with stereotypes of Blacks. Black teachers made sacrifices to bridge the gap, while they worked with less and inferior materials. Another thing that I liked about my school was that it had indoor toilets and hot and cold water and, oh yes, gas heaters.

I made good grades at Reed and was promoted to the seventh grade. My junior high school, Lincoln Road, now Phoenix, was even better. The teachers were great, and the student body was made up of a whole group of new people. There were lots of pretty girls. Junior high included grades 7-9. Many of our textbooks were old, and some had missing pages. We were happy to be given new textbooks and be the first to write our names in them.

My years at Peabody High are the most memorable ones. Preparation for graduation was the highest moment of my public education years. Peabody held a traditional baccalaureate worship service prior to graduation to honor graduates. It was held early on a Sunday morning. A preacher would be invited to speak, and he would end up preaching. Some people would shout, cry and praise God Almighty.

I graduated from Peabody High in May 1968. Peabody had prepared me for the world.


## THE BLACK MEDICAL EXPERIENCE

I, like all other Black babies in or near Alexandria, was born at the Huey P. Long Charity Hospital in nearby Pineville. This hospital was established in Louisiana to serve the indigent. The treatment we received was sometimes inhumane. I'll never forget my visits to the hospital. We lived five miles from the city bus stop, and we would walk those miles to catch the 6 a.m. bus to make a 7 a.m. medical appointment. If you were not at the bus stop on time, the driver would pull off even if you were a fourth of a mile away. The bus ran every hour and half. The last bus ran at 6 p.m. When we would miss that last bus we would have to find another way to get back home. Sometimes, we just had to walk all the way back home. Very few Blacks in the 1950s and early 1960s had their own transportation. Sometimes, we would hitchhike.

We had to be at the hospital by 7 but would not see a doctor until about 2:30 p.m. The wait was long, and children would get hungry and cry. Some parents could not afford to buy food for their children because sometimes they either had no money, like us, or the cost was too high. Sometimes parents had to take a child to use the restroom and would miss when their name was called and would have to wait until all other appointments had been completed. Sometimes parents would have to reschedule and return the following month.

Many parents would resort to using home remedies because of the poor professional medical care. Sometimes we were given a spoon of sugar with three drops of kerosene on top to treat ailments. Parents believed that a dose of castor oil was a cure for all ills. If you were to cut your foot or stick a nail in it, the wound would be washed, a piece of salt pork would be placed on top of it, and then a wrap. For upset stomach, there was lime water (same white powder used on streets before concrete is poured), castor oil and/or Black Draught, a bottled liquid laxative found in many Black homes at the time. The home remedies were mixed with prayer and a little superstition. Somehow those remedies did the job, and I felt a whole lot better.

Some of the nurses and doctors would treat Black parents and their children like they had no feelings. We loved it when a nurse or doctor had a special treat for a child. Health insurance was nonexistent. The worst thing that could happen would be to get sick at night. I remember my mother telling us on several occasions to go find a ride during the late hours of the night. Sometimes it took two hours before we found someone to take a sibling to the hospital. The wait lasted until doctors started arriving about 7 a.m. Emergencies were given consideration only if one was in a serious accident, cut, or shot.

As a boy growing up, I saw Black adults who had sustained some serious wounds return to the cottonfields to work in the hot sun. Black mothers who had given birth had to return to the fields to work immediately after. Given such inhumanity, as a child, I could only reason that whites believed that Black people did not feel pain. I witnessed some Blacks attempting to impress whites by showing no signs of discomfort and pain. Blacks would not reveal their fear of losing their jobs.

There was a saying among Blacks who lived on plantations: "If a mule dies, buy another, if a Nigger dies, hire another." When an adult Black male got sick, white overseers would say he was faking. Black parents would do what they had to do to protect the men from the scorn of white men. Black mothers would curb the assertiveness of young Black males and put a cap on their expressions of anger. That move would spare their sons from getting cussed, fired, or sent to jail. If your son got labeled as a troublemaker, he could no longer live on the plantation with his parents. He had to find shelter with other family or friends who lived in town, another city and sometimes another state. Many Black males looked for escape to a better life in the city and especially the U S Army. Parents would encourage their daughters to finish public school and go to college.


## CALL HIM FATHER

Life on plantations during the 1950s and 1960s was hard living and full of challenges. There were single parent families, broken homes, abuse, abandonment, addiction, runaways, teen pregnancy, poverty, disease, and even mental health problems. Incest was a problem. Adultery and infidelity created problems for the kinship matters. Many children, like myself, grew up not knowing who either one or both biological parents were.

I never really knew who my biological father was. I learned to call my younger siblings' daddy my father. Their father and I had somewhat of an estranged relationship.

There was little communication. We did not spend any time together. I do not ever recall sitting on his knee nor receiving a smile of approval. To me, he was just another adult male.

I really liked the old Model T Ford he owned. We had to crank it to start the engine, and sometimes we had to push it to get it started. Once the car started, we would run and jump in, and off we went down the road. When he bought a new Model I, we helped him push the old one into the bayou. The car wasn't totally submerged in the water, so my siblings and I would use it like a toy. Sounds from our mouths were the engine, and our imaginations were the fuel. We drove to places, and the car never left the bayou.

I had a twofold fear of my father. I wanted his love, attention, and approval, and I feared his whippings. My younger siblings got his attention and love because they looked like him, and like him, they were light skinned. I was a dark chocolate kid. I felt at times that I did not belong in that family. I was shunned, picked over and seldom chosen. My comfort and encouragement came from my mother. She sought to comfort me by saying, "Blacker the berry, sweeter the juice." My experiences and realities were so powerful, her words brought little or no comfort. I would often hear the old adage, "If you're white, you're right, if you're brown, stick around, and if you're Black, get back."

I was in the ninth grade before I learned that my father had another legal family. My siblings and I gladly welcomed our new discovered siblings. Even their mother opened her hands and heart to us. The closest that I ever got to my father happened during a visit to his house in the city. He and I were there alone. He told me that he was not feeling well. I do not know how it happened, but I ended up placing my hand on his head and praying for him. I somehow found the words to lead him to faith in Jesus Christ. He asked me why we had not talked before. I could not answer, and I did not answer him. That experience was so beyond my ability to make any assessment as to what had transpired between us.

I later learned that my father had been baptized at the Antioch Baptist Church by Rev R. B. Bennett. I was not there the morning my father passed away. There were some conversations that I wished we'd had during the living years. When I became a father with children, I had to give my children something that I never had.

## MY PREACHING AND MINISTRY EXPERIENCE

The Baptist church that I grew up in and where I received my spiritual nurturing was both a people and a place. It was a people of praise and protest, a place that provided a sense of identity and community and room for empowerment. Worship was multidimensional. It touched every aspect and dimension of the worshipper's total being. We got something for the head, heart, hands, and feet. There was no sitting quietly listening to a song or sermon. Worship was a trialogue, not a monologue. One was animated by the music and the message. I remember my elders saying they had received enough from that experience to last them all week. They would leave that service equipped to deal with the blue and brutal forces of Monday morning. The structure for worship was simple and routine. Sunday School at 9:30 a.m., followed by public prayers led by the deacons. Some of the prayers were memorized, and the young people recited the words to such prayers before a certain deacon would utter them. Many worshippers would wait outside until prayer time was over.

One of the most memorable and moving moments was when the choirs would march in to render the special music. One could tell and identify with the issues and the challenges that Black people were dealing with by the music they would sing. Our pastor served several congregations at various locations. He would arrive about 1:30 p.m. and then there would be more singing rendered by the Senior Choir. Rev G. C. Jacob would preach a high-spirited sermon. The church would catch on fire! By the time worship ended, it would be 3 p.m.

I really loved the times when baptismal services were held. We would have a host of candidates waiting to be baptized. The baptismal services held during Easter Sunday were incomparable in their impact on the lives of people. It was not unusual to see an assortment of expressions of praise — the responses of shouting, crying, fainting, running.

I was baptized at the age of 9. I heard the gospel preached. My heart was strangely warmed by the presence and power of God. I enjoyed my home church, Second Union, located between Moreland and Inglewood Plantations. I especially appreciated and enjoyed the saintly elders. There were people in my home church born between mid-1880s and 1890s. They would tell stories about their parents and grandparents. We were so taken by those stories. I spent many weekends in the home of a lady who was born in 1893. Miss Dixon would talk about the times she plowed with a team of oxen for 50 cents a day. The work was hard, and the pay was small.

I was considered what people called a "boy preacher". I started preaching at the age of 9 but did not make it known publicly until four years later. No one was surprised when I announced my call to the ministry. I was shackled by a shame-based personality, and I was downright afraid. The formative years of my journey as a preacher are marked by two pivotal events: my initial public sermon at Galilee Baptist Church, pastored by the Rev. Edward Jones Jr. (no relation), in August 1963, the summer before the assassination of President John F. Kennedy, and my ordination to the ministry of preaching in May1968 after the assassination of The Rev. Dr. Martin Luther King Jr.

I faced many changes and challenges growing up through the developmental stages of my life. The expectations imposed on me were high, unrealistic and, to some degree, and, in hindsight, unfair. I never got a chance to live a normal life of a child, teen, and young adult Black male. I was placed under restrictions. Certain child and teen loving activities were off limits. People, including my siblings, would often remind me of my need to avoid participation in certain worldly activities.

I did not have a girlfriend. I ended up spending most of the earliest years of my life as a loner. Oftentimes, I would leave home and go to the woods and preach. My congregation consisted of animals, cows, birds, chickens, and insects. When I would raise my voice, my congregation would take flight or run off. Ms. Edna B. Jones Whitney, a biology teacher at Peabody High School, lived near the plantation and said many times she could hear "that little boy down in the lower pasture having church because I see the cows running."

I preached a gospel of negativity and separation from worldly affairs. Mind you, the sins that I committed, I had to commit them while I was a preacher. Such preaching was popular back then, and it drew crowds. Churchgoers were highly fascinated by a child preacher. I was a Boy Wonder. I had to stand on a box behind the pulpit to see and be seen.

Preaching opened many doors, and I often was invited to preach. I took my Bible everywhere, even to school. At school, classmates would jokingly ask me to preach. I was teased by such things as playing cards, dancing, drinking alcohol, listening to worldly music, cussing, smoking, sex, and females who wore short and tight skirts. Sometimes guys would physically push a female on me to check my response. Despite the jokes and funny and embarrassing moments, my classmates would show me respect. I often was asked by classmates to pray for them. There were times I offered them counseling and encouragement. I got put out of the school library once for sharing the Bible with students.

The renowned principal of Peabody High, Mr. D. F. Iles, would invite me to address the student body and faculty during general assembly. I would stand in what Danish theologian Soren Kierkegaard called "fear and trembling" and deliver my message. One day after making my exit from the D.A. Anderson Auditorium, Ms. Johnnie M. Sampract, English teacher, caught me by my arm and told me that she enjoyed my speech and that she would help me improve my communication skills. I accepted her help because I had struggled for a long time with a series of crippling speech impediments. I worked hard at improving those skills, and it really helped my preaching. I was chosen by my high school drama club to serve as its president.

I fell in love with serving the churches through preaching. An honorarium or pay-for-preaching was not to be expected. I was told by some preachers if I was offered money to turn it down. I never followed that advice. After I preached my first public sermon, I was given $1.75. I stayed at the $5-$10 level for many years. A deacon would at most times give a collection and say that the gospel was free and one could not pay for it. He would further say that the church was not trying to pay me but was just giving me a little token of appreciation. I would say to myself, "The few pennies that you're offering me is a sure sign that y'all *aint* trying to pay me."

I served as pastor for the first time at age 19 at a salary of $45 per month. I rapidly became a popular and sought-after preacher. I was invited to preach in many churches of various denominations and no denominations. I was one happy itinerant preacher. My lodging was often in some segregated motel, and the rooms in some of those places were poorly insulated.

Opportunities to preach have taken me across America to Europe, Russia, and South America. I have served as pastor of congregations of various sizes, demographics and locations. I have served as a facilitator in numerous conferences and conducted workshops across America. My ministry of preaching has been influenced by so many able stewards of the Divine Story. Dr. King was a tremendous inspiration for me and many Black preachers in search of biblical and theological competence. I enrolled in New Orleans Baptist Theological Seminary to obtain a Master of Divinity degree back in the early 1970s, and I was among the first class of Black preachers allowed to take residence in their dorms. My seminary education opened many other doors for me. I have served as both a college and seminary instructor, in hospital and prison chaplaincy positions, and as president of a nonprofit organization.

## A FINAL WORD

I have seen a great deal in my lifetime and now am at a point at which I have great concerns about recent threats to civil rights for Black Americans. After the successes for the fight for racial equality in the 1960s, we decided that we no longer would rise every morning and ask whites and their system for permission to love. As African Americans, we continue to see racism and white supremacy as ungodly. We are determined now in this 21st century to make democracy work for all people. And, we will continue to push to humanize all institutions, change racist policies, and push to overturn unjust laws. There now is a strong will to create and build an America that is based on inclusivity and not exclusivity. As a race, we have lived with illusions of freedom far too long. The Black Lives Matter Movement was founded to remind the country that the serpent of racism is alive. The whole world looked in horror while George Floyd was publicly "lynched". The lynching was a painful reminder of what living Black in America can look like. We are now witnessing, on the part of some, an attempt to level the playing field for justice, equality, fairness and open access to wealth and resources. Right on the heels of that effort came an insurrection. Evil does not know when to quit.

I am pleased to share and pen my own narrative. I have witnessed many changes in this country for the well-being of all. Those changes came about at the price of suffering, sacrifices and the shedding of blood. I can somewhat explain as to why my life turned out to be what it is today with the following: "The Road Not Taken" by Robert Frost, *Born to Rebel* by Benjamin E. Mays and this statement from George B. Shaw: "Some people see things as they are and ask why, I dream of things that never were and ask why not."

On a personal level, there is no event nor experience that made the most radical difference in my life than marriage and the birth of my five children and nine grandchildren. It takes a life to change a life. I have traveled through life trying to answer the following: Why was I given? What does life want from me? I hope when I come to the finish line of life that my response was one of Commitment, Compassion, Integrity and Service. As I move on and heal from the wounds of that dehumanizing system, the scales of distortion and deception are slowly falling away. I can now see with much clarity and understanding the old molds that tried to hold me captive in a dimension and place of "non-being". I'm empowered by my family, friends, community and culture to work at self-analysis and self-knowledge, reject the distortions and live a life that is open to truth, love, justice and service.

# MY JOURNEY: EMPOWERED BY HIS GRACE AND FAVOR

*"Now unto Him that is able to keep you from falling, and to present you faultless before the presence of this glory with exceeding joy, to the only wise God our Saviour, be glory and majesty, dominion and power both now and ever. Amen."*

JUDE 1:24-25 (KJV)

## Emma L. (Jones) Gray, CPC

*"My father (a chef) had walked off his job because his white supervisor called him, 'boy'. I heard my dad declare to my mom... 'I am not a boy, Maxine. I am a man!' I was proud of my dad for taking a stand.*

I WILL SEEK TO tell my story from my "window sill" or "front porch" of the Black experience/dynamics while growing up in the South in Rapides Parish, Louisiana in the City of Alexandria. My goal is to provide an opportunity to peer into my life as a Black citizen of this town by taking a look at my community and culture and how it affected my outlook on life moving forward, as well as a reflection of a people determined to thrive by doing and being the best, they could in spite of obvious and unjustified challenges.

There comes a time in your life when you begin to wonder if your life mattered. What will be the story or legacy told about you? Questions swirl around in your head such as, did I live a life of purpose, did I help somebody, did I finish my purpose? These reflective questions are especially important to me because I am in the "seasoned citizen" time of my life. I realize that my actions and how I did life can have an effect on my children, future generations and society. This matters to me.

Well, I must say being a part of such a historic book project as this one truly fit my desire of telling my story, at least in part. It is indeed an honor and blessing to be asked to participate, and it's especially exciting to partner with my Peabody High School classmates. Although in the beginning I was not fully aware of the hardship that discriminatory Jim Crow practices placed on my parents and our community at large, I will seek to pull back the curtains and allow a glimpse of what life was like for me in "the Black" experience and how my eventual awakening to such unfair practices and norms helped shape my life by preparing me to face such realities.

This momentous body of work is certainly needed today at a time when the call and cry of "BLACK LIVES MATTER" is seen as something new for some but clearly understood by Black communities everywhere. This movement is a sum total of the fact that Black lives and Black life have always mattered to our enriched heritage and community of African descendants in Alexandria that continues to contribute to "the diaspora of a people" and their resilience.

## FAMILY BACKGROUND

My dad would come up from Colfax, LA to work in the "big city" of Alexandria (Alex) that was considered more developed and perhaps offered a little more pay. He worked in Alex on a weekly basis and rented a room at the boarding house that my grandmother managed. It was in this setting that my mom and dad met.

I was born to the union of Calvin Jones and Maxine Woodard Jones on November 3, 1949, the fourth of six siblings (Cecile, Calvin, Jr., John/deceased, Emma, Marion/deceased and Angela). We lived in what is known as the Lower Third section of Alexandria, parcels of land attributed to the "Negroes/Colored." My family lived within the "George Jackson" parcels in the 700 Block on Applewhite Street between Seventh and Eighth Streets in a distinctive green colored three-bedroom house with white trim surrounded by "hurricane" fencing.

My mom was an only child who lived in Alexandria for most of her life, as far as I can tell, with my grandmother Lucille Welch Woodard and grandfather, John Woodard, a businessman and skilled carpenter, who happened to be "half white" (called "biracial" today). Her parents later divorced, and her mother married a man who became a wonderful stepfather to her.

My grandmother Lucille was a domestic worker (The Help) who worked for a white employer. Although my mother did not talk much about her upbringing, she did share with me what was a norm at some point in her life. She would go to work with her mother and be placed in a closet while her mother did her job. And it was under these circumstances of loneliness and isolation that she created an imaginary friend as a coping mechanism. That saddened me.

*My Grandfather, John Woodard Sr., Owner of John D. Woodard Sr. Construction,*
*building a home on Harrison and Vance St. in Alexandria (Circa 1925 - 1935)*

My mother attended South Alexandria School and later attended Walls-Hammond Trade School, owned and operated by Blacks, in Houston, Texas, where she trained to become a seamstress. She practiced her trade and became a skilled seamstress in the neighborhood until she had to enter the mainstream workforce to help make ends meet. She worked at Alexandria's St. Francis Cabrini Hospital for over 37 years, rising from housekeeping to a surgical instrument technician before retiring.

*My mother, Maxine Woodard (Graham) Jones, pictured with her class in 1945.*

My dad, Calvin, "Coot," came from a large family of 15 siblings born to the union of Lonsby Jones and Hattie Williams of Colfax in Grant Parish. I did not know very much about my grandmother, Hattie Williams, other than she and her sister, Lucille, married the two Jones brothers (Josh/Lucille and Lonsby/Hattie), all from Colfax. My grandfather, Lonsby Jones, attended Coleman College in Gibsland, Louisiana, about 20 miles from Grambling State University. The school later relocated to Shreveport. According to *lostcolleges.com/coleman-college*, the college, established in 1890 for freed slaves, is believed to have been the first of its kind in North Louisiana. Oliver L. Coleman served as founder and president. Unfortunately, my grandfather's quest for higher education was cut short due to a family emergency that required him to return home to help on the farm.

## FAMILY TIES/DYNAMICS

There was a definite rhythm in the daily life in the Jones household: my parents working, coming home, and expecting us kids to have followed the rules set in place. We had to complete household chores, do homework and help the younger siblings with their homework. We were not allowed to open the door to anyone. Weekends were for more chores, any homework assignments, attending church, fun with friends, and visiting family.

If the household rules were not followed, there would be the strong hand of discipline to pay. One rule I believe that was common for children throughout the Black community was to "be in the house before the street lights come on." This was the rule I tested most because of my love for the swings on the schoolgrounds. Swinging was the highlight of my life every evening. It was always my intent to make it home. However, the call for just one more swing would win out. It was only when I heard my mother's voice aimed in the direction of the schoolgrounds and calling my name with a familiar cadence that I knew there would be an inevitable outcome. I would snap out of my fantasyland and run toward the voice. By the time I set foot on the front porch, I knew I was in trouble. Needless to say, my mother did not disappoint, as she commenced to the punishment I deserved. Oftentimes the lecture that came along with the discipline was more than I could bear. "Just do it."

## WORK ETHICS/VALUES

Mom and dad were hardworking people. I witnessed their work ethic early in life, as I observed both of them being responsible in their individual lines of work. This helped me formulate the importance of integrity, trustworthiness, showing up, doing your part and more. The two-income household afforded the family the ability to own an automobile, which made life a little easier. However, my parents had different work schedules. My mother would always have to catch a ride from a fellow coworker in the mornings around 6. She would always be ready when coworkers arrived and blew the horn. I took note that they never had to blow the horn twice because she was either sitting on the porch or in the chair by the door, depending on the weather. But before leaving, I would hear her in the kitchen preparing her breakfast and routinely preparing enough for us kids to have breakfast before leaving for school. She would always leave instructions to the older person in charge, stopping by the bedside and giving directions on how to heat it up and strong precautions on how to safely put out the fire.

My dad (Calvin) was a baker, a short-order cook, and a chef who worked at many establishments around Alexandria, including the famous Cotton Brothers Bakery on MacArthur Drive, which sold my favorite Holsum Bread. (I could still smell the scent of fresh baked bread, when he came home from work each day or night depending on his shift). Cotton Brothers Bakery back in the day was the site of employment for many Afro-American citizens of Alexandria. It was a source of income no doubt unequal to their Caucasian counterparts, I would imagine. He also worked at popular places around town such as the Holiday Inn, Ramada Inn and eventually the historic Bentley Hotel located in downtown Alexandria. I would often watch my dad happily preparing his chef uniform for the day's shift as a cook. I enjoyed watching him in the evenings or weekends starching the white ensemble that consisted of the white chef's hat and jacket. His routine of ironing the jacket and chef's hat became a spectacle to me — especially the hat! He was most proud when after ironing it, he would try it on. When it would flop over, that seemed to give him all the pleasure, as I observed the reaction on his face.

It wasn't uncommon on Sunday afternoons to visit family members in and around town. It was routine that when my dad rested up a little before the weekend was over, the family would pile into the car and travel to visit family members, alternating every other weekend between visiting my mom's relatives and his relatives. On his days off during the week, I could find him taking a neighbor or family member to and from a doctor's appointment or grocery store. People loved "Mr. Calvin" for his caring and willingness.

I was a "daddy's girl" during a time when I was the youngest and believed my dad could do no wrong in my eyesight. How he got put on this pedestal was because of his playfulness and generosity. A couple of incidents shot him over the moon for me. First thing was an unspoken game we played when I would offer to clear out his workpants before washing and me being surprised that pennies were left in the pockets for me to buy rubboard cookies from Mrs. Taylor's store. The second was when he surprised me with the hula-hoop I had asked for. One day, my dad asked me to go to the car, and when I opened the back door of the car there was this pink hula-hoop with a white stripe and bells all around it! My little eyes stretched as far as they could, and there was a big smile on my face. I was the happiest little girl that day, as I hula hooped throughout the neighborhood.

## EMPHASIS ON EDUCATION

Education was a big deal in our household; getting my homework was very important (no excuse). Although, I did not understand at the time the correlation between getting my education and the type of life I could afford to live, I got the sense that it was very important for me to do my best. The evening routine my parents established laid a good education foundation for us. For the most part, this routine and intrinsic norm proved to be one of the greatest legacies of my parents' persistence. For the most part, the oldest to the youngest of my siblings (six children) went on to higher education and/or gleaned achievements from nursing, engineering, prominent minister/civil rights advocate, business owner, social worker to a published poet. My parents were not the bragging kind about their children. However, I know that they were proud of their children and most of all what their successes meant to their survival.

## INFLUENCE OF SPIRITUAL GUIDANCE

Beyond my understanding at the time, it was the norm in the Jones household to acknowledge God. Forever etched in my mind is the little blue velvet/felt sign posted over the threshold leading from the living room to the middle bedroom. The words, inscribed in gold glitter lettering, read, "The Lord Will Provide." I often reflect on that signage today when I need a reminder of God's provisions in my life.

I would often see my mom as she sat on the side of the bed reading her small *New Testament Bible*, focusing mostly on the "Book of Psalms". She had favorite verses that she would read over and over again, and when she needed some comfort and peace, she would lean on several Psalms depending on the situation. As I grew older, when I would tell her of a situation going on in my life, she would refer me to a specific Psalm for clarity and relief from the concern.

My dad sang in a quartet that performed in Alexandria and surrounding towns. I loved when rehearsal was at our house on some Friday evenings. I could hear the guys tuning up their voices (acapella) while the guy on the guitar would adjust the strings. I was excited to watch it all come together. And when they would begin to sing, I could hear the harmony of the voices, as they all would slap the side of their thigh to the beat of the music. Wow! What precious memories, for sure. This was the style of the "Black" or "soul" music in the gospel realm, and it was repeated and admired throughout the Black community. I often find myself, too, slapping the side of my thigh when I hear a song that reminds me of that time in my life.

## THE BLACK CHURCH IMPACT

The neighborhood was able to support two historically Black churches, Mt. Triumph Missionary Baptist Church and True Vine Missionary Baptist Church, established in 1897 and 1900, respectively. We were members of Mt. Triumph. Members in attendance at both of the churches were Blacks that represented every walk of Black life from schoolteachers, school dieticians, and attorneys, to working moms/dads and fellow classmates.

Although I lived somewhat in fear of what would happen to me if I was not good, I found it joyful and a pleasure to attend church regularly from Sunday school, 11 o'clock service, BYTU (Baptist Youth Training Union) and ending in Sunday night service. In other words, just about all day this was the norm for me on any given Sunday. As I began to mature, I participated in church activities and even held different church positions (e.g., church secretary, choir director, etc.). I even sang as a member of my church's original gospel group, The Trumpeters, all of which I enjoyed.

There were many traditions in the Black church. Attending a "Black" Baptist church in particular is where I learned to have a healthy respect for the House of God, about appropriate and inappropriate behaviors, including not chewing gum, eating or drinking in church. The one I followed for a long time was the protocol to hold up the index finger and walk tiptoeing when leaving the sanctuary while service was in progress and the one about not allowing the unbaptized to take communion. I was able to embrace some of these traditions and glean for myself some basic foundational truths and respects that have laid the framework for my spiritual growth throughout my life. As Maya Angelou titles her book *I Wouldn't Take Nothing for My Journey Now*, I, too, make that declaration.

## THE NEIGHBORHOOD/BLACK COMMUNITY INFLUENCES

There were two major incidents in my life, as I look back and realize that it does "take a village" and what it means in real time how important community can be. In my case, it even helped saved my life.

The first incident was shared with me by my mother. I was two or three years old and had ingested something that was poisonous to my body. I was rushed to one of the most prominent Black doctors in town, Dr. James Hines, who was responsible for saving my life. He prescribed a series of antibiotic shots and continued care for me with a follow-up treatment over a period of time. The care he offered showed how important the Black professionals were to the community. There were times, however, when I would hear an adult say, "I'd rather go to the white man." I have come to realize that for some reason we (Blacks) had or still have trust issues with Black professionals, questioning their levels of competency/quality. This attitude perhaps is a holdover from the propaganda of white superiority passed down by the slave masters and needs to stop.

The second incident occurred when I was about 4 or 5. I was disobedient to my father's order to me and my slightly older brother John to stay in bed, as he made a quick run to Mr. Albertson's store. I was the youngest sibling at the time and rambunctious. I proceeded to get out of bed and head to my favorite spot, the mirror, where I applied Dixie Peach to my hair, ignoring the cries of my brother for me to get back in bed. At some point, I realized that I was cold and got the hidden matches to light the heater but stopped by the mirror to declare myself the queen by lighting a match and holding it over my head of hair. My hair caught on fire. I ran, first through the house, then outside, screaming for help. Our neighbor (the local midwife) three doors down heard the screams and could see the flame. I was told that she was outside feeding her chickens and dropped the whole bag of feed to come to my rescue. Before the neighbor got there, my brother, John, was able to move beyond his fright and mustered up the courage to douse the fire with a pale of water. Between my brother's dousing my head with water and Mrs. Edith's quick action, my life was saved that day. I thank God for the sense of community for looking out for one other. I lived with burn treatments and bandages for several months until the skin healed from my third-degree burn. I'll say the Dixie Peach also saved my life because it was a slow burning petroleum fire.

Our community consisted of Blacks from all walks of life from schoolteachers, dieticians, seamstresses, domestic workers, sanitation workers, small business owners, cooks and more. Seeing the range of the workforce that contributed to our community really connected me to an understanding and appreciation of my parents' emphasis on education. In addition, most of the neighborhood was a two-parent household that ranged from two or three children to as many as 10 children in the household.

## FORMATIVE SCHOOL YEARS (GRADES 1-6)

It was somewhat of a short walk from my house to Peabody Negro School, and I can still remember the excitement I felt as I entered the campus. And to be honest, I thought nothing of the name of my elementary school at the time because I had never heard any displeasure about it from the adults in my life. It was routine to line up every morning outside at the foot of the stairs in a row, as the bell rang, to enter the school. As I climbed the stairs and entered the school hallway, in my mind this was a time for no nonsense. The smell was even different, which is the only way I can describe it. I was fortunate to have Miss Elizabeth Williams as my teacher in first and second grades. I loved her. I admired the way she dressed, smelled, and wore her hair, her confident walk and overall demeanor. She had a way about her that has stuck with me to this day. I especially admired her confidence and determination and the way she focused on each child in her class by meeting them where they were.

Though she would divide the class into groups from advanced to the not so advanced, I did not feel less when I found myself needing attention in an area. She gave equal attention to every student, and she inspired me to do better. Each child received a special handwritten name card and a napkin full of animal crackers on their desk on their birthday. How cool was that? As I continued to advance from one grade level to the next, some classes seemed to be a little harder than others, but I managed to make decent grades overall. In sixth grade, I enjoyed when I was chosen to help those that needed a little more support understanding a concept.

My days were filled with the routine of classroom work and recess when I would get the opportunity to play with classmates until the sound of the bell when we would return to class. I vividly remember the school celebration of May Day when we got to wrap the maypole. I did not understand the custom or the full meaning at the time, but I got to dress up that day. It was a special place of honor to be chosen to wrap the May Pole, and it was a big event to look forward to each year. I loved lunchtime. The meals were balanced and often similar to the meals I ate at home. The cooks and dieticians in the cafeteria were people from the neighborhood. Some were the mothers of my classmates. I was a cafeteria helper and my job was clear tables after lunch. The downside of the job was eating last, the upside was having all you wanted to eat, including extra milk.

I enjoyed my elementary years. However, my school taught me nothing about the "Negro experience." The books I had were sometimes new, sometimes old, though not worn. If they were hand-me-downs from the white schools, I did not know it. The books taught me about Columbus discovering America but nothing about slave ships that brought my ancestors to America.

## JUNIOR HIGH (GRADES 7-9)

By the time I completed sixth grade, Jones Street Junior High had been built. Junior high was notably different because I had different teachers and classmates, as I moved from one class to the next throughout the day. The routine of changing teachers and having to adjust to different styles of teaching somewhat hampered my efforts to keep up. However, the routine established in our home of having the older sibling act as a tutor to the younger ones proved to be a valuable resource for me. By the time I made it to the eighth grade, I was even an Honor Roll student.

I remember this incident as though it was recent. Mr. William C. Marcus was the Supervisor of Negro Schools during our era. He often visited the schools. I happened to be in the school's office one day and was talking to the school's secretary when Mr. Marcus stopped by and interrupted our conversation. He looked at me and then asked me to spell "biscuit." I froze because I was caught off-guard and became nervous and could not get this simple word to come to my frontal lobe. I did not want to make the mistake of spelling it the way I pronounced it (biskit). I couldn't trust my southern diction that had proven to be wrong in the past. I was able to spell it correctly eventually with a little help from the secretary in the background using hand gestures. As I walked away, I was feeling a little embarrassed, but he was kind and patient, as he challenged me. I will never forget him. It was sometime after this incident that I felt it necessary to come up with some technique to help me with spelling. I developed a latent technique that would help me not spell words the way I heard them. I began to spell words by closing my eyes and using an imaginary screen to visualize where I had seen the word written. This technique has proven to be successful for me over the years, and I still use it today especially as I have entered into my "seasoned citizen" years. By the way, you could wake me up in the middle of the night and ask me how to spell biscuit.

As I came to the end of my years in junior high, I believe they were eventful, as it had prepared me for the next leg of my educational journey to senior high. I was able to become an honor roll student, develop a technique that helped me to be a better speller and writer. I was able to gain more confidence with the help of a classmate who was outgoing and engaging. (She had been stricken with polio at an early age.) She encouraged and challenged me to stand up against the rude insults of a school bully that I had been facing almost on a daily basis. Her help and kindness forever changed my life from that day forward.

## Unrecognized Incidents of Racism

Up to this point, my life was routine with a few bumps in the road. There was nothing up to this point that really stood out as a problem in because of the color of my skin. There was food on the table, my parents had jobs, I loved my community, my teachers looked good, smelled good, had beautiful homes and we had a car. The principles my parent taught at home were more about integrity and honesty than preparing me to face discrimination. I now understand that my parents either deliberately had me stay in my place as a child, or they thought that racial disparity was grown folks business, as they lived through unjust treatment during the Jim

Crow era on the job and elsewhere. In any case, I was totally oblivious to the plight and the extent of what was going on in the adult world of coping with discriminatory practices in a system designed for inequality. There were, however, a few unrecognized incidents and eye-opening events of discrimination that helped me at a young age connect the dots on my own and help me to become aware of the times I was living in.

## THE BUS RIDE (LITTLE MS. ROSA PARKS)

I was probably about six or seven years of age when this incident occurred. I remember waiting with my mom at the bus stop for the bus to come. As the bus was about to stop to pick us up, I could hear the sound of the brakes as it pulled up. I walked behind my mom and stopped, as she carefully put the monies in the slots to pay our fare. I then saw my mother do something very strange. She began to walk straight to the back of the bus, passing all those empty seats in the front. Well, in my mind, I thought perhaps she did not see them, so instead of following her, I sat down in the long seat across from the driver and began to swing my little legs while holding onto the pole. I thought that mt mom would surely come back up to join me. The driver glanced over at me but did not say a word (I did not notice that the bus had not taken off). Suddenly, my mother rushed to the front of the bus where I was and without a sound, but with an angry look on her face, gave me the Froggie hop pinch that caused me to follow her immediately to the back of the bus. There was silence on my mother's part, and, of course, on my part, as I rubbed my inner forearm for some relief. And she never spoke about the incident after returning home.

I knew not to ask any questions about the matter, so I just assumed I needed to follow her and not strike out on my own. I did not learn until later that this was part of the Jim Crow era practices of discrimination. The historical Rosa Parks bus moment in December 1955 likely had already occurred, making tensions and awareness even more heightened. Who knows what could have happened in Alexandria that Saturday afternoon on that bus ride uptown if it were not for my mother's quick actions?

## "I'M A MAN, MAXINE!"

As mentioned earlier, my father worked at several establishments (restaurants, hotels, inns) in Alexandria. It never dawned on me that there was a reason for the many changes in venues in his employment. I thought the world of my dad's cooking I had so often enjoyed. And besides his talent, I never sensed any uneasiness in him as he prepared to go to work. During this time in my life, I had no clue of his dismay because of unfair norms and practices aimed at "the Black" men.

On one occasion, I happen to overhear a heated debate my parents were having about my dad walking off his job. It was apparent on my mother's part that she was not happy with his decision no matter what. My father had walked off his job because his white supervisor called him, "boy." I heard my dad declare to my mom in an emphatic way, "I am not a boy, Maxine, I'm not a boy! I am a man!" Based on my mother's response, I got the feeling that it did not matter because she believed he shouldn't have been so quick to walk off the job without considering our family. "But, Calvin, we have six children," my mom said with such passion.

At this point in my life, I had begun to be more sensitive to these types of practices and norms that affected my race. And I knew at this time that the word used by a white person toward a Black man was derogatory and disparaging and was meant to make one feel less. And although my mother had a valid point, I was proud of my dad for taking a stand. His action laid a groundwork that stuck with me for the rest of my life. He found another job not too long after the incident.

## HIGH SCHOOL YEARS (1965-1968)

My years at Peabody Senior High were some of my most eventful and productive years. There were challenges, distractions, eye-opening realities of life as a person of color that brought some sadness, hope for the future, determination and a sense of pride and responsibility for the sacrifices that I made. As a sophomore, I was determined to maintain good grades throughout my time there, and although it became increasingly difficult at times, I managed to stay clear of failing grades. I participated in extracurricular activities, and I, along with fellow members, represented the Science Club in Peabody's Homecoming Parade. On the weekends, I found the time to enjoy a house party with friends and cousins.

Our high school principal, affectionately known as Professor David "Prof" Iles, was either loved or hated because of his knack for showing up unannounced and catching students off-guard. He had no problem calling you out to either shame you or to encourage you to do better, seemingly for the sake of your family's legacy. I believe he was a man who cared about Black students and wanted to do his part in preparing us for the world we were going to face after leaving Peabody.

I recall an unusual occurrence around Thanksgiving in my sophomore year. The cafeteria prepared excellent meals. Our Thanksgiving meal that year was no exception. That evening at home, however, I became very ill with an upset stomach that I'd never experienced before. My father made a concoction of flour and water at a thick consistency for me to drink. It was not easy getting it down, but it did the job. Home remedies were the norm in the Black neighborhood, with remedies passed down from one generation to another. That same night coincidentally when my mother returned home from work, she shared news that the school librarian had been admitted to the hospital and was not doing well. When I returned to school the next day, I learned that many students had become ill and that our librarian had passed away during the night. It was a sad beginning to our Thanksgiving holiday break that year.

## CIVIL RIGHTS, THE AWAKENING

By the time I reached my junior and senior years at Peabody, the Civil Rights Movement had already begun to intensify elsewhere in the South, and there had been a growing awareness of the desire for equality. I watched the TV news where reports showed clashes between the police and students seeking to conduct sit-ins in different parts of the South to break the discriminatory practices of Jim Crow. Their determination and dedication for equal rights inspired and challenged me to keep change alive in me. Although most of the Civil Rights Movement was driven by and focused on the philosophy of The Rev. Dr. Martin Luther King Jr., who led non-violent and peaceful protests, there was a conflicting element driven by Malcolm X, who believed that violence was necessary to bring about change. Even though my dedication was to the philosophy of Dr. King, I was saddened when Malcom X was assassinated in February 1965, and I began to fear for Dr. King as well. When Dr. King was assassinated in Memphis on April 4, 1968, I was shaken, saddened, and I wondered what was going to happen next.

The signing of the Civil Rights Bill by President Lyndon B Johnson in 1964 was slow in manifesting equal justice. After the death of Dr. King and Robert Kennedy in 1968 (only months apart), a shift in the momentum of breaking down the walls of discriminatory practices occurred. Black pride really began to increase in me so much so that the song, "Say It Loud, I'm Black and I'm Proud," written by James Brown several months after the death of Dr. King, became my personal anthem. Despite the dark shadow of pain and uncertainty and racial issues that existed elsewhere my senior year, I was left with a greater appreciation for the sacrifices of those that came before me. I had a determination and a sense of responsibility to not waste opportunities that had been opened up for me. As I left the halls of Dear Ole Peabody, I was on a mission.

## Life after High School

After graduation, I had a personal charge and determination to show the world that I am not inferior to white people and that I am worthy and deserve to pursue life goals and dreams like anybody else. I took several actions upon graduation. Because my older sister was pursuing a nursing degree at Dillard University, I determined my parents would not be able to send me to college. In the summer, I participated in the Miss Alexandria Pageant (all Black participants) under the direction of Mrs. Herbert Allen and took a receptionist job at a Black-owned funeral home. In the fall of 1968, I started classes in the secretarial/stenographer program at Alexandria Trade School. The student body was integrated, but the instructors were all white. I vowed to keep the silent commitment I made to always be a credit to my race.

All of my classes were integrated except for the business accounting class, and I found myself the only Black in this class. All of the white students sat together, and I sat alone. The white teacher recognized me as a member of the class and would politely address my questions when I raised my hand. Being in this atmosphere, however, caused a large degree of anxiety for me. I made up my mind that if there was going to be a failing grade made in this class, it wasn't going to be my grade. The anxiety continued, as I allowed myself to think about what they thought about me.

The rest of my classes were made up of familiar faces and white students. I never told anyone about my anxiety, and I felt all alone. I continued to do well in all my classes except the business accounting class. I was beginning to feel a little tired and stressed out but ignored it. I later suffered a panic attack and was put on bedrest because of the stress and lack of sleep. After a few days of rest, I returned to school with a new attitude and a whole new outlook on life. I graduated a year later with good grades in my entire subject and excelled in shorthand in such a way that I believe it helped me land the first real job on my career path.

What I learned from that experience was you can't take the whole world on your shoulders. You are only responsible for yourself by making sure you take care of yourself and do the best you can. And, it's alright to ask for help. In looking back over that experience, I had set myself up to fail by looking at the struggle for equality in a wrong way. It should have been all about taking advantage of and focusing on the opportunities and nothing else.

## FIRST PROFESSIONAL JOB

By 1969 desegregation efforts were in full swing throughout the South. By then you could eat at the Walgreen's counter if you wanted to. I have no doubt that there were still some pockets of resistance. It seemed, however, that my hometown of Alexandria was onboard to comply with the statutes. During this time, attorney Louis Berry, a Black community leader, was actively leading the charge to ensure that local blacks would be integrated into the school systems and workforce in Rapides Parish. A family friend encouraged me to integrate the predominantly white sheriff's office. She had recently learned of my certificates from the trade school. After some preparation, I applied for and received a position in the Records Division as the Secretary for two detectives, Detective Bolden (Crime Scenes) and Detective Harding (Check Fraud). My duties consisted of answering the phone, filing arrest records (rap sheets), taking dictation (in shorthand) from both detectives when they returned from investigating a crime scene, etc. I enjoyed my employment there at the Sheriff's Department and was treated with respect by staff and my immediate supervisors. At one point, I developed aspirations to become a fingerprint expert because I was so impressed by the process of this technique. However, I worked there for almost a year, then decided to move to Los Angeles.

## ADULT REALITIES OF LIFE

In the early 1970s, I moved to Los Angeles where I became a wife and mother and would spend the next 40 years of my life. That experience contributed to my diverse outlook on life. Before moving to California, I had heard rumors that there was an absence of the southern hospitality that I had been accustomed to and that people were rude. That was not the case. I made friends with a variety of people of all races and even picked up a bit of Spanish through those relationships. I worked in a series of temporary positions before settling in a permanent position. I learned a couple of lessons from those experiences: (1) Keep the amount of money you earn to yourself. (2) Everybody is not your friend. (Watch your back!). We lived in two different neighborhoods in Los Angeles, one racially mixed and the other predominantly Black.

When I began to look for a permanent position in line with my chosen field, I wanted to work as close to home as possible so that I could be home for the boys. There were major companies within 15 miles from where I resided. I applied for a job with a nationally known insurance company that fit my criteria of being close to home. I interviewed and was not selected for the position. Based on my exchange with the interviewer, I knew that I would not get the job, nor would I want to work under the circumstances presented in the interview. I also recognized what had happened in the interview process. Several weeks later, I received a notification from the Department of Equal Employment Opportunity Commission letting me know that there was a "Class Action Suit" for hiring discrimination practices brought against the company I had interviewed with. I followed the instructions to become a part of the lawsuit, which included giving a narrative of my interview experience (including the interviewer's name). Several months later, I was employed by the same company, working closely with the man who had interviewed me. We had a good relationship. I worked for the company for 25 years.

Institutionalized racism (covert attempts at Jim Crow practices) by this time had already been recognized and called out by the Black community. While working in this corporate environment, I got a snapshot of how institutional racism played out in the workplace. This well-established company had a long history of being white male dominated. Women employed there were mainly in clerical positions. No doubt the company needed to loosen its grips of the stereotypical atmosphere due to the Civil Rights laws and the changes it demanded.

During my tenure, I was able to witness and call out covert behaviors designed to hinder the advancement of African American employees. At the risk of losing my job and with the support of my husband, in my administrative role at the time, I took actions to work on behalf of Black employees who were being discriminated against. I conducted extensive research on how other companies dealt with similar issues. My efforts were successful and made a difference in how employees were treated and viewed.

While employed with this company, I did not abandon my desire to obtain a college degree. I attended the University of Phoenix on campus at night in pursuit of a bachelor's degree in Business Management, which I obtained at age 55.

Since my retirement, I have moved to Austin, Texas and obtained my certification for Life Coaching (Certified Professional Coach/CPC). Today, I am the sole proprietor of Personal Life Strategies LLC, a Life Coach and Christian Mentor Service. On my creative side, I love to crochet and have been practicing this art for over 40 years or more. In line with my goal to become a businessperson, I am the owner of

Sassy But Classy Crochet Fashions by Ms. Em, and I sell my designs by consignment and retail.

## CONCLUSION

At the time of this writing, I am 71 years old. The most important thing I've learned from the ebbs and flows of life is nothing lasts forever. They just don't. Life is ever-evolving, how or where I started does not dictate where I'm going or how my story will end (that is true for everyone). And every now and then, I must take the time to celebrate the blessings, forgive myself for the missed opportunities and remember that life isn't over until it's over.

In conclusion, from my humble beginnings in that green colored three-bedroom house at 716 Applewhite Street in the city of Alexandria, to my present residence in Austin, I acknowledge that God has been by my side and has guided me through all my imperfections and wrong turns and has blessed me with His grace and favor on many occasions. He is faithful. I am so appreciative to my parents, Calvin and Maxine Jones, who, although not perfect, they have taught me guiding principles that have been mainstays in my life. And, as I began to establish my own style of creating a home life, being a wife of more than 47 years to Charlie, and parent to Kevin and Theron, I was able to make adjustments from my upbringing to create an environment that included awareness and inclusion for my sons, and their input, as well.

I say, "To God be the Glory!"

# CHANGE GON' COME

*"Let go, and let God."*

## Pearlie Mae Lewis Carter

*I remember each morning my entire (elementary) school would meet on the campus to sing the National Anthem and recite The Pledge of Allegiance to the flag that would be blowing in the wind. Now, however, I know the anthem, pledge and the flying flag were not for all people.*

I WAS BORN ON August 5, 1950, the first of five children, to Silas and Rosemary Lewis at Huey P. Long Charity Hospital in Pineville, LA. The hospital was segregated, and the staff were often rude. But we were always told to never speak.

My mother and her family migrated from Simmesport, LA; my father came from Bunkie, LA. My father worked as an ironworker at Alexandria Iron & Metal. He did not earn much, and my mother did not work at all, so we were scraping, to say the least, but happy. My father always taught me and my siblings the value of a dollar and to always try to own a piece of land. He and my Aunt Virginia bought property on Seventh Street and Palmer. We lived on the Palmer Street property, which was in the back of Seventh Street.

Growing up in those days was good. We were allowed to visit friends after we had done our chores, and all would be well as long as we got back home before the corner light came on. The neighborhood was rich with games to play and things to do, like 1-2-3 red light, hopscotch, baseball, racing, marbles, and climbing trees. We did not travel far as a family, only biweekly trips to Bunkie, LA to visit my father's family. I loved those trips.

My friend and I often would play in canals. One particular day, as we were playing in the canal, or on our way from the Ritz Theater, in front of the Casson Street Community Center, I noticed a Black man hanging from a tree. My friend saw this as well. At first, I thought it was a dummy (someone playing around), but after hearing and seeing people coming over and screaming, I knew it was real. I felt fear, and we ran home, not crying, but afraid. I overheard my parents talking about it later, and from what I overheard, it seems this person was hung due to him being caught with a white girl. We should have received some type of counseling after this type of exposure but, of course, that was unheard of in those days. I have never forgotten that scene.

In our household, the love of God was an absolute must. I was an active member of Mount Triumph Baptist Church, baptized there at age 9, attended Bible School in the summer, and all other events were through the church. I was taught to tithe early, but sometimes I held back for my favorite two-for-a-penny cookies. We were taught about fire and brimstone. Lying and stealing gets you to Hell. If I would get into trouble in an area where the person knew me and my parents, they would punish me and then take me home with the reason for the punishment, and for my parents that was not a problem. Looking back, I appreciate all the discipline I was given.

I spent my first six years of school at Peabody Elementary, my neighborhood school. A few of my favorite teachers were Mr. Leon, Mr. R. Hall, Mr. Duell, and Ms. Gauthier. I was always an honor student even in elementary school. I remember each morning the entire school would meet on the campus to sing the National Anthem and recite *The Pledge of Allegiance* to the flag that would be blowing in the wind. Now, however, I know the anthem, pledge, and the flying flag were not for all people.

At the end of elementary school, I was promoted to the seventh grade at Jones Street Junior High. I was active. I became a member of the Office Helper Club, Glee Club and the concert and marching bands. I wanted to play a clarinet. However, my father could not afford to purchase one, so I was offered a school instrument and ended up with a French horn. I learned pretty quickly under the direction of Mr. Williams. I actually would buy manuscript paper and write my own music, *Swing Low Sweet Chariot* and *She'll be Coming 'Round the Mountain*, in my free time. I quickly realized that I wanted to major in music. My first solo concert piece, *Green Sleeves*, was awesome. Those days at Jones Street were good. A park and a public swimming pool were located in the area. My friend, Mary Ann, and I would often go there, and we also took swimming lessons.

One of our favorite places was the ice cream parlor inside Redmond on Third Street. We would often ride our bikes there and peek in the window and wish we could enter and sit on one of the swivel green stools and have a sundae. Of course, a huge sign hung out front, "No Coloreds". But one day (I think the year was 1962), we were in school, and the principal made an announcement concerning desegregation. He said we could now go in by the front entrance to businesses and could now be allowed to go anywhere.

Mary Ann and I were excited to hear that news. We ran home, got our bikes, and made record speed to the drugstore. We did not park our bikes; we were too excited. We just ran through the front door and jumped on one of those beautiful green swivel stools and ordered a sundae. We did not notice how the parlor was emptying as we ate. When we finished, it was quiet and completely empty. I remember being a little puzzled but still so happy just being in there. Mary Ann and I talked about this incident decades later when President Barack Obama was elected, and we cried happy tears.

After graduating from Jones Street to Peabody High, once again all was new. I was engulfed in music, so I began under the direction of Mr. Andrews. He was a very nice instructor, but I missed Mr. Williams. However, Mr. Andrews moved me around on different horns besides the French horn. I also began to play the E# horn and finally the trumpet, which I fell in love with and am owner of one today. My algebra teacher, Mr. Simmons, was awesome, and I excelled. I was an honor student at Jones Street and Peabody.

After graduating from Peabody High, I moved to New York with my Aunt Pearlie. She had been there for 10 years at the time. She felt I would have better opportunities there, and she was so correct. After living there for two months, I was hired by the New York Telephone Company as a TSPS (Traffic Service Position System) operator, which was awesome. I was told to walk fast and give good eye contact. Coming from the South had its glitches. Ironically, I did not experience the culture shock as expected. I blended right in. I was always into fashion/trends, and WOW was I in the right city. I met some nice white and Black people, mixed into Black Power. I joined the Harlem Lenox Avenue Marching Band, and, unlike in Alexandria, was able to move around a lot. There was so much to do and so many places to go. I also was hired on with AT&T Long Lines (strictly overseas calls on a switchboard) during my eight-year stay. My baby daughter was born in Harlem Hospital.

I would visit Alexandria at least once a year, and each time I saw no changes. However, I had changed tremendously and felt so free. I wanted to share everything I knew with everyone I cared about. I let them know how many opportunities were available to them outside of Louisiana. My aunt passed away in 1972. Even though I had friends there, I decided to move back to Alexandria. In 1975, I returned with all of New York in me. I do not know how I thought I could live at home again. There were no opportunities for Blacks, and you could tell the racism was as thick as ever. Because of the way I dressed and the confident way I carried myself, I got rolled eyes from the whites. But I knew I could not stay and did not want to go back to New York right then. Fortunately, I was hired by South Central Bell Telephone Company as an operator. After a year, we were informed that the office would be closing, and we had the option to transfer to Austin, Dallas, or Houston. I transferred to Southwestern Bell to the Heights location in Houston in 1978 and have been here since.

It has been a struggle dealing with racism, which is still alive and kicking, just in a different form. But we have a good God, and He is still in control.

*Pearlie mom and sibs*

# COMING OF AGE IN ALEXANDRIA, LOUISIANA

*"I thank God for placing my family in Alexandria where it was possible to live in a village of caring people. During this period, I learned life's concepts of respect, honor, patience and compassion while becoming a young man. The confidence instilled in me by the instructors at Peabody and Lincoln Road gave me the courage to challenge the world."*

## Michael Milton

I WAS 2 AND the baby of the family in 1952 when my parents relocated to Alexandria from Jackson, Mississippi, looking for employment opportunities. My stepfather's brother who already had settled there recommended the move.

My mother, Lillie Mae "Miss Lillie" Pinkston, was a product of the Mississippi Delta and had spent the early years of her life on a farm in a small town called Marks, about 135 miles north of Jackson. My stepfather, Frank Pinkston, aka "Daddy," was raised on a farm in Yazoo County, in Holly Bluff, MS. In 1952, he met my mother in Jackson. At the time, she was a single mom with three kids, my older brother and sister, Leroy, 6, Diana, 4, and me. They got married in Jackson and shortly after moved to Alexandria.

*Our teachers were extensions of our families because the teachers looked like us, and it was clear to us how much they cared. They looked at us as the next generation on the battlefield for racial equality*

After a short stay in our new town's Woodside neighborhood, we moved to a community closer to my Daddy's job at Foote's Lumber Yard on Monroe Street near the Upper Third area. Foote's was a family-run mill company and one of the major employers in the Oil Mill Quarters. We lived at house 95 on Upper Third Street, the second house on the right at the top of the hill. The house had four rooms (front room, two bedrooms and kitchen) and outdoor bathroom plumbing. There weren't any children nearby, so we entertained ourselves.

We had a large enough yard for a vegetable garden and area for a chicken yard and coop. The chickens were our source for fresh eggs. When a hen no longer produced, it became the main dinner menu item. My Daddy would go into the chicken yard and grab the animal by the neck in a chokehold. He would then whirl it around until its neck broke, then drop it on the ground. Death was eminent. It was not uncommon to pass by other homes and see a chicken coop. If you were raising chickens, there had to be a rooster keeping things in order. We fed our chickens two types of food. There were "chops," dried corn cut up into bits small enough to be eaten by chickens, and "pellets," also small and easier to handle and store.

During the Upper Third period, the new baby in our family, Frank Pinkston Jr., was born. It also was the time I began my education journey. In 1956, I started first grade at Reed Street Elementary School, a newly built campus in the Oil Mill Quarters. Because I had not gone to kindergarten, that made my first-grade teacher, Miss Emanuel, very special. She was my introduction to the learning process, and she inspired me to want to be a good student. I walked the short walk to Reed Street with my older brother and sister. Every day we would meet up with other kids from the area and walk together.

We lived at house 95 until fall 1958. It was at that time, shortly before the start of my third-grade year, that my family moved to the house on Parker Street in Carver Village. The area of the city was known as "the projects," and Carver Village bordered The Sonia Quarters, another of the city's historic Black neighborhoods. Our house was on the Wise Street end.

It was during this period in the projects that I began to learn the facts of life. My local community would grow exponentially, as I became acquainted with families from all walks of life. Households with children who would become lifelong friends. Up and down Wise Street, around the corner on Houston, at the end of Harris and in the projects, there were ministers, hairdressers, mill workers and many other decent adults trying to make life better for their kids.

With the 1958 school year in progress, I entered third grade at the old South Alexandria Elementary School on Vance Street between Overton and Mason Avenue. Miss Walker was my teacher. I began new relationships with kids from the Sonia Quarters.

During that time, the Big Event was grocery shopping with friends and family at the A&P on Bolton Avenue. The store back then stood right next to the Don Theater, which I learned was for whites only. I could not understand why "colored" people were not allowed. When I asked, I was told that colored folk went to the Ritz Theater downtown on Lee Street.

I began in those days to learn by word of mouth from friends and family about many race customs that I later grew to know were racist customs. When I was in elementary school, Nehi Bottling Company began a special summer marketing campaign for RC Cola. If you collected six RC bottle caps, you would earn free admission to the Paramount Theater Wednesdays at 10 a.m. during the school summer break. Because of the segregated laws, Black children were only allowed to sit in the balcony level, which had far fewer seats than the main floor for white kids. Not only were we separated by race, but only a handful of us first in line benefitted from the campaign.

Religion was vital to our Black community and especially important to my mother. The family joined Rose of Sharon Baptist Church. The church's renovated building stands today at its original site near Downtown Alexandria on Martin Luther King Drive. I was baptized at 9 in the baptismal pool located underground near the front of the sanctuary. Man, that pool water was cold.

I made lots of new friends growing up in the congregation. We attended vacation bible school every summer. The city would provide free public transportation to all students presenting a "Bible School Tag." It was during these bus rides in 1959 that I learned that the front seats on the bus were reserved for white people. This was way after the 1955 Montgomery, Alabama bus boycott started by Rosa Parks.

I began to grow more responsible while living in the projects. I learned the value of hard work. Mrs. Lela White was the projects property manager, and her job was to collect rent and ensure the proper maintenance and upkeep of the units. During spring and summer months, management provided residents with a manual lawn-mower, rake and a lawn edger. My brother and I had the job of lawn upkeep. There were periodic property inspections, and Mrs. White was no joke when it came to performing inspections. If you failed, she would send her husband, Sergeant White, a commanding World War II veteran, to collect the penalty fee.

Sergeant White was well-connected. Through his contacts with pecan orchard owners, during pecan season he would help boys in the community get our hustle on every Saturday in October and November. We were hired as pecan pickers, but we had to sacrifice half of our bounty to the owners. It was called picking on "shares," not the best situation, but still better than no income if you're a kid. The money I earned (20 cents per pound) allowed me to go to the movies and have money for a chili dog at the Ritz Theater.

Working the pecan picking business prepared me later for summers in junior high as an independent laborer at a fresh produce farm outside the city. The father of a neighborhood friend would take four of us boys including his son to the farm to pick crowder and purple hull peas. At three cents a pound, we were underpaid, but we made up for it by eating our share of free watermelons (knots). Picking vegetables also kept us out of trouble.

Looking back, those were innocent days. Some of the simplest activities were the best. Like being lucky enough to pass by the Noah's Potato Chip building at the same time chips were being cooked. Wow! That aroma seemed to hang in your nostrils the rest of the day. Or, coming upon the Dr Pepper Bottling Company at the corner of Texas Avenue and Lee Street Extension and checking out the observation window in front where passersby could view the entire process of filling, bottling, and crating the product.

I would be sure to save some pecan picking money for fireworks during Christmas vacation. We traveled in groups of 5 or 6 for safety, plus the conversations kept our minds off the long walk to the fireworks stands on MacArthur Drive. Our limited funds only allowed us to buy the basic firecrackers, sparklers, roman candles. Sometimes someone in the group would have enough to purchase a cherry bomb. Oh boy, we all had to be present when it was ignited! We eventually would spend all day New Year's Eve ringing in the new year because we were not allowed outside at midnight.

The late winter/early spring rains in March raised the water level in drainage ditches around town and signaled the beginning of crawfish season, which lasted about a month in Alexandria before the banks became overgrown with new weeds. We would spend hours walking along the banks, looking for a good spot with crawfish. We started off using raw salt pork for bait but soon learned that with chicken liver or guts, you could catch two to three at a time. Me and Frank Jr. would bring our catch home and our mother would boil them. It was never a big deal in Central Louisiana. It wouldn't be until college at Southern University (in Baton Rouge) that I learned that the crawfish boil was a "Big Deal".

The big playground/field right outside our house provided the backdrop for all types of sports from baseball and football to foot races and kite flying. As neighborhood kids, we took advantage of it all.

My years at Aaron Street Elementary were some of my best. I achieved academic excellence and was given the high honor of sixth grade King of May Day. It was fifth and sixth grades when I first had classes under male teachers. Mr. Calvin Cook taught science class, and Mr. Amos Wesley taught arithmetic. Both were excellent teachers and role models for all the boys.

Mr. Cook even organized the little league team where I played for two years. My experience from playing baseball on the projects' playground served me well during my little league period. Playing little league also created a platform to building friendships with kids beyond the classroom who played on other teams in the city. Little league season ended summer after sixth grade. Before the start of junior high, I spent summer 1962 swimming at the public pool in Cheatham Park on Jones Street and making multiple ice cream stops, mostly after swimming, at the Dairy Queen at Broadway and Jones. It was at the end of that summer in August that my parents left the projects and for the first time became homeowners.

The house wasn't as large of a space as we needed, but based on customs at the time, the youngest kid would be grown in eight years, and it would be the ideal size for what's nowadays called empty nesters. We were now in a secluded Sonia Quarters neighborhood across the tracks off Dallas Street. We lived on Cedar Street, which was one block long. The immediate area was a nice mixture of longtime property renters and property owners. My family would hold special connections to this location and the great families that lived on our block and surrounding streets throughout my adult years.

Junior High meant you got to the bus stop on time, or you took a three-mile hike to Lincoln Road's campus. Junior High turned out to be the place where all the fun memories were stored. Ordering pork chop sandwiches during lunch because we could. Boys with crushes on Miss Barnes, the French teacher, trying to impress her by greeting her speaking in French.

Junior high was also the place where new nicknames were attached, and for some, old ones updated. Willie Frank Norris, a friend from Aaron Street, tagged me with the nickname "Big Bruiser" after Mattel Toys came out with its wrecker truck that year. A beloved classmate, James Perry, as a younger kid started off being "Underdog," but by teen years was promoted to "Dawg," and Calvin McClintock, who started off being "Tic Toc", later on was just "Toc." All three of those friends have passed away.

Junior high was a preview of life yet to be experienced. Our teachers were extensions of our families because the teachers looked like us, and it was clear to us how much they cared. They looked at us as the next generation on the battlefield for racial equality. In hindsight, I cherish those moments more today than at the time growing up in adolescence. These strong Black men and women would become powerful forces in my success as an adult.

We were introduced to classes designed to address real life and stimulate our imagination. There were home economics classes. There were fine arts classes, where Miss Guillory gave us glimpses of the great painters, while also exposing us to pottery making and 3-D drawing. Mr. Briscoe taught industrial arts, which included identifying mechanical equipment and safe handling of wood, band and circular saws.

It was my eighth-grade year when my parents bought the family's first set of encyclopedias. I believe every niece, nephew, and friend that visited our home spent time turning the pages and discovering new knowledge. I went through the entire alphabet before the end of that school year. Reading was important and further opened the world around and beyond me.

The summer before the final year of junior high ended up being a year like none other. I took my first solo trip by bus to visit kinfolk in Chicago. The trip was very involved, trying to keep up with when I would get to Jackson to change buses. I had no idea that Greyhound and Continental Trailways shared riders. I was so excited about the trip, and I guess I was so focused on when to change buses, I don't remember where I sat on the bus or the skin color of other riders. It was my first time visiting such a large city. I will never forget the ride along Lakeshore Drive when I got my first sight of Lake Michigan and the excitement of seeing skyscrapers in real life.

My ninth-grade year in 1964 brought more big family changes. My Daddy left his Oil Mill Quarters Foote Lumberyard job for better work at Alexandria Scrap Iron and Metal Company in Lower Third. In April 1965, he bought the family's first car, a 1958 Plymouth Savoy, to get back and forth to work. My mother, who had worked years as a maid for well-off white families, that same year began working as a maid for James and Frances Bolton. My mother called the new job "a blessing." James Bolton was the President and CEO of Rapides Bank & Trust, and his wife, Frances, was a Texas oil company heiress.

The Bolton family lived in a sprawling beautiful white mansion across the creek along City Park Boulevard. The couple's only child (a daughter) was married with her own family, and their other employee, a houseman, took care of the home's interior cleaning and the yardwork. My mother primarily prepared family meals and did the family laundry. The Boltons were decent people. When the engine on the Plymouth blew, Mrs. Bolton told my parents to go to the Southern Chevrolet dealership in town, pick out a car, and they would take care of everything else. My mother worked for the Bolton Family until 1989. Concurrent with her employment at the Boltons, my mother got her driver's license and successfully emerged as an Avon Products sales consultant. She gave new meaning to "Avon Calling" and was a natural with people, cultivating a dedicated clientele across Alexandria that would continue for 30 years.

Having a new family Chevy when I was in ninth grade motivated me to begin driving practice. In the '60s, Louisiana issued driver's licenses to persons 15 who passed the written and road tests. I was 14 when Daddy's good friend, Mr. Percy Snowden, allowed me to practice on his 1951 Chevy standard shift. Having a driver's license would come in handy in high school when I got my first real job.

The Peabody High School years will always be special. I entered Peabody (Magnet) Senior High under the administration of Professor David F. Iles, principal, in the fall of 1965 as a 10th grader. Professor Iles had the utmost respect of the entire Black community and hovered over the students like a mother hen. No student ever wanted word to get back to his parents that he was sent to the principal's office for cutting up in class. Professor Iles would cruise the halls, making sure you were authorized to be out of class.

Oh man, what a thrill to be walking the hallowed halls of such a great institution while moving closer to becoming an adult! The teachers would address the students as Mr. and Miss. It was amazing to see the young ladies all dressed up with hairstyles that were 'outta' sight! Peabody was the only public school attended by Blacks, so it became a reunion of old friends from elementary school, separated by junior high, and now back together.

Peabody had great caring teachers who, like my junior high teachers, gave me a great feeling of comfort, again, like having extended family. My sophomore year was spent getting adjusted to multiple class schedules, socializing, and focusing on personal hygiene and appearance.

During spring of my sophomore year, after attending a presentation on campus, I signed up for and was accepted into the Distributive Education Clubs of America, Inc. program (DECA). DECA is a national non-profit organization designed to help high school students 16 and older prepare for careers in business and entrepreneurship. Participants attended classes at school the first half of the day, and afternoons worked part-time for local businesses, learning on-the-job skills. A bus picked us up at school and dropped us off at our worksites. Students accumulated enough class credits to graduate on time and make money in the process.

Six of us from Peabody participated. I worked for Sears, Roebuck and Company in the Shipping and Receiving Department. I unloaded merchandise from trucks, reviewed packing slips, tagged them, and delivered them to the sales floor. Sears was the first exposure I had to white people in a workplace. My supervisor was a white guy in his 50s, the clerks were white women and the sales guys on the floor were white. A Bolton student in the program also was white.

By the end of senior year when the job was ending, I felt like it had been a Big Deal, learning up-close how business operated. It wasn't until years later, though, when I accepted my first professional job out of college, that I would clearly appreciate what I learned from the experience.

The biggest moment of my junior year had to be November 23, 1966, the time The Rev. Dr. Martin Luther King Jr. made a stop in Alexandria. Dr. King was guest speaker at an open meeting of the Louisiana Educators Association (LEA), the statewide Black organization for black teachers, at the Rapides Parish Coliseum. We were so excited. My parents and I, joined by two of their friends, arrived at 5 p.m., two hours before the event started. The coliseum was packed to capacity that evening.

We were seated in the nosebleed section waiting, and when Dr. King stepped to the podium, you could have heard a pin drop. His speech, "Remaining Awake through This Great Revolution", was powerfully delivered and reminded me of a church revival. He bellowed out unbridled words of wisdom, while those in attendance sat at the edge of their seats, taking it all in. I remember feeling God's presence and an anointing that left goose bumps.

Those high school years provided adventures outside of school as well. Downtown Lee Street offered a world of excitement to a 15-year-old looking to see what made the world turn. I had always heard my older brother (Leroy, aka Duck) say that he had been to the pool hall. So, I was excited to make my appearance. I began stopping by the pool hall to watch and learn how the game was played. It seemed easy enough. Use the cue stick and cue ball to sink the numbered balls into the side or corner pockets. It cost 25 cents a game, and it was more fun to have an opponent. The old hustlers were more than happy to play free off your money. Usually, you somehow managed to win the first game; afterwards, the loser pays. Guess who lost the next three games?

Lee Street had always been the focal point of business in the Black community during the mid-1970s and earlier. You could find law and dental offices in the same block, A&P groceries and beauty salons together, and funeral homes on a separate block. The Ritz Theater, Cave Lounge, and the Big Wheel Lounge were two blocks apart with Paul Caesar's Clothing Store across from the city bus barn and Ms. Leona's café right after you crossed the railroad tracks on Lee Street heading downtown. If you were going downtown, it was tradition to cruise down Lee Street to see what was going on. Ms. Leona was a friend of the family, and we would occasionally visit her at the café. I swear, she made the best homemade burgers and fries in Alexandria!

It became for many a rite of passage once you became a teenager, to go downtown on Third Street at the corner by S.H. Kress and hang out on Saturday afternoons, joking with the fellas or trying to get a word in with one of the beautiful females shopping. Afterwards, you would walk up the street to Woolworth or stop into the Walgreen's Pharmacy or continue window-shopping by Caplan's Men Store.

When I turned 16, my parents would trust me driving the family car so everyone would ante up gas money in order to ride. Our little posse (Spock, Milt, Charlie Ray Thompson (Smooth) and I) began to hang out on Sunday afternoons after church because we all were working on Saturdays. William Milton III (no relation) even started us wearing the same color (olive green and baby blue) jump suits with our names embroidered over the pockets. I must admit "we were clean", wearing jump suits with box-toe Stetson shoes, or a pair of Stacy Adams or Johnston Murphy, shining so bright you could see your reflection, ha, ha, ha! My job afforded me to visit the barber shop every week and a half. My barber was Mr. Alfred Rue on Houston Street. As a young teenager, I learned a whole lot about activities in the community, listening to the grownup conversation.

Sometimes, we would contact our female friends and take a road trip down Hwy 1 to Mansura and visit this juke joint called the Hole-in-the-Wall where most of the teens hung out. We would have the most fun when we would bring our female friends, so the local boys had some new action. We visited a few other towns, but none compared to the Hole-in-the-Wall in Mansura.

My junior year high school experience was a wakeup call. Adjusting to being an upperclassman and settling into my work schedule required some time. Leaving school for work after lunch rather than attending class resulted in my being out-of-touch with social activities taking place during my absence. I had to play catchup on the weekends, contacting friends and riding around. I am so thankful that Kathlyn Giles extended an invitation to attend her annual Christmas parties. Being involved with DECA limited my socializing, so I was so happy that Delores Jiles, a friend from my math class, accepted my invitation to the Junior-Senior Prom of 1967 held at the Alexandria Convention Center.

It was at the beginning of my senior year that Jerry Joubert played matchmaker with me and Toni G. Scott. It felt good to be going steady that year. And yes, it is true that when you went visiting your girlfriend's home, the front room light remained on! My Senior Prom in 1968 was much more enjoyable being with someone special. Good looking out, Jerry! For me, the social highlight of our senior year was the graduation dance held at the Casson Street Community Center. Percy Sledge was the headliner of our dance. A lot of classmates let off a lot of steam. I will not mention any names, but those in attendance had a good time and memorable outing.

We got through high school almost unscathed until that day in April, the month before graduation when Dr. King, the greatest civil rights leader ever, the first Black man to be awarded the Nobel Prize for Peace, was murdered on that balcony at the Lorraine Motel in Memphis. He had delivered a speech there the day before to sanitation workers on strike for stronger union laws and overall workers' rights. His death was deeply upsetting. He was just beginning to do other great things.

After graduation, I spent summer having fun with my posse before we prepared to go our separate ways come fall. There was a lot of uncertainty among us with the Vietnam War in full swing. Most of my immediate friends had yet to make up their minds about college or the war. I entered Southern University A& M College in the Fall 1968. I still recall the Continental Trailways bus trip to Baton Rouge and being amazed at the numbers of Peabody classmates on the bus heading there, too. Oh, what a time we had on that ride! I would later discover that there was a nice group of Peabody graduates registering that semester.

College life, although exciting, came with challenges. I have to admit I went wild with my newfound freedom. I made some mistakes. Missed my high school teachers, missed the nurturing. Adjusting to my new independent life, learning under white professors for the first time and the many other distractions and extracurricular activities that come with college life. It took a while to become steady. Thanks to my parents' teachings and the firm love and life lessons my Peabody instructors gave to me, I eventually prevailed and got my degree.

Only a few weeks before graduation, however, on November 16, 1972, tragically, two SU students, Leonard Brown and Denver Smith, were killed at the hands of the East Baton Rouge Parish Sheriff's Department while attending a nonviolent rally for state education funding rights. It was the saddest day of my college years. Classes immediately were discontinued the next day, and school remained closed until January 5, 1973.

On Jan. 31, 1973. I graduated, thank you laude, managing a B.S. Degree in Accounting, then immediately accepted an entry level position as an inventory accountant with the Honeywell Corporation in Minneapolis, Minnesota. Honeywell turned out to be an ideal start to my career. I was in my early 20s, from the deep South, and I had a lot to learn about the workplace and a different region of the country. Things went well the first year, especially after I changed managers. My second manager was not much older than I, late 20s, maybe 30? He and I got along very well.

As our work relationship grew, I learned a lot under his leadership. He even invited me to his home for steak dinner to introduce me to the wife and kids. It was the first time I had such a personal social interaction with a boss or coworker. His family was lovely, and the evening was enjoyable. He had a good sense of humor, too. He overheard me use the '70s slang "jive turkey," and when I explained the meaning, he picked up on it and would use it in conversations with others, but he would always change it to "jivin' turkey."

I stayed at Honeywell for 15 years and received numerous promotions and recognitions. Years later, I ended my professional corporate business career, formally anyway, at Wells Fargo Corporate headquarters as Administrator of Financial Reports.

Growing up in Alexandria taught me how to deal with overt racism, but my childhood fell short of preparing me for the perils of the *Smiling Faces* such as those mentioned in the song by the '70s band Undisputed Truth. Living up North most of my adult life, it would be my obligation to become more keenly able to distinguish between the "good" and the "ugly." Looking back, I guess I can say I made a success out of reading faces.

*Alexandria Town Talk coverage of Martin Luther King Jr. visit to Alexandria in November 1966.*

(Town Talk Staff Photo)

**Dr. Martin Luther King (left), president of the Southern Christian Leadership Conference, and J. K. Haynes, executive secretary of the Louisiana Education Assn., before King's speech to an open meeting of the association here Tuesday night.**

# Remain Awake, King Tells Delegates to LEA Meeting

White backlash is not new, Dr. Martin Luther King told an audience that filled the Rapides Parish Coliseum here Tuesday night.

King, in his speech to the open meeting of the Louisiana Education Assn., said, "They're talking like white backlash is something new. You only have to study the history of the Negro to see there's nothing new about it."

He called the "myth of the white backlash" one of the myths the Negro must get rid of if he is to "remain awake during the present revolution."

King also called for solution of the economic problems of the Negro, saying that today three times as many Negroes as whites are unemployed.

He said that until this problem is solved, chaos will remain in cities across the country.

King added, however, "I will stand up with all my might against riots. They only create problems. But I will condemn also conditions which engender the despair that makes people engage in such activity."

Non-violent resistance, he told his audience, "is still the most potent weapon available in the Negro struggle."

King said the subject of his talk was "Remaining Awake through a Great Revolution." He used Rip Van Winkle as his analogy, pointing out that Irving's character not only slept 20 years, but he slept through the American revolution.

All too many people today fail to achieve the new attitudes the situation demands and tragically are sleeping through a revolution which is sweeping away the old order, King believes.

He listed three ways to stay awake, one of which is the achievement of excellence.

"We must achieve excellence in our various fields of endeavor," said the president of the Southern Christian Leader-

(Turn to Page A2, Column 1)

ship Conference. "This is more important for us on the oppressed end of the old order than for any other The dilemma is that he who is behind must run faster than the man in front "

He urged teachers to inspire their students with this desire for excellence. to try to do a job so well nobody can do it better

"If you set out to be only a good Negro teacher or janitor or lawyer or whatever you are, you have already flunked t h e matriculation exam in the university o f integration'" declared King

'If you're a street sweeper. sweep streets like Michelangelo painted pictures. sweep them so well everyone will have to notice." he said

To remain awake, according to King, Negroes must engage in a massive, continuing action program to get rid of the last vestiges of segregation and discrimination

'If you think racial injustice will just pass away, you're sleeping." he told the applauding crowd

His third means of staying awake King called achievement of world perspective — "any nation which thinks it can live alone is sleeping."

He cited the achievements of science which have made the world a neighborhood and called on the moral and ethical genius of people to make it a brotherhood

"We must learn to live together as brothers or perish together as fools," said King.

In this context he criticized the U. S government for spending "too much of the budget on military bases rather than bases of understanding."

### Hits War Costs

At another point his speech the Baptist preacher and Civil Rights leader criticized the government for spending more on the war in Viet Nam and the space grogram than it is spending "to put God's children on their own two feet."

Two more myths which the Negro must rid himself of King listed as those of exaggerated progress and time.

"We are freer, but not yet free," he declared "We have a greater sense of dignity but we are not yet equal. . .We still have a long. long way to go."

He ridiculed the "don't push too fast now" theory, saying that "in one or two hundred years the problems will work themselves out if we don't move faster than we are now "

"Time is neutral," said King 'It can be used e i t h e r constructively or destructively. But the time is always right to do right."

He reminded his listeners to remember their brothers and sisters still in it when they have won their war on poverty

King said if Negroes hope to achieve peace and brotherhood, violence isn't the answer, "you can't kill lies and hate through violence "

### 'Become Involved'

He urged teachers and leaders to whom he spoke "to be involved in the struggle. Not all of you can go to jail — leave that to me — but you can march. picket, c o n t r i b u t e,

there's something all can do "

Difficult times still lie ahead, King said, but "we know we will get there because the ultimate goal of America is freedom "

"But." he warned, "some of us may go to jail, lose a job or even face death as the price we pay to free our children from psychological death."

"We will win freedom because the Bible is right when it says 'you reap what you sow,'" the speaker repeated

Before King's talk, an offering estimated at $1500 was taken for the Southern Christian Leadership Conference.

King was introduced by J K Haynes, secretary of t h e Louisiana Education Assn.

Dr. John W. Davis, director of the Legal Defense a n d Education Fund. NAACP. New York City, substituted for Wm J Dodd, state superintendent of schools, at the afternoon session

Dodd was unable to attend the meeting. Haynes told t h e audience.

A. Maceo Smith, zone intergroup relations advisor of the Federal Housing Administration, Dallas, Tex., one of the LEA convention program leaders, is in St Frances Cabrini Hospital, following a heart attack during the Tuesday afternoon session.

His condition was listed as "good" this morning by the hospital.

# DEBT OF GRATITUDE

*"Train up a child in the way he should go; even*
*when he is old, he will not depart from it."*

PROVERBS 22:6

## Roderick Newman

*When the slaves were freed, my great grandfather was named Charles Eddy after the slaveholder. He decided when he was freed that he was a new person and a "new man", and he changed his name to Newman.*

PRIOR TO THE Civil War, there was a large number of plantations established in what is now Rapides Parish that used slave labor to grow cotton, sugarcane, and other crops. The timber industry also grew because of the extensive forests that exist to this day around Alexandria. The area grew to be the most prosperous area in Louisiana. The Black population was larger than the white population. During the Civil War, Union Army soldiers destroyed many of the plantations and burned most of Alexandria to the ground. Many lives were lost during this period, and there was dramatic social upheaval with the economy destroyed and the newly freed Blacks living in squalid camps. The Union Army mistreated the former slaves, and many died. During Reconstruction, however, Blacks began to settle on the edge of town and prosper in these new freedmen's communities. These areas evolved into the neighborhoods we know today as Sonia Quarters, Oil Mill Quarters, Rock Island Quarters, and Lower Third.

*Great grandparents, James and Sarah Newman*

## FAMILY BACKGROUND

My family, the Newmans, came to Alexandria in the 1890s, settled in the Lower Third area and became successful carpenters, painters, and homebuilders. My great uncle built his home in Duck Alley, which became Church Street and is now Newman Street, and he was able to help his brother, my great-grandfather.

Great-grandfather James Newman moved to Alexandria from Baton Rouge where he was a sharecropper. My great-grandfather settled on Carr Street, and with the help of his brothers, bought a lot, built his home, and raised his family. My family became involved in the founding of three Baptist churches in Alexandria: Mt. Triumph, True Vine, and Pilgrim. My great-aunt told me that she was six years old when they moved from Baton Rouge to Alex, and she remembers the trip by mule drawn wagon. The trip took almost three days for the entire family, including my grandfather, Horace Newman, who was a baby at the time. My grandfather graduated from Peabody in 1925, and my mother graduated from Peabody in 1950, the year I was born. I found out later that one of her teachers was Mrs. Locks-Stemley who taught me history and ignited my interest in the subject.

I was raised by my great-aunt who lived in Shreveport. When her husband died, we moved to Alexandria, and I was enrolled at Jones Street Junior High. It was during this period that I began to recognize racism for what it was: traveling between Shreveport and Alexandria on segregated trains and buses, sitting in the back of buses, waiting in separate waiting areas, drinking at separate water fountains, and using bathrooms that were labeled "colored". I recall an incident at the old Kansas City Southern Railroad station where I drank at a water fountain for whites only. The white ticket clerk screamed at me. My aunt intervened and knocked me upside the head, sat me down, and explained segregation, which did not make sense to me. She told me that we would be moving to Detroit where it was not segregated, and things would be better.

*High school graduation day with Great Aunt Sarah Evelyn Newman Hardeman who saved my life*

My experience in Detroit was a culture shock. Compared to the South, it was a completely different world. I found out the meaning of the saying "when in Rome do as the Romans do". I attended Durfee Junior High in Detroit, a tough, gang-ridden school where the teachers were afraid and/or did not care about students. My grades dropped, and I was skipping school and doing things I had never done before such as stealing and rolling drunks. I had to join a gang for protection. Even though the school was integrated, there were very few whites at the school. President Kennedy was assassinated in 1963 while I was at school in Detroit, and I remember there was a riot. We burned cars and set buildings on fire. I came home one day from being out all night, and my aunt told me that we were leaving Detroit and moving back to Alexandria. Even though she told me that this move would save my life, I did not want to leave. My aunt told me it did not matter what I wanted, so in 1965, we moved back to Alexandria. Looking back on it all these years later, she was right.

## THE PEABODY YEARS

I enrolled at Peabody in the fall of 1965 and did not know at the time this was the best thing that could have happened to me. In Alexandria, I had a large safety net with so many family members living in the city. They became my village, and everything began to change for the better in my life and at school. My grades improved, and I learned the value of education and being responsible. I also realized the value of church and family. With so much family in Alex, my aunt began to inform me about our family history. My World History teacher at Peabody was Rev. Perry, who also happened to be the pastor at Mt. Triumph Baptist Church. I remember a conversation with him about most Blacks taking the surname of the former slaveowner. I looked up my surname Newman and learned that it was German/Jewish. I remember asking my aunt if this was how we got the name Newman. She told me that our family surname was given to us by her grandfather, Charles Newman, in the 1870s. When the slaves were freed, my great grandfather was named Charles Eddy after the slaveholder. He decided when he was freed that he was a new person and a "new man", and he changed his name to Newman.

Upon learning this, I took a lot of interest in researching and learning my family history. It was in Alexandria that I began to change my way of thinking regarding school. My grandfather, who was a painter, taught me how to paint and made me his helper during the summer months. I got my first job working at Walgreen's as a dishwasher and later at Piccadilly Cafeteria working, part-time making $1.65 an hour. I have many memories from my time in Alexandria and at Peabody. I cannot include all of them, however, I have listed below the moments that stand out:

- Going to The Shack on Sixth Street where I learned how to dance and began chasing girls.

- Hanging out at the concession stand on Broadway where I tried to perfect my dancing skills (I wasn't that good, but I had a lot of fun trying.)

- Sneaking into Bracey's on Lower Third, trying to be grown, and buying loose cigarettes for a quarter from Paul Dupree's store.

- Playing daredevil on the Kansas City Southern Railroad Bridge over the Red River when a train was coming.

- Going to the old Paramount Theatre and sitting in the balcony, throwing soda and popcorn on the white patrons below. (This was my way of protesting segregation.)

I remember well my first girlfriend, who shall remain anonymous, and my first jobs that gave me the means to go shopping for myself at Caplan's Men's Store, Wellan's Department Store and other businesses in town.

My high school experience at Peabody was great. I took the driver education course from Mr. Curtis and got my driver license. I also participated in extracurricular activities and competed in the statewide LIALO (Louisiana Interscholastic Athletic and Literary Organization) competition and won medals in history. I was on the track team, tried out for basketball but did not make the team. I also attended the junior and senior proms. I owe a debt of gratitude to the numerous friends, relatives, teachers, and classmates who helped me turn my life around.

Although I was aware that Alexandria was segregated, and racism was rampant in the 1960s, I am proud of the progress that Blacks have made politically. I now look back at that period in my life and realize that it prepared me to deal with racism and the world after high school. Upon graduation from high school, I left Alex, moved to Houston, got drafted and joined the U.S. Air Force. After four years in the USAF, I attended the University of Houston and earned degrees in Sociology, Social Science Teacher Education, and a certificate in African American Studies. I went to work for the City of Houston Human Resources Department and retired after 35 years of service. I credit my family and my village, Alexandria, with providing me with the foundation that shaped my life.

PART FOUR

# OUR COMMUNITY'S FIGHT
# FOR CIVIL RIGHTS

*"The problem of the 20ᵗʰ century will be that of the color-line, — the relation of the darker to the lighter races of men in Asia and Africa, in America, and in the islands of the sea."*
— WILLIAM EDWARD BURGHARDT DUBOIS,
*The Souls of Black Folk, 1903*

D R. DUBOIS' MADE his prediction that race would be the problem of the 20th century at its beginning. He was accurate about race, not only for the 20th century but for the 21st century, as the struggle continues. Though federal and even state legislation in Louisiana allowed for freedom of African Americans at all levels, freedom was withheld well into the 20th century, and African Americans and other people of color experience a lack of ability to exercise the rights and privileges espoused in the U.S. Constitution. The narratives accompanying this overview cover discrimination in employment, the military, one's neighborhood store, workplaces, classrooms and a lynching.

Two of the contributors to this volume, Pearlie Mae Lewis Carter (Narrative 16) and Rev. Larry D. Smith (Narrative 22) share their reaction upon seeing a lynched Black man hanging from a tree when they were children around seven or eight years old in the 1950s. That was not the first time a person had been lynched in the Parish. Bryan Stevenson's Legacy Museum and National Memorial for Peace and Justice in Montgomery, Alabama has researched and documented victims of racial terror lynching across the United States between 1877 and 1950. Their work reveals the lynching of the following individuals in Rapides Parish in that period. We memorialize them here as well as the man our classmates saw hanging from a tree at the Casson Street Community Center.

| Name | Date | Name | Date |
| --- | --- | --- | --- |
| Champe Rendon | 10.08.1880 | Frank Pipes | 05.09.1904 |
| Louis Bush | 04.05.1893 | Henry Johnson | 06.01.1907 |
| Henry Harris | 05.12.1900 | Mathias Jackson | 06.27.1907 |
| Thomas Amos | 08.29.1900 | David Blackman | 06.02.1928 |
| Frank Dupree | 06.11.1903 | Lee Blackman | 06.02.1928 |

## OUR COMMUNITY'S FIGHT FOR CIVIL RIGHTS

The fight for civil rights in 20th century America was played out in different ways across the United States. The fight for equal rights in Alexandria was not a series of dramatic events as experienced in some other southern towns and cities. Alexandria's

*Attorney Louis Berry*

fight occurred slowly, over time, and continues to this day. The city's active chapter of the National Association for the Advancement of Colored People (NAACP) played an important role in the integration of schools and public facilities. In the 1960s, the Congress of Racial Equality (CORE) also sent three of its workers to Alexandria to assist with integration efforts. Attorney Louis Berry gave them office space.

Louis Berry, the second Black attorney in the state of Louisiana and the first Black attorney in Rapides Parish, was Alexandria's civil rights champion. Feature articles in the *Alexandria Town Talk* in 1983, 1992, and 1998 share his astonishing trailblazing story. Born in Alexandria in 1914, Attorney Berry gave up a potentially lucrative career to fight for civil rights in his hometown.

A Howard University graduate who studied under U.S. Supreme Court Justice Thurgood Marshall, Attorney Berry filed numerous civil rights lawsuits not only in Rapides Parish but other parishes in the state and at the state and federal levels. Fearless and determined, his actions made the difference in the fight for equality in Alexandria and throughout Louisiana from the 1940s until his death in 1998. His work resulted in educational, social, and economic opportunities that Blacks had been denied for decades because of Jim Crow practices.

## VOTING RIGHTS AND OTHER CIVIL RIGHTS ISSUES

One of Attorney Berry's first victories in Alexandria occurred upon his return to Central Louisiana after completing his law degree in the early 1940s. The voter registration process in Rapides Parish, and throughout the South, was known for its discriminatory practice of requiring only Blacks to answer questions pertaining to ridiculously obscure details of the state or federal Constitution to prevent Blacks from meeting voting eligibility requirements. Mr. Berry and 10 others had prepared for the test, however, on the day he appeared at the courthouse to take the test, only three of the 10 were present. He was armed with a copy of the Supreme Court ruling overturning legislation that would allow only whites to vote in Democratic Party primary elections in southern states. The voting official relented, and the four in the early 1940s became registered Democrats that day, according to a 1998 *Alexandria Town Talk* article on Berry. Fifty years after the incident, Attorney Berry said upon reflection, "We left the registrar's office happy, knowing we had knocked down a barrier from slavery."

In another Black Alexandria historical note from the Jim Crow voting era, C.O. Compton Jr. was the focus of an October 2, 1979, news article in which he pointed out that he was one of the 17 Blacks who registered to vote in 1944, making him a part of the first group of Black citizens in Rapides Parish to register since Reconstruction.

Even after the bravery of Attorney Berry and others who registered to vote in the early 1940s, the right to vote for Alexandria Blacks was slow to come. In the featured vintage photo, Black voters are seen lined up, patiently waiting to receive their election ballots at what used to be a farmer's market located on Third Street near the tracks that crossed the Red River. According to the caption for this photo contained in *Alexandria (Images of America)*, the 1952 opportunity to vote for most Black Alexandrians was a first since the end of Reconstruction in 1877.

In 1947, Attorney Berry also filed the first civil rights lawsuit in Rapides Parish with The Rev. J.M. Murphy, then president of the NAACP, as the plaintiff in a case against the city regarding the closing of the Casson Street Community Center, purchased by the city after the war. The facility had been erected by the federal government as a USO (United Services Organization) for the exclusive use of Black soldiers during World War II. The facility closed after the war ended in 1945. In 1947, Blacks requested use of the center and were denied because whites living nearby objected, according to an April 8, 1947, *Alexandria Town Talk* story.

With Attorney Louis Berry as their legal counsel, members of the community brought a suit against the city and presented a petition signed by 500 Blacks asking for use of the all-white center three days a week. That request also was denied. After Mr. Berry's suit was denied twice, however, the city renovated the center and reopened it for exclusive use by Blacks.

From 1980 to 1990, Attorney Berry capped his legacy, as he continued legal work for educational equality, championing the fight against white flight, and working on school busing and the parish's massive desegregation plan. Attorney Berry's impact on the lives of Alexandrians can be felt to this day.

Upon his passing, a 1998 tribute in the *Town Talk*, looked back at Attorney Louis Berry's commitment to the law and to his people. Throughout his career, he undoubtedly loved the law and fought for Black causes, filing an abundance of civil rights suits at all levels of government in areas including housing, employment, business, school integration, higher education, professional sports, and healthcare. He considered himself a social engineer who used the law for justice the way a surgeon uses a scalpel to cut away the malignant parts, a description he learned in his Howard University days.

## School Desegregation

Desegregation of schools in the South was fraught with danger for all involved. For whites, having their children attend the same schools as Blacks was intolerable "race mixing." It was the most feared occurrence of all. For Blacks, desegregation was a conflicting equal opportunity that could damage the esteem of their children but simultaneously open a world to them they would otherwise likely never fully know. For many Blacks, it was an acceptable risk or sacrifice. The Peabody Class of 1968 never sat in a class with white students and were among the last in the parish to make up all Black class. Highlights of the community's desegregation history to 1968 follows.

1952    New Peabody High School for Blacks opens on Broadway for grades 9-12. Old structure on Third Street becomes Peabody Elementary and serves grades 1-8.

1954    *Brown v. Board of Education of Topeka* U.S. Supreme Court ruling passes, declares that state laws requiring racial segregation in public schools unconstitutional even if the segregated schools are otherwise equal.

1960    Two new, modern public junior high schools (Jones Street and Lincoln Road, Grades 7-9) open for Black students, some believe to ward off integration of schools in Rapides Parish by establishing "equal" Black schools. The addition of these two schools restructured the Black schools. Students in the six Black public elementary schools attended one of these junior high schools once reaching seventh grade. Peabody High becomes Peabody Senior High School, Grades 10-12.

1961    With Louis Berry as his attorney, Rev. Sylvester Valley files a discrimination lawsuit against the Rapides Parish School District. U.S. District Judge Edwin Hunter orders integration of the schools. The School Board responds with enactment of a limited school choice plan. This case was not resolved until 2003.

1965    In January, NAACP President, the Rev. Joseph Rax and Congress of Racial Equality (CORE) representative Judith Rollins[6] attempt to enroll 11 students at Bolton High School for the spring 1965 term and are met with rejection. The superintendent argues that midyear would not be a good time for students to enroll in a new school. The following fall, Black students quietly enroll at all-white Bolton.

Suit filed to desegregate all Rapides Parish public schools

1966    Three Black former Peabody High School students (Carolyn Armstrong, Claudia Davis, and Linda Torry) pictured in the Bolton High School 1966 yearbook with the senior class, graduate from formerly all-white Bolton because of the efforts of Rev. Rax and Ms. Rollins. In November, Dr. Martin Luther King Jr. speaks at the opening meeting of the Louisiana Education Association in Alexandria's Rapides Parish Coliseum.

1967    Rapides Parish School District offers **total** "freedom of choice" plan, and 14 students accepted.

1968    Four Black former Peabody High School students (Gussie Davis, Sherrie Dunn, Donald Owens, and Jacqueline Towels) pictured in the 1968 Bolton High School yearbook graduate from the formerly all-white Bolton High School.

---

[6]    Ms. Rollins was a Congress of Racial Equality (CORE) worker, who, along with scores of others, worked for civil rights in Louisiana. She and two other workers lived in the home of Mrs. Odette Hines. The work of CORE's integration efforts in Alexandria are described in detail in Mrs. Hines' biography, *All Is Never Said: The Narrative of Odette Hines*, written by Judith Rollins.

# Sanders to Discuss Bolton 'Mixing' Only With Parents

Two Negro leaders Thursday asked the Rapides Parish School Board to transfer 11 Negro students from Peabody High school to Bolton High school and received no answer.

Supt. C. R. Sanders said the administrative office, which handles transfers, does not discuss the problems of individual children with anyone other than the parents or legal guardians.

The Negroes were Judy Rollins, a representative of the Congress of Racial Equality, and Rev. Joseph Rax, a Rapides parish leader in the National Assn. for the Advancement of Colored People.

Sanders said it would be an "irregular proceeding" to discuss any matter relating to children with anyone other than the parents of the children involved.

Sanders told the pair that he would listen to any problems presented him by the parents.

The Negro representatives were with the group of 11 children from Peabody, a Negro high school, who sought Monday to transfer to Bolton, a white high school.

They approached the Bolton offices but were told all transfers are handled by the administrative offices. The new term begins Monday and the students are seeking to enter school then.

*Alexandria Daily Town Talk, January 31, 1965*

As noted, civil rights action in Alexandria was lowkey. Integration of schools, employment, and public facilities were slow in coming. Many of the first Blacks hired in public places were mulattoes who were plentiful and looked more white than Black. Whites in Alexandria put integration off as long as they could. But there were leaders in Alexandria who would not let them prevail. Those along with Attorney Berry who pushed tirelessly an honorably for civil rights, sacrificing their privacy and taking risks, will never be forgotten.

Miss Georgia M. Johnson                              Miss Maud E. Scovell
Directress                                           Secretary

CASSON STREET COMMUNITY CENTER
"Finest in the South for Negroes"

815 Casson Street
Alexandria          Louisiana
Dial 2-2786

September 21, 1951

Hon. J. Howard McGrath
Attorney General
Washington, D. C.

Dear Sir:

As you may know Dr. W. E. B. DuBois is known
as an ardent worker for over half a century for the
advancement of our race group. Being an aged man now
that has been so outstanding, it is sad that now he
is considered a criminal.

In view of this fact and others too numerous
to mention, we ask that charges against him be
dropped.

Thanking you in advance, I remain

Yours very truly,

mes

*Copy*

*I am enclosing $1.00 This small but
is best I can do just now.
Wishing you success
G M Johnson*

The letter (above) from Casson Street Community Center was sent to the
National Committee to Defend Dr. W. E. B. DuBois and Associates in the Peace
Information Center, September 21, 1951. This is an example of the awareness of
Blacks in Alexandria on national issues.

*"Those who forget history are condemned to repeat it."*

—GEORGE SANTAYANA

# NO ERROR

*"For I know the plans I have for you," declares the Lord, "plans to prosper you and not to harm you, plans to give you hope and a future."*

JEREMIAH 29:11

## Doretha Perry Wyatt

MY GIVEN NAME is Doretha Perry (Wyatt). I was born in Pineville, Louisiana (LA), in 1950 to Sidney and Ruby Perry. My father's birthplace was Franklin, LA, known for its sugarcane and rubber production. My mother's birthplace was Bunkie, LA, known for its sugarcane and cottonfields.

*I did not have the funds to attend college. I applied for jobs, did interviews and passed (work) requirements for employment, but I was told repeatedly, there were no positions available.*

At the time of my birth, my family was living on a farm in Morrow, LA. My father was a sharecropper (tenant farmer). As a sharecropper, he plowed the farmland and performed all the physical labor. The yields from the crops would be shared between the owner of the farm and the sharecropper/tenant. The tenant would be the one being shortchanged and receiving less from the harvest. In addition, the cost of farm tools, seeds, fertilizer, and family provisions were deducted from the sharecropper's portion. Therefore, after several years of sharecropping in Morrow, to prosper, my parents decided to move to Alexandria for better opportunities.

My father's work in construction took him out of town for weeks at a time, building roads. After many years in this position, he was promoted to cement mixer from which he retired. My mother worked at the Bentley Hotel as a maid to help with the family income. In my family, it was a practice to name their children after other family members: sisters, brothers, uncles, aunts and parents. I was named after my father's sister, Doretha. It was also customary to have a nickname, and mine was "Fat", believe it or not?! I was given this name because I was chubby from birth to about age 12. To this day, some people only know me by my nickname "Fat". Funny, isn't it?

My parents taught us to always take care of each other. The oldest was responsible for the

*My mom*

younger siblings. I am the fourth born of nine siblings. Since I was the next oldest after my older siblings left home, I was left alone with five younger brothers to care for. My mother worked and did not get home until after 5 p.m. Caring for them was difficult until I learned how to manage chores and new responsibilities.

We were raised in the Baptist faith. We attended Sunday services and other church programs. Saturday was washday, and housecleaning chores also had to be done. Sunday dinner was prepared on Saturday evening. No cooking was done on Sunday (church day). All businesses were prohibited from operating on Sundays (Blue Law). Entertainment was going to the park, going to the movies, and playing games with friends in the neighborhood.

We lived in Samtown. Most of the families in the neighborhood had large families with six to 12 children per household. The community as a whole was very support- ive of each other. If someone needed support (such as food, childcare, etc.), the com- munity would provide help. We lived near the railroad, and many times hobos would walk through the neighborhood asking for food. My mother would feed them. She would say, "You never know who you're helping — could be an angel in disguise." The hobos were not considered dangerous or perceived as a threat to us. During this time, many people did not lock their doors because we trusted each other.

I remember the time my parents would buy many things from the traveling door- to-door salesman who sold products from the Watkins Company. We called him the Watkins man. He would drive around the neighborhood selling different items (such as vanilla extract, clothes, etc.). These were items that most Black people could not buy in the store on credit. A Black family, the Franklins, ran a neighborhood corner store that allowed us to buy on credit.

The main grocery stores were at least five miles or more away from our communi- ty. At the time, we did not have a car. We had to ride the city bus to the grocery store and ride back with bags of groceries. At that time, we had to sit in the back of the bus only because the front seats were for whites only. When we went on family road trips, my mother would prepare food because many restaurants would not serve Blacks or would send us to the back kitchen area to pay for food.

I attended several elementary schools in Alexandria because we moved quite a bit: J.B. Lafargue, Silver City, and Aaron Street. I remember one teacher who would make you stand in the back of the class on one leg while holding a book, as a punishment for bad behavior. I especially remember Mr. Wesley, who told us many stories about his military experiences as a soldier. He encouraged us to follow our dreams and never give up — he didn't. He achieved his goal of becoming a teacher.

When I started seventh grade, I attended Jones Street Junior High School. There were many things I wanted to participate in (choir, track) but couldn't because they all met after school. I couldn't stay after school because of my home obligations. I remember Mrs. Kelso, who was a very compassionate and caring teacher. She would listen attentively and assist as needed. She even took our class to *her home* for a science project.

In 1965, I graduated from Jones Street and began my studies at Peabody Senior High School. At that time, it was the only high school available for Black students. Some surrounding towns did not have a high school for Blacks, so students commuted by bus to Peabody. I remember the football team was one of the best in the state because of the talent from other towns. All instructors encouraged us to continue our education to reach our goals in life.

I was a member of several school clubs, such as Science and Future Nursing Clubs. The nursing club helped me explore the aspects of becoming a nurse. The club gave me the opportunity to volunteer at the Huey P. Long Charity Hospital. I worked Saturdays and some Sundays as a candy striper. Candy Stripers are hospital helpers without pay in a variety of healthcare settings, working under the supervision of staff nurses. Our senior year was marked by tragedy with the death of Dr. Martin Luther King Jr. on April 4, 1968, a month before I graduated. Dr. King had led the struggle for equal rights for all people. Our graduating class theme was "Lest We Forget". We all were inspired to enroll in higher education and reach our goals.

Unfortunately, I did not have the funds to attend college. I applied for jobs, did interviews and passed (work) requirements for employment, but I was told repeatedly, there were no positions available. White people, however, also would apply and would get the job. I contemplated joining the army, but my parents wouldn't let me. They were afraid because many people told them horrid stories about treatment of Black women in the army. I continued to apply for numerous jobs with no luck. My friend and I decided to attend Alexandria Trade School. She chose the secretarial curriculum, and I chose nursing. Before the courses started, I got a job at the local chicken processing plant. My job was collecting the innards (heart, gizzards, liver, necks), wrapping them in a special way, and inserting them in the inside of each chicken, as they all moved quickly on an assembly line. You had to be quick. The job paid well for the time, and it should have. It was a tough environment that inspired me to stay in school. I worked for two months on the 7 a.m. to 2 p.m. shift, then changed to the 3 p.m. to 11 p.m. shift after starting classes from 7 a.m. to 1 p.m.

Many times, I had to change clothes in the car to be on time for work. The courses were intense because of the necessity to learn a lot of material in a short period of time. But I was determined to do my best to finish. The work at the chicken processing plant was eye-opening. I realized I did not want to spend the rest of my life in such an environment, doing that kind of work. I worked at the plant for eight months. I had to make a choice. I knew I could not do both. I decided to continue the nursing courses, quit my job, and focus on my studies. It was the best choice I ever made. That decision changed the direction of my life.

At the beginning of the trade school classes, the director announced to all students that whatever happened in our classes, he would not change or question the instructor's decision about any problems/questions we would encounter. This was an intimidating statement to the Black students. That meant whether it was right or wrong, he was going to be on the side of the instructors. The class consisted of approximately 50 students and only eight were Black; the remainder, 42, were white students. We (Black students) all realized that we had to really work hard to complete the courses. The first six-week period evaluation report had the same comments on all the Black students' progress reports: We all had "interpersonal relationship problems" because we formed a clique (according to the instructors) by being together during breaks. We did not associate with the other (white) students. Of course, we did not know the white students, and they didn't know us. In the end, all the Blacks passed the courses except one. She had passed all the courses, but it was stated that the student had had an unacceptable attitude during classes. She was very outspoken and had displayed an arrogant attitude toward the instructors.

Upon completing the nursing curriculum, there was a pinning ceremony for which I was asked to do the prayer. I was surprised to have been selected. I chose the Serenity Prayer: "God grant me the serenity to accept the things I cannot change, the courage to change the things I can, and the wisdom to know the difference." I chose this prayer because it gave me inspiration to conquer my fears and persevere toward my goals.

After graduating from trade school and passing the state board for practical nursing licensure exam, by God's grace, I secured a job at Rapides General Hospital. I married in 1970, and from this marriage, I have two children, a boy and a girl. After working there for approximately one-and-a-half years, I worked at Central State Psychiatric Hospital. While working there, I applied to Louisiana State University at Alexandria to pursue an Associate Degree in Nursing. I was determined to succeed and worked different shifts to realize my goal. It was difficult, but with prayer and God's grace, I completed the required courses as a parttime student and graduated in 1979 as an Associate Degree Registered Nurse.

After my divorce, in 1981, I moved to Houston, Texas, with my children for better economic gain. I worked in several hospitals in the Houston area and experienced and observed job discrimination there, as well. You literally could count the number of Black nurses on one hand. As a Black nurse, I frequently would get the most difficult patients to provide care. Private hospitals would not promote Black nurses to certain positions. One facility, for example, would not allow Black charge nurses to work the day shift, we would have to work the evening/night shift.

In 1983, I applied to the Houston Veteran Affairs Medical Center for a nursing position. The Veteran Affairs Medical Center is an equal opportunity employer. The process for acceptance took at least three months to complete. I was very excited about the acceptance. The benefits were an improvement by comparison, including paid holidays, a retirement system, opportunities for advancement, and, lest I forget, more Black nurses in higher positions.

The Veteran Affairs Medical Center began offering assistance to nurses who wanted to advance their education. I took advantage of their offer for advancement and started the Bachelors of Science in Nursing (BSN) program as a parttime student at the University of Texas in nearby Galveston. This was a difficult time because I drove to Galveston two to three times a week for two years. But with much prayer, studying and God's grace. I completed the program in 1990.

As time went on, advancement in nursing care continued, and southern states began to offer the advancements at the universities. I was accepted for Advance Practice Nurse in the master's degree program at University Texas Health Science Center. The environment was conducive for learning — and the white instructors, as well as white students, were helpful. I did it again, succeeded at working fulltime and attending school parttime. I completed the course in 1998 and earned the Adult Nurse Practitioner with master's degree in Nursing. No Advanced Practitioner Nurse positions were open at Houston VA at that time, so working with my supervisor and staff, we developed a position to apply my skills during this time. In 2010, I was awarded "The Daisey Award", and honor given to nurses who provide above and beyond patient and family care.

Reflecting over my past, I realize I have been a caregiver all my life. Case in point, starting as a babysitter for my younger siblings, neighbor's children, all family members and friends. Caregiving is my calling and profession. My earliest personal healthcare story also linked me to the medical and nursing field. When I was a toddler in the early 1950s, I developed pneumonia. My parents took me to Huey Long Hospital for treatment. They were told that there was nothing they could do for me. There was no specific medication or treatment except an experimental drug. My parents agreed to let them give it to me. The medication was successful. The rest is history! I am still here. Part of God's divine plan.

# MY FIGHT FOR EQUALITY

*"The Lord is my shepherd; I shall not want."*

PSALM 23:1

## Freddie Price Sr.

*It would not be until adulthood, my junior year in college, that I had person to person interactions with whites my age....*

I WAS BORN OCTOBER 4, 1950, at the Charity Hospital in Pineville, Louisiana, a small, segregated town outside of segregated Alexandria. Charity was where most of the African American children I grew up with were born. I was reared in Samtown, an all-Black community located right outside the city limits of Alexandria. I grew up in a house at the end of a dirt road in a family of 12 children and a loving father and mother. I was the tenth born and the last of six boys.

My father was born in Ward, Louisiana, and my mother was born in nearby Carson. Both were small sawmill towns not far from Alexandria. We were a close-knit family. My father and mother were strong, God-fearing good people, and they raised me to be the same.

I have warm memories of my early childhood. One of the earliest was my mother taking me with her when I was 3 to visit our neighbor, Mrs. Rachal, who lived across the street. The Rachal family structure was similar to ours with young boys close to my age. These two mothers were more than neighbors, they were good friends. I was the youngest at the time, and my fondest memory of Mrs. Rachal was her beautiful smile when she would look at me.

Being the last boy in a large family, I was spoiled and enjoyed a safe protective up-bringing. My mother, father, older sisters and brothers made it possible for me to not want for anything. My two younger sisters enjoyed the same benefits.

Life as I knew it was good. My father was the head of the house, and my mother was his partner. The folks in my all-Black community protected one another. At the time, there was no television showing real relations between colored people and white people. We were two groups separated in every meaningful lifestyle way.

As a young boy, when I had the opportunity to go to downtown Alexandria with my mother, it was a treat. My mother would take me to the S.H. Kress five and dime to shop. When I wanted a drink of water or needed to go to the restroom, I had to drink from an old and dirty water fountain, compared to the newer clean ones for whites. I also had to use the "colored people only" toilet. That was the way it was, and there was to be no questioning why.

My first stop for learning was my immediate family where I learned the core values of life. Then came religion, going regularly to church and Sunday school class, Baptist Training Union (BTU) and summer Vacation Bible School. The church I grew up in was located at the beginning of the street that I grew up on. My father was a deacon and mother a deaconess. My parents were highly respected members and overall pillars in the community.

I received my formal education in the Rapides Parish School District where colored people went to their school and white people theirs. I attended my all-Black neighborhood elementary and junior high schools, and ultimately graduated from the historic Black Peabody High.

Growing up in an environment of segregation, I could not then appreciate that colored people and white people operated in two separate worlds. It was the way of life. My parents never owned a personal car. When we needed transportation, there was either someone in our extended family to give us a ride, or there was the city bus that stopped and picked up at the beginning of our dirt road.

As it was in the segregated South, when riding the city bus, Black people had to sit in the back of the bus. It was not questioned. It was the given and acceptable practice. When the law was passed that allowed for the desegregation of the buses, I could not wait to sit in the front seat.

In the solidly segregated world I grew up in, there was no direct intermingling with white people. In the environment of those days, my parents' interactions were strictly with the white insurance salesmen who came to our house to pick up the monthly life insurance premium payments and the white man, who we called Mr. Jack Block, who would pick up the mortgage payment for the land that my father had purchased from him. There also was the white lady who hired my mother to do her laundry. She would bring the dirty clothing over for my mother to wash, iron and neatly fold and would return for pickup after the job was finished.

It would not be until adulthood, my junior year in college, that I had person to person interactions with whites my age during Army ROTC summer camp at the U.S. Army installation at Fort Riley, Kansas.

In fall 1968, I became the first in my family to attend college, entering Southern University in Baton Rouge as a freshman at age 17. It was at that time that my eyes became wide open to what was going on with race relations in America. Although Congress had passed the Civil Rights Act in 1964, the Civil Rights Movement did not impact me until I left Alexandria late summer in 1968 on a Continental Trailways bus heading to Baton Rouge.

As a college freshman on the campus of one of Louisiana's oldest HBCUs, the movement became real. The campus at that time, like other campuses in the country, still was reeling from the assassination of Dr. Martin Luther King Jr., and angry about the Vietnam War. It was then that I participated in my first boycott. The student leadership and other student body groups organized protests, pushing for and demanding racial equality and equal justice.

In the unrest, while students marched, the police authorities stormed the campus in riot gear with their weapons. They fired guns at us and lobbed teargas at us. I was teargassed, and several students were injured. Fortunately, on that day, there was no loss of life.

In fall 1972, my last semester before graduating, student demonstrations took a more direct approach after learning that there were inequities in how state elected officials in control of funding for public colleges and universities distributed the money. It was then that I learned that only half of the total dollar amount spent on a single white student at Louisiana State University was spent on a single Black student at Southern. I supported the protests. The demands were the basics — improved curriculum, more professors and equal spending. Students were arrested, but no one expected students to die in what started out as basic and fair student demands and peaceful demonstrations.

After talks with the administration eventually went south, and reports that an anonymous call to the police misrepresented the campus situation, Governor Edwin

Edwards sent hundreds of law enforcement officers and State police officers to campus. That's when the protest turned deadly. Police were in riot gear with weapons. Two students were killed. I was again teargassed. A tree limb fell several feet in front of me, briefly stopping me in my tracks, just missing me after a police officer fired his gun into the tree.

The traumatic event became a big national story and nearly drove me to a point emotionally where I was ready to quit college in my last semester without graduating. I believe it was God who sent three women from the Alexandria community who were Southern University alums to talk to me. They advised and encouraged me to not drop out. When campus reopened, I returned and, as planned, graduated January 31, 1973.

The campus unrest of my college years was significant. My college life for the most part set the stage on how I would see the world in all its rawness. Freshman year, I was fortunate to bond quickly with a group of likeminded young men and women. We called ourselves, Alexandria Main Dudes, and together we were able to help each other navigate college life.

I joined two fraternities — one military (Association of the United States Army), one social (Omega Psi Phi, Inc.). These groups of men were instrumental in my development as a young man.

The military experience was a life changer. As I mentioned, I participated in the Army ROTC program and graduated college as Second Lieutenant in January 1973. In my junior year, I attended ROTC summer camp at Fort Riley, Kansas. First time in the Midwest. It was at the summer camp that I experienced firsthand peer to peer racism, and it came from my fellow white soldiers from the bigger schools — Alabama, Mississippi, and Texas A&M. There were two other African American cadets in our relatively large size, predominantly white platoon.

There were daily drills and exercises, and through a random rotation, I eventually was put in command of my unit. At first, a group of the white cadets ignored me. They did not want to follow my orders for what appeared to be no other reason than my skin color. Ultimately, I firmly stood my ground and commanded my unit in such a way that the unit fell in line and began to comply. My white training officer witnessed the event and complimented me on how I handled the situation. This incident taught me how to hold my ground and stand up for myself when handling future racist situations that I encountered.

*1971 letter to my friend about ROTC summer camp incident*

In February 1973, I began my military career as Second Lieutenant and spent 11 years of serving my country overseas in Seoul, Korea and Stuttgart, Germany, and stateside in Indiana, California and Louisiana. I applied for and was granted an early retirement from active-duty service, ending my Army duty with the rank of major while serving at Fort Polk in summer 1984.

At the time, as I prepared for transition to civilian life, a headhunting firm head-quartered in San Francisco fortunately was on post at Fort Polk, recruiting officers for jobs in corporate America. After I was vetted through their interview process and interviewed with several corporate recruiters for employment, I accepted an offer as a Team Manager for the Proctor & Gamble (P&G) paper plant in Green Bay, Wisconsin, where I lived for six years.

It was the collective core values of my parents' upbringing and growing up in a supportive Black community, coupled with my active-duty military career that helped create a smooth transition to civilian life in Green Bay. At that time, the city's Black population was less than 1 percent. I found myself in a community where the largest African American population for the city came from three major local sources: Black managers working at Proctor & Gamble, the football team for the Green Bay Packers, and Black people at the Green Bay Correctional Institution, an adult male maximum-security correctional facility.

Since the P&G start in my civilian career, I've journeyed from corporate America to entrepreneurship. In June 1994, I opened a One Hour Martinizing Cleaners fran-chise in West Chester, Ohio, and now own an Information Technology company in Alexandria.

As a small business owner, when I see the world today, I think about how the fight for racial equality changed things for Americans like me. While there were challeng-es for African Americans when I was young, in many ways important progress came from the Civil Rights Movement of my youth. Dismantling Jim Crow segregation in the South, the passing of federal legislation in education, housing and employment, and implementing affirmative action policies in public and private institutions have significantly impacted mostly for good the lives of many persons of color. We have come a long way, but African Americans cannot become complacent when there are many more steps to achieve the full equal rights that our brave ancestors and role models fought for to get us here. The struggle continues.

As a father of three children, I have attempted to model the way I was brought up as best I could. I learned from my parents' many examples what it means to love, enjoy, and support family, to strive to be honest and to do good for others as often as you can. Parents never know how core values impact children as they grow up. I held on to a social media post I once read on my son's Facebook page. It was an exchange with his sister pertaining to me and their dear mother, who we lost to cancer in 1996.

Son: I miss our library and all of those books. I spent a lot of time in there.

Daughter: We were blessed to be raised by two highly educated thinkers. We were taught to think for ourselves. Taught to look for the answers.

Son: Momma used to say, "If you don't know, ask."

I am optimistic about the present and the future only if we stay on this battlefield of racial equality, each one of us doing our individual part in fighting systemic racism in this country. For our children and their children.

# AN UNEXPECTED JOURNEY

*"We often don't realize that where God puts us is the very place we need to be to receive what He wants to give us."*
— PRISCILLA SHIRER

## Gloria Roberts Sadler

*...I had a good childhood growing up on the farm. We didn't have a lot, but we had family and everything we felt we needed to survive. My grandfather's ownership of the farm made the difference for us.*

As the saying goes, we are powerless to change our past, but we can change how we look at it. Nothing happens out of order or by chance. We must look for the lesson that can be learned from each of our experiences.

My father was born in Alexandria, Louisiana and raised on Bayou Rapides, and is the youngest of seven kids. My paternal grandparents are Roberts/Innis. My mother was born in Mansura, Louisiana, in Avoyelles Parish, the fourth child of five. My maternal grandparents are Guillory/Baptiste. My mother's parents divorced when my mother was a teen. After the divorce, the family moved around a bit before settling in Alexandria.

My parents would often talk about how they met at a movie theater in Alexandria. My mother went with her sister, and my father went with his cousin. When the movie was over, as they were leaving the movie theater, my father saw my mother and flipped a coin to the ground. As my mother bent down to pick up the coin, my father caught her by her elbow and introduced himself. They started dating a few months after that and eventually married.

My mother grew up Catholic and attended Saint James Catholic Church. My father was Baptist and a member of First Evening Star Baptist Church on Bayou Rapides. Growing up, we (the children) went to catechism every Saturday evening, and the family went to Mass every Sunday morning. Coming back home from Mass on Sunday morning was one of the highlights of my week as a kid because we would always stop at a store in town to buy some goodies. One of our favorite places to stop was at a donut shop owned by the family of one of my classmates, Dennis Smith.

We would always attend my father's Baptist church every fourth Sunday. I remember the pastor of the church would always come to our house for Sunday dinner. Marrying someone of Christian faith different from one's own was discouraged during my parents' time. However, my parents defied the rules, married, and lived happily. No problems surfaced in our household as a result of their decision. They made it work. The way I see it, we got the best of both worlds.

*Adults from left to right are my mother, grandmother, and aunt.*
*The children are my cousin and another aunt.*

My parents had four children. I am the second born. My older brother and I are one year apart. My younger brother and I are five years apart, and my younger sister and I are nine years apart. We lived on Cooper Road on Bayou Rapides until I was 15.

Information obtained from rapidesgenealogy.org describes Bayou Rapides as an island surrounded by lakes and bayous. It emerges from the Red River at Cotile Landing and reenters the river at Alexandria. Bayou Rapides thus formed, is about 15 miles long and varies between two to five miles in width. Along both sides of Bayou Rapides is the unusual tier of fine plantations. Within the island is a low, swampy basin, with cypress brakes and several small lakes scattered through it.

Bayou Rapides is known for its rich farmland, bayous and lakes. Black and white families owned land on Bayou Rapides with white families owning the majority of the land. Others were sharecroppers. Early on, all the roads on the bayou were dirt and gravel. Though landowners included Black and white families, it was still segregated. There was no such thing as a next-door neighbor unless it was your family members living next door on your property. The bayou was racially segregated. You could always tell the difference in land ownership by the size of the houses. The whites had large plantation homes on their property, while Blacks owned small wood framed homes.

Those had to be trying times for my parents. Money was tight in our household, but we made do with what we had. My mother was a domestic worker for a white family for many years until she decided to quit working and be a stay-at-home wife and mother. She was a talented and resourceful person. I remember when we had the rare opportunity to go into town (Alexandria) to shop. S.H. Kress was the spot. Very seldom would we buy anything other than underwear. I didn't realize it at the time, but our main purpose for going there was for my mother to look at the dresses hanging on the clothes racks. She would often buy fabric and thread before leaving the store. We didn't have the money to buy the dresses, so my mother would come home after looking at the clothes, create a pattern using newspapers, and sew the dress using her foot propelled sewing machine. I think all the dresses I wore until I was in seventh grade were made by my mother. Females did not wear pants during those times.

I couldn't wait for those Montgomery Ward and Sears & Roebuck catalogs to come. Those were our wish books. As a kid, I would flip through every page and dream and say to myself, "One day". Not being exposed to too much other than what was going on in the Bayou Rapides, we didn't wish for too much. But for Christmas, we got everything we wished for. For me, it was doll and doll clothes. I think my mother even made the doll clothes. We always got one of those red mesh Christmas stockings filled with candy, toys, apples and oranges.

Let's not forget those S&H Green Stamps. My mother would get them from the merchants when she went shopping. We loved collecting them and pasting them in the green stamp book so that we could "buy" stuff later.

My father was industrious. Although he did not have the opportunity to attend school regularly because he had to work in the fields picking cotton, he served in the U.S. Navy. After he left the military, he was determined not to go back into the fields to pick cotton. He was hired by a machinery company on MacArthur Drive in Alexandria. I was told that with him being such a hothead, that particular job didn't last long because someone said something to him that rubbed him the wrong way. My father's family describes him as being "spoiled" and accustomed to getting his way as the youngest of his six siblings. Eventually, he was hired by the U.S. Post Office and worked there to retirement. After retiring from the post office, my father started his own transportation business, and, in doing so, found his passion. The business became very lucrative.

I was born in 1950 at the charity hospital in Pineville, Louisiana, and raised on Bayou Rapides on my paternal grandparents' farm. As far as the eye could see, there was other farmland owned by whites, growing mostly cotton and corn. Everything raised/grown on my grandparents' farm was for sale. There was always a variety of food for the family year-round.

*My grandfather, Waddell Roberts Sr.*

My grandparents' farm had rows and rows of cotton and corn, different types of animals, cows, pigs, goats, chickens, roosters, ducks, geese, turkeys and different types of produce such as watermelons, cantaloupes, beans, tomatoes, cucumbers, okra, etc. My grandfather also had a fruit orchard where he grew pears, grapes, berries, persimmons, figs and peaches. We would help harvest and preserve fruits and vegetables for the winter and even make wine from the berries we picked. He told us not to go in the orchard and pick any of the fruits before harvest. Of course, we didn't listen. We loved picking and eating the fruit off the trees and vines, never bothering to wash any of them before eating. One day my grandfather went out to the orchard and started sprinkling white powder on the fruit trees and told us it was poison to prevent us from messing with the fruits. That worked. We never touched another fruit in his orchard. Later, we found out the white powder was flour.

I remember my grandfather would start out early in the mornings to plow the fields. He had an old mule he named Bob. He'd hook up his plow to Bob and work in the fields for hours creating straight rows for planting. He would come home before it got too hot and sit on the front porch in his rocking chair and drink a pot of coffee. But I never heard him complain. I spent as much time at my grandparents' house as I did my own.

The only items I remember my parents buying were flour, corn meal, sugar, and seasonings, and, of course, they would get that free government cheese. Sometimes they would purchase various ointments from the Watkins man on his visits. We definitely lived off the land.

The most difficult times for me were during slaughter. To me, the wringing of the necks of chickens and the way they killed the hogs was cruel, but I enjoyed eating the cured ham, bacon, cracklings, fried chicken, roasted duck and all that good stuff. On weekends, sometimes family members who lived in town and around Bayou Rapides would come to the farm for weekend celebrations. We all would sit under a big tree at our grandparents' house, have cookouts, and it would be one big party.

In addition to my grandparents and our family, some of my older cousins moved in with my grandparents to help them with the farm. My brother and I were close in age, we only had each other as playmates. Later on, my aunt and her family and my great aunt and her family also lived on the farm. Their children became our playmates. We would play from dusk till dawn most of the time. I remember us making walking stilts and racing each other to see who could run the fastest on the stilts. We made slingshots and would have a contest to see how many birds we could shoot from the trees. We'd ride our bicycles up and down the road and in the fields. Most of my cousins who lived on the farm were boys, which meant the activities I had to participate in with them were baseball or football. I was somewhat of a tomboy. Otherwise, I would be playing with my dolls. My father even bought my older brother a quarter horse and told him he was responsible for keeping the horse fed and watered. We would spend hours riding that horse in the pastures and on the trails. When my brother started neglecting his duties with feeding and watering the horse, we ended up selling it to the Alexandria Police Department. I remember other fun times when my parents would take us to rodeos and wrestling matches. As I write about my early years on Bayou Rapides, I realize I had a good childhood growing up on the farm. We didn't have a lot, but we had family and everything we felt we needed to survive. My grandfather's ownership of the farm made the difference for us.

Without my grandfather's knowledge, during the '60s, some of my teenage cousins got a little bored and started growing a few patches of marijuana plants in his cotton-fields. When my grandfather found out what they had done, he was beside himself. The punishment they received is something they said they would never forget. They thought picking cotton was hard, but when he made them chop down a huge tree with an axe after they'd had a full day of picking cotton on the farm, they said that was worse than picking cotton because every time they would hit the tree with the axe, the axe would bounce back, making it very difficult to cut down the tree. I think they were able to chop down the tree after about three weeks.

There was a country store on Bayou Rapides that we would frequent to buy sodas, candy, cookies, and other stuff. The store had a "Colored" entrance and a "White" entrance. I remember going to the store one day with my cousin. I did not know she had a pistol with her because she was determined she was not going to use the "Colored" entrance. I think I was about 12 or 13 at the time. My cousin had to be around 17. That day, she was determined to be bold, take her chances, and challenge the establishment. As she was approaching the "White" entrance, I told her she was going the wrong way. As she entered, a white man yelled at her and pushed her out and told her to go back out and go through the other entrance for colored. She pulled out her gun and held it where no one else in the store could see it. At that moment, I was scared to death. Luckily for both of us, she came to her senses and relented, and we both left the store. Needless to say, we never went back to that store again.

There were no highway lights in the "country" other than maybe porchlights on the homes with electricity. If you ventured outside at night, you had to use either oil lamps, flashlights or one of those hunting headlamps and, of course, a gun, which we always had in the house. Eventually, my parents and grandparents had two dusks-to-dawn lights installed on the property. But that didn't deter any of the undesirables from roaming on my grandfather's farm. The thickets were massive across the road from where we lived. There was no telling what would come out of there. You had to be careful going outside day or night. It wasn't unusual for us to encounter wild hogs, snakes, raccoons, armadillos and opossums. I shiver, as I did then, just thinking about it.

I remember an instance when my father was coming home from work one night. He said he was just down the road from our house. I heard him tell my mother that some white guy tried to run him off the road, as he got closer to our house. My father always carried a pistol with him. I heard him tell my mother nobody is going to have to worry about that guy anymore. It took me a while to figure out what that meant.

As far back as I can remember, while living on the farm, we always had a television, our first being a black and white. We didn't know of anyone with a color TV early on. When my grandparents told us that they had a color TV, we couldn't wait to see it. Come to find out, the color TV they had was the one where you place a film over the screen to change the picture color. We eventually got one of those black rotary dial telephones installed in our house. The phone lines were party lines, which meant you could pick up the phone any time someone else was talking on their telephone and listen to their conversation.

My family loved listening to rhythm and blues and gospel music. We couldn't wait to buy the latest 45 R&B records and dance to the music on Saturday evening. Back then, all music was cut on vinyl records. The gospel records would be played on Sundays, especially when the preacher would come to dinner. I still have a large collection of 45s in my possession from back in the day.

My family was faced with significant losses in 1965 when tragedy hit our home. We were in town one Saturday evening visiting one of my mother's sisters. As we were driving home on Highway 28, we could see flames, thinking at the time it was trash being burned. As we got closer to the house, we could see that it was our house up in flames. It was a blessing that no one was home at the time. Since we lived in the country on Bayou Rapides, there were no fire stations nearby. All we could do, as we drove up, was to stand there and watch as our house burned down to the ground with everything we owned. It was devastating. I get emotional now thinking about it. After our house burned down in the country, we moved to Alexandria and rented a house for about a year. My parents decided not to move back to Bayou Rapides and in 1966 built a house in the suburbs of Alexandria.

My grandparents and a few of the older adults passed away while living on the farm. Eventually, all the other family members moved away and started another life of their own and never returned. I reflect often on how things have changed since my childhood in the 1950s and early 1960s.

- We used rubboards with an oval tin tub to wash clothes. Some people called it a washboard. The same rubboards have been repurposed by Zydeco musicians who use them as instruments in their bands.

- We graduated from the rubboard to an electric wringer washing machine with tub base and handles.

- Washed clothes were hung outside on clothes lines. That was our "clothes dryer".

- Woodburning stoves provided heat during the winter.

- Electric floor fans were placed in the windows during the summer months to keep cool even though the fans were blowing in hot air from the outside. That was our air conditioner.

- Cast-iron (Sad) irons that had to be heated on the stove were used to press clothes.

- There were only three television stations to watch and those stations signed off the air at midnight and TVs would go static.

- To get TV reception, television sets had indoor antennas/rabbit ears. Wrapping aluminum foil around the rabbit ears could improve reception.

- Lots of our family members used outdoor toilets/outhouses.

- Public telephone booths, requiring coins for usage, were on the streets/street corners and in some businesses throughout the city.

- No clocks in the house? No worries. If you had a telephone, you could dial a specific telephone number for the time.

On Bayou Rapides, we had only one school for Blacks, C.E. Robinson Elementary. It was for first through eighth grades. When my brother started first grade, I remember feeling lost and couldn't wait to go to school. However, when I started school the next year, I would cry every day. I was very timid and shy. I was so overwhelmed by the number of people there. My brother came home one day and told my mother not to let me go to school because I would cry too much. She asked me why I was crying, and I remember telling her it was because people were looking at me. Eventually, I got used to it because I remember her telling me if I didn't stop crying, she would not let me go back to school. I put my big girl panties on because I knew I didn't want to stay home. Looking back on it, those were some of my best years, without a care in the world.

In my first four years attending C.E. Robinson, we had to walk at least a mile from our house to catch the school bus. We had to be diligent walking to the bus stop because sometimes white boys would try to give us a hard time by calling us out of our names. Thankfully, we had our older cousins to walk to the bus stop with us. If we missed the bus, we'd have to walk another two miles to school. Eventually, the school started sending a bus to our location on Cooper Road.

My time at C. E. Robinson was some of my best and most memorable school years. There was lots of comradery. We were like family because all the families knew each other and would support all the school activities. We were encouraged to broaden our horizons and participate in any and all extracurricular activities, school plays, choir (whether or not we knew how to sing), art and science projects, boys' baseball, etc. No one except had to stay after school except for the boys with sports activities. All activities other than boys' baseball games were practiced during school hours. Boys' baseball games were played on Friday nights. All parents attended open house and participated in parent-teacher meetings.

When I completed eighth grade, I had a much longer ride for ninth grade to Jones Street Junior High School in Alexandria. We had to ride the bus approximately 10 miles a day. My time at Jones Street Junior High, meeting new friends, was an exciting time. But I felt a little isolated, coming from Bayou Rapides and being unable to participate in any after-school activities because I had no way to get home if I missed the bus. For 10th through 12th grades, I attended Peabody Senior High School, which was a block from Jones Street. Participation in after-school events at Peabody or seeing school friends on weekends also was a challenge. Since the houses on Bayou Rapides were miles apart, I looked forward to the beginning of each week to see my friends on the bus and at school.

After we moved to Alexandria from Bayou Rapides, I was able to enjoy some of the fun after-school activities. I joined the drill squad, played tennis, and went to some of the dances/sock hops after school. I even had the opportunity to attend some of the football games since my parents didn't have too far to drive. I attended the junior and senior proms and even had the opportunity to be part of the Queen's (Miss Warhorse) Court my senior year at Peabody.

It is true when they say some parents live through their children. I couldn't enjoy the experiences of being involved in a lot of extracurricular activities, so I bent over backwards to make sure my children got the experience. When they were growing up, they got involved in Girl Scouts Inc., the school band, gymnastics, ice skating, synchronized swimming, ballet, tap, cheerleading and almost everything I missed out on.

During the Christmas holidays in the 11th grade, I worked in the toy department at Sears & Roebuck in Alexandria, and during the summer of my senior year of high school, I worked for the Head Start program in Alexandria. After graduating high school, my desire was to get a college degree in Early Childhood Development/ Elementary Education.

I attended all segregated schools from first through 12th grades. My first experience in an integrated educational environment was immediately after high school at Louisiana State University at Alexandria (LSUA). I attended the fall and winter semesters at LSUA, along with a few of my Peabody classmates. I dropped out after the first year. Going from a segregated school to an integrated college was an eye-opener for me. According to some of the white students attending LSUA, the courses we were being taught during the freshman year at LSUA were actually repeat/refresher courses of what they had been taught at their high school. As the professors were lecturing during classes, I realized most of the lessons they were teaching were foreign to me. It was very evident to me that we as a segregated society had been cheated. I got really frustrated and stayed in the union hall most of the time playing dominoes with some of my classmates. My parents tried to encourage me to stick with it, but I felt so overwhelmed. I thought it best that I get a job and see where life would take me from there.

I applied for a job at Guaranty Bank in Pineville in the bookkeeping department. I was so excited when I got the job. I can remember being the only person of color at that time at Guaranty Bank. I was in the file room filing signature cards, checking obituaries to determine what accounts had to be flagged, and sending out monthly bank statements with checks. Never in my wildest dreams could I have imagined this first job at Guaranty Bank would open up a world of opportunities and become a steppingstone for me and guide my career as a banking professional.

After two years at Guaranty Bank, I got married and had my first child, a beautiful baby girl. We moved to Los Angeles, California, and that's where I started working at Security Pacific National Bank. Los Angeles was a more diverse and integrated society.

Even though my mother and I visited Los Angeles quite often during summer months as I was growing up, it was nothing like living there and making it my home. I felt like a kid in a candy store when I moved there as a grownup. Walking or driving down Sunset Boulevard, I would see celebrities in person who were in movies and shows on TV. Some would enter the bank to do their banking transactions and have conversations with the staff. Being in my 20s and from a little town in the South, I never thought I would experience the excitement of meeting so many celebrities in person. I even tried getting on one of my favorite shows, Soul Train. After standing in line for hours to get on the show, it was determined that my dance moves weren't good enough. But after a while, all the excitement of meeting celebrities wore off. It became just another day in the life of living in California.

I continued my education by enrolling in a few accounting courses at a junior college in Los Angeles. My career in banking continued at Security Pacific National

Bank in Los Angeles as a paying and receiving and collections teller for eight years. Many times, I thought about getting out of the banking industry while in Los Angeles because of the numerous bank robberies. There were bank branches in the city on every corner. One day, the Security Pacific National Bank branch where I worked was robbed at gunpoint. We were all told to put our hands up while the robbers went to each teller and emptied out each till. By the time the policeman came, they were long gone. To our surprise, those bank robbers had hit three nearby bank branches the same day in the same neighborhood. After leaving California, I moved to Dallas and started working for Wynnewood Bank as a teller. Wynnewood Bank eventually went into receivership. As a result, I took a hiatus from banking for a year and gave birth to my second beautiful baby. I decided the next job would not be a frontline worker and began working for Mercantile Bank in their Mortgage Banking/Document Custody Department as a clerk. There were only six people in the department when I started. At that time, I had no idea what mortgage banking was and enrolled in banking classes to grasp as much as I could about the business. That decision helped my career. I hit my stride and thought to myself, this is where I belong.

Through a host of mergers and acquisitions, Mercantile Bank eventually became Bank One, then JP Morgan Chase Bank. After about a year, the mortgage banking area started growing at the bank. I was promoted to Supervisor and Banking Officer and started building the department and adding staff. Though none of the clerical positions in the department I managed required a college degree, all positions required some type of college background. In the Human Resources Recruiting department, there were no recruiters that looked like me. After they would screen applicants' resumes based on my job postings, very seldom would I receive applications of individuals that looked like me. Most of the candidates sent to interview for open positions were either someone with no experience or people who didn't look like me. That changed after I demanded they send all applications for open positions in my department to me and allow me to screen, interview, and make the decision for the best candidates.

I eventually worked my way up to the department manager position and became Assistant Vice President at Bank One. My job also included auditing all our mortgage banking clients. Before long, I was collaborating with the attorneys on clients' Commercial Loan Agreements. After a few years, I was promoted to Vice President/ Operations Manager at JPMorgan Chase Bank and did a lot of traveling during those times, visiting clients and preforming audits of their mortgage loan department.

My career at Chase/JPMorgan was rewarding. I had the opportunity to travel to many different states on their dime. Though my travels were work-related, I would take an extra day or two and explore the cities and do some shopping. Sometimes I was able to take my children with me as a mini-vacation. I am proud of my two daughters. There were sacrifices during those years being a single mom raising two children. Both have college degrees, successful careers, and are working in their respective fields. I retired from Chase Bank after 30 years of service. During my tenure, we grew from a staff of six people to four assistant vice presidents, a staff of 50 and more than 50 temporary employees.

Six months after retiring from Chase Bank, I got a call from a former coworker. He had resigned from Chase Bank and partnered with a group of investors as the CEO to open a bank in Highland Park, Texas (in central Dallas County). I went to work for them as the VP/Loan Operations Manager. After about five years, the bank was taken over by another group of investors. They appointed another CEO and then started hiring other Highland Park people to take over various departments within the bank. I worked there until the group merged with another bank, and afterwards, I fully retired.

I decided it was time for me to let loose and have some fun. I joined a performing line dance group in the Dallas area. We perform at various events and venues throughout the Dallas area: The State Fair of Texas, Juneteenth Celebrations, Dallas Police Department events, wedding receptions, church nursing home ministries. I also partnered with an acquaintance who had a nonprofit organization geared toward tutoring elementary students in reading and math. That program allowed us to partner with the City of Dallas in their STEM program. I had a flashback to my early goal of becoming an elementary schoolteacher. I must say the children nowadays are nothing like the children back in the day. God drove my footsteps and knew where my destiny was headed.

# BLESSINGS WRAPPED IN STRUGGLES

*"But they that wait upon the Lord shall renew their strength; they shall mount up with wings as eagles; they shall run and not get weary; they shall walk and not faint."*
— ISAIAH 40:31, KJ

## Rev. Larry D. Smith

B LESSINGS ARE GOD'S favor and protection bestowed upon His children. Thankfully, all of us are the recipients of God's favor in some form or fashion. Regardless of our personal issues, it is a blessing just to be alive. Think about it. God did not give us all the same talent, but without a doubt, He gave us all something, and whether we realize it or not, we can make it on what He has given us. Blessings do not always appear to us as blessings. Sometimes they show up at our doorsteps wrapped in packages of stress and strain or sickness and sadness. Sometimes blessings appear to us in the form of hardship, pain, poverty, and struggles.

*To our surprise what we thought was a scarecrow was a Black man hanging from a tree. Before our bus arrived, police were everywhere. Afterwards, silence covered the community like a quilted blanket. No one was ever charged with the crime, but the message was clear...*

When our ancestors realized that struggles were a part of their daily routine, or as frequent as the morning sun, to help them get through the hard days and long nights, they sang, "I'm So Glad Trouble Don't Last Always". When our mothers and fathers could not see their way, and it was dark most of the time, they forged ahead despite overwhelming odds and held on to the belief that "The Lord will make a way somehow." A firm belief in God was all they had, and God was all they needed. I am both a product and benefactor of heritage, and since every day was a struggle for my parents, over the years, I learned to adjust to abject circumstances as though they were normal, believing, as they did, that The Lord would make a way.

I am a native of Alexandria, LA born April 28, 1950, at Huey P. Long Charity Hospital in nearby Pineville. Although the name of the hospital is self-explanatory, as a kid, I had no idea that the Charity Hospital was for poor folks because everybody I knew was either born there or received treatment there. I am the oldest of eight born to Laney Mae Smith and Charles M. Kay. My siblings are Janice, Marilyn, Elizabeth, Kim (deceased), Sonny, Greg, and Brian. Laney was from Oberlin, about 65 miles south of Alexandria, and Charles was from Powhattan, about 67 miles north of Alexandria. Both migrated to Alexandria in the 1940s in hopes of finding a better life. I suspect they were running from the farm, but little did they know, they were jumping from the skillet into the frying pan.

## ALEXANDRIA, LOUISIANA

Alexandria is a medium-sized city in central Louisiana with a population of 49,000. Between 1940 and 1968, it was primarily a sawmill town with a large commercial chicken processing plant, two private hospitals, several nursing homes and low paying city civil service jobs. Blacks migrating from the surrounding parishes, farms and plantations jumped at these jobs because they provided relief from plowing mules and picking cotton. In their minds anything was better than the cottonfield. To ensure that employees were at work on time, Kellogg Mill, Arkansas Oak Flooring and Roy O. Martin Lumber Company, the three primary employers, sounded a loud whistle or horn that could be heard all over the neighborhood at 6 a.m. every workday. Anybody sitting outside at that time could see droves of Black men headed for the sawmills. Some were bright-eyed and bushy tailed, some had been up all night, and some were hungover, but they made it to the mills. Snapshots of these images are etched in my mind. The sawmills provided employees with shotgun houses, as well as a get-out-of-jail-free card for those misbehaving during a weekend drinking binge. Looking back at the sawmill operation, it was nothing more than a system of indentured servitude that made other folk rich at a workingman's expense. Minimum wage in 1950 was 75 cents an hour, equivalent to $8.17 in 2020, and yet, there were Black mothers and fathers, who came early, stayed late, and worked their fingers to the bones to provide for their families. They demonstrated to us that you can make it if you try. What a blessing they were.

## THE NEIGHBORHOOD

Black neighborhoods were surrounded by railroad tracks, scrap iron yards, sawmills, or sewage pumping stations, and, if you looked hard enough there was a big ditch close by. I grew up in the Sonia

Quarters neighborhood, one among several quarters. Other areas included the Oil Mill Quarters, Rock Island Quarters, Sam Baker Quarters and the White Quarters. In addition to the quarters, a large concentration of Blacks lived in other communities such as Upper Third, Lower Third, Samtown and Woodside. Although it was not within the city limits, Blacks also still lived on Inglewood Plantation. The landlords or Slumlords in the Sonia were typically Jews or Italians with a few Blacks. Generally, if you had a plumbing problem, a leaking roof, or hole in the floor, you had to fix it yourself to keep the landlord from increasing the rent. As a kid, I learned a lot about fixing old houses. I could take a commode apart and put it back together blindfolded.

During those days if you had an indoor toilet, you were fortunate. Until the late '50s, many homes around town had outhouses nearby. For poor Blacks like us, indoor bathtubs were a rarity. Slop jars, Number 3 tubs, and foot tubs were kept inside to prevent us from having to brave the elements at night and in inclement weather. Heating bath water in a dish pan and pouring it into a Number 3 tub for bathing purposes was commonplace, and it was not uncommon for children to share bathwater with siblings. If such conditions were not bad enough, people who lived outside of the city limits had outhouses with a hole in the ground.

Most homes in the Sonia Quarters were wood frame with an occasional brick house. Brick houses were symbols of affluence. Some of the residents were homeowners, though most were renters. Families for the most part lived in structures white folks did not want. There was a church on every other corner in the Sonia, and a gambling shack, bootlegger, or nightclub not far away. If you lived close to a club, you could hear the music well into the night.

There was no guessing in the Black community that Lee Street was the center of nightlife in Alexandria. On Friday and Saturday, it was *the* place to be. The area was a four-block strip with a smattering of nightclubs, eating joints, pool halls, mercantile stores, shoeshine parlors, an ice cream stand, the city bus barn, and the Ritz Theater. On both sides of Lee Street, neon lights stretched from one end to the other like a scaled down model of the Las Vegas Strip. In my youth it was the most festive place I had ever seen. It also was the place you could find some of the best dressed men in town. I was always impressed by their sharkskin suits, knit shirts, Stetson Hats and Stacy Adams Shoes. I learned how to dress by watching some of the fellows on Lee Street.

On Lee Street, professional gamblers and pool sharks honed their skills daily, while waiting on working stiffs to show up after laboring all day. A working man could lose a paycheck in a few minutes. Many had families to feed and had to face their wives empty handed after a gambling or drinking binge. I worked with a few of those fellows at the Alexandria Water Department, and by Monday morning, they didn't have lunch money.

As colorful a place as it was, Lee Street was also a dangerous place. Stabbings and cuttings were frequent and every once and a while somebody got shot. Ice picks, straight razors and 38 caliber pistols were weapons of choice. When I was old enough, I made my way to Lee Street only to find out that "all that glitters is not gold." I learned a lot about life on Lee Street, but mostly how I didn't want to spend the rest of my life there.

Most Blacks in Alexandria were poor. As children we did not have a grasp on the full magnitude of a parent's plight. As poor as families were, they shared what they had. If you needed baking flour, you could borrow a cup from the neighbor without being put on "front street." If your pantry was bare, or neighbors knew you were struggling, extra food might show up on your doorstep. Mama and the rest of the neighbors would even feed the hobos that wandered off the railroad tracks into the neighborhood begging.

Uncle George Brooks, a family friend, liked to hunt, and every once in a while, late at night or early in the morning, you could hear a loud boom on our front porch. It sounded like a home invasion. The first time I heard it, I leaped out of bed and grabbed my baseball bat to defend the family. It was Uncle George throwing a couple of coons on the porch to help with the evening meal. Oddly enough, he threw them on the porch and disappeared. I never understood why he never gave us a heads-up.

Despite a meager existence, people in our Black community found pleasure in the simple things of life — a cookout, a ride through the park, Friday night football, high school basketball and church on Sunday. People really cared for one another and looked out for the children in the neighborhood. My mother, along with Ms. Willie Mae Carter, Ms. Dora Edwards, Ms. Annie B. Wilson, Ms. Katy Green and Mama

Chew were the anchors on our block. They were the judge, jury, and the executioner. Obviously, there were men present, but these women controlled the ebb and flow of events, and nobody challenged them. There was always some old lady, usually housebound, who saw every misdeed in the "hood" regardless of the time, day or night. And she was sure to rat you out.

If you were caught doing something wrong, anybody could whip your butt, and if they did, you prayed that your parents did not find out because they would whip you again. In those days, calling child protection on adults was unthinkable, and if you did, you surely would regret it. The favorite weapon for whippings was a switch, a slender, long branch broken off a tree. The sheer terror before the punishment was magnified when a parent would order the child to select the switch. To minimize the pain, I tried sneakily to get the smallest switch I could find, but Mama would say, "I sent you at a switch, not a twig. You don't want *me* to go get it, do you?" I was a veteran of many whippings because I pushed limits in a mischievous way. That said, with few exceptions, I never caught a whipping I did not deserve.

## THE WHITE QUARTERS

Our close-knit charitable community knew how to stick together and where to draw the line when it came to race and lifestyle. Lee Street was the demarcation line between the literally named White Quarters and the Sonia Quarters. In the early years, segregation was king. To avoid harassment, or physical danger, Black children were told to stay out of the White Quarters. If you were in that area, it was in your best interest to be hanging off the back of a garbage truck or pushing a lawnmower. Put simply, you needed a reason to be in the White Quarters. The houses in that area of town looked much better than the ones we lived in, and the yards were well manicured. Early in the morning you could see proud looking Black women wearing aprons and heading to the White Quarters for domestic work.

As a young boy, I was employed by an old man named Mr. Ray, who cut grass in the White Quarters. He was a small man, not more than 125 pounds, and he had a lucrative yard business. Mr. Ray was an ornery old cuss with more tricks up his sleeve than The Great Houdini. I did not like working for him because he kept up more mischief than I did. (Later in life, when I would run into ill-tempered abusive supervisors, I remembered Mr. Ray, and like the Apostle Paul, I learned to adjust to difficult circumstances.)

On those workdays with Mr. Ray, Mama would fix my lunch and tell me not to come home until the job was finished. Obviously, it was easier to put up with Mr. Ray than to disobey Mama. One day on a job, Mr. Ray went to the back of these White folk's house and knocked on the door. A lady came to the door and in an abrasive tone asked, "What do you want, Ray?" He said, "Ma'am, can you give me something to feed this boy. His old mammy turned him over to me because he's unruly, and I'm trying to help her out. He's hungry." Mr. Ray was lying. He was hungry, and because I had been taught to respect my elders, I did not say anything, but I could not believe my ears. The lady said, "Wait a minute, Ray," and slammed the door. Later, she returned with a banana and pimento cheese sandwich. "Here Ray, give this to that rascal," she said. After she closed the door, Mr. Ray turned to me and said, "Give me that damn sandwich boy, you already have one." I did not tell mama about Mr. Ray's outrageous antics because she respected him and would have thought I was trying to get out of work. Unfortunately, I was stuck with Mr. Ray that summer.

## MAMA, WORK ETHIC, AND FAMILY VALUES

Ms. Laney Mae Smith Speed Hunter (Mama) was the undisputed head of our family. Obviously, there were male figures in our lives, who helped along the way, but Mama was always there calling the shots. Laney Mae was an interesting case study. She worked hard, took care of us, fed the hungry and would give you the shirt off her back. She did not finish high school but demanded that we finish, and to make sure we did, she kept up with our progress by monitoring our report cards. I learned early that if you wanted to get along with her, or have a few extra privileges, bring home a decent report card. You didn't have to have all As, but she had a tremendous disdain for Ds and Fs. Some of my siblings learned that the hard way.

Like many mothers, Mama had an abundance of mother's wit, and you couldn't run a game on her. She loved reading and her prize possessions were a huge collection of books and a HiFi stereo. On Friday and Saturday evening, the sounds of Nat King Cole, Ray Charles, Dinah Washington, Brook Benton, Sam Cook, Aretha Franklin and Bobby Bland filled the air. On Sunday mornings, the lineup changed to Rev. C.L. Franklin and other notable gospel preachers.

When it came to conventional jobs for Black women in the 1950s and '60s, Mama refused to follow in my grandmother's (My Me) footsteps as a domestic worker. My Me was employed as a maid by the owners of Foley's Department Store Chain in Pasadena, Texas, until her retirement. I overheard the conversation when Mama turned down my grandmother's recommendation. Put simply, there were some things she was not going to do, and domestic work was high on the list among them. Given that kind of boldness, Mama was forced to consider alternative jobs for women. So, she convinced a foreman at Arkansas Oak Flooring Sawmill to hire her. When my male friends found out, I got teased every day about Mama working at the saw mill.. She eventually left the sawmill for a job with Mayflower and later Wheaton's Allied Van Lines. There, she learned the moving business, and moved up in the company. Eventually, they gave her a pickup truck, a gas card, and a clipboard, and she made calls on prospective customers to estimate the cost of their moving expenses. The company moved airmen in and out of Alexandria every day which created job stability. Without a formal education, coupled with her negative view of domestic work, I watched mama struggle financially. The moving business was a blessing in disguise with an opportunity to earn better pay.

## SCHOOL AND WORK

Mama's high standard for her children's education stayed with me throughout my learning years. I started school at Silver City Elementary in 1956. Elaine Ford Provost and I were in the first grade together, and we remain friends today. Our first-grade teacher was Ms. Chambers, a kind and gentle lady, who treated us like her own. I transferred from Silver City to South Alexandria Elementary in the third grade when my family moved across town to 918 Saint James Street. Our little three-room shotgun house was directly across from Berry's Grocery Store, Rose of Sharon Baptist Church and about two houses from the Big Wheel Nightclub. Music blasted all night, but somehow, I learned to focus on homework and managed to sleep through the noise.

On school days, we caught the bus near Newman Methodist Church and the Casson Street Community Center. One morning in 1959, we were waiting for the school bus when someone said, "Look at that scarecrow over there in the tree." To our surprise what we thought was a scarecrow was a Black man hanging from a tree. Before our bus arrived, police were everywhere. Afterwards, silence covered the community like a quilted blanket. No one was ever charged with the crime, but the message was clear, "Niggers, stay in your place, or the same thing will happen to you."

The teachers were great at South Alexandria. Ms. Tillman, the music teacher in particular. She was skilled at playing the piano and had a voice that sounded like it

came straight from heaven. She introduced us to patriotic songs such as "My Country 'Tis of Thee", "This Is My Country", "America The Beautiful", "The Star-Spangled Banner", and many more. We were taught ironically to sing "God Bless America" amid racial segregation, Jim Crow, and the lynching of Black folks.

As I developed an appreciation for curriculum content, I realized that certain songs were designed to assimilate Blacks into white American culture. So, as a bonus lesson, Ms. Tillman threw in some Negro spirituals and the Black National Anthem among others. Those old songs are indelibly etched in my mind. She was a dynamite teacher, and I credit her with inspiring my excitement for learning.

During those South Alexandria Elementary days, in 1962, I played on the best Little League team in the city. What a memory. To this day I think about the good times and successes we had under our coach, the Rev. Robert Berry. My teammates, Willie "Stick" Goff, Michael Johnson, Robert Dixon, Claudius Jones, Bobby Andrews, Richard Chew and I defeated Silver City in the preliminaries and faced C.E. Robinson Elementary in a winner-take-all dogfight for the Elementary School Championship. The score was tied until the ninth inning. D. Ray and "Stick" got on base ahead of me. When I stepped to the plate as the "cleanup hitter," I did not recoil under pressure because I was right where I wanted to be. I could hear the taunts and heckling coming from one side of the grandstand and cheers from our fans. I hit a game-winning triple, cleared the bases and it was all over. My teammates hoisted me to their shoulders and packed me off the field. Michael Johnson received the championship trophy for our team. For most of us, at age 12, this was our first real taste of victory.

Between elementary and junior high school, I developed a speech impediment, a severe stutter. The condition left me feeling like I was trapped inside a body that could not talk. In friendly, informal settings, I would barely stutter, but if the teacher called on me to read, I was in trouble. If I got caught talking in class when I was supposed to be listening, a few of my teachers would deliberately call on me to read. My peers laughed the whole time, as I struggled to get the words out. When the teacher had sufficiently proved her point, she called it off. I thought it was cruel for teachers to impose that kind of punishment, but from the pain I learned how to keep my mouth closed in class. I was eventually assigned a speech therapist to no avail. Stuttering hounded me through high school and released me finally from its vicious grip in my early 20s.

In 1965, I started at the legendary Peabody High School. The school was known for educating standout graduates who would go on to make a positive impact across the United States. Every school district in Louisiana was familiar with Peabody's high academic standards and its athletic superiority. In the early days it was the only high school for Blacks in Rapides Parish. The U.S. Supreme Court Brown v. Board of

Education decision in 1954 ruled that school segregation was illegal, however, Blacks did not integrate Alexandria's all-white Bolton High School until 1966.

Peabody Principal, Professor D.F. "Prof" Isles, was determined to make Peabody a beacon in the community, and he did. He kept bad characters from invading the campus, walked the halls daily to ensure that everybody was where they were supposed to be and doing what they were supposed to be doing, including teachers. Prof was everywhere. He even chased wayward students from behind the buildings smoking cigarettes, including yours truly. I did not realize it at the time, but all Prof Isles wanted was for us to become productive citizens. He was loved by some and hated by his detractors, and he ran Peabody with an iron fist. I was delighted to be invited back in 1993 as the Law Enforcement Day speaker.

*Coach Smith, Coach Charlie Baker, me, Professor Iles, April 30, 1993*

There are many schools in Alexandria named in honor of Black educators, but none in honor of Prof Isles. What a travesty! It is not my intent to denigrate anybody's accomplishments, but no one left a larger footprint on the education of Black students from 1950 to the early '70s than Prof Isles. Perhaps, it is the price you pay for standing your ground.

By the time I got to Peabody, I was working every evening after school. Mama had a solid reputation among business folk in the community, and she used it to keep us out of the cotton fields. I picked pecans, stocked and bagged groceries, worked at George Cruise Mill, loaded furniture, and drove a moving van. I was a decent athlete and really wanted to play ball but decided to help Mama, as she struggled to care for the family. We needed every penny we could get, and I could not stomach the idea of her facing the financial stress and strain alone.

Failure, especially when it came to academics, was not an option, so I learned how to balance school and work and enjoy my high school years. I was not the best student because I was balancing getting an education with work and staying socially involved. I maintained decent grades, doing enough to keep Mama off my back and managed to have fun, too. How could you not have fun at Peabody? For me, it was a teenager's heaven.

Teachers took their jobs seriously in those days, and some even made home visits. Two of my teachers, Ms. Marguerite Baker and Ms. Georgia Foccia, came to our house one day. I saw them coming before they saw me and ran out of the back door of the old townhouse on Turreganno Street. I didn't know the reason for the visit, but I knew it couldn't be good. By that time, I was prone to fistic encounters and cheap port wine. I was "ear hustling" by the window on the side of the house when I heard one of the teachers say, "Laney Mae, if you can keep that boy of yours out of the penitentiary or the graveyard, we can send him to Southern University. He is an eagle, but he likes to hang out on the chickenyard."

"What do you mean?" Mama asked. "He can fly higher than those fellows he's hanging out with, but he dumbs down to run with them, and worst, he's the ringleader," one of them replied. Maybe the two teachers were on to something. When I graduated from high school, I did not give college a second thought. Like many of the guys I admired, I wanted to go to the Marine Corps. Ms. Baker, who was our

English teacher, told me that she had nothing against the Marine Corps, but she really thought I was college material. She set out to find the financial resources to make it possible.

I later got a call from Mr. Jimmy Atwell, a Vocational Rehabilitation Counselor, advising me that I had been scheduled for a series of diagnostic tests at Central State Hospital. Everybody in the "hood" called Central State Hospital the Crazy House. So, naturally, I began to think that maybe they were trying to have me committed to the Crazy House. I, nonetheless, went over to Central, took the test and later I was informed that I had been approved for a four-year Vocational Rehabilitation Grant to attend Southern University. As it turned out, the blessing came wrapped in a struggle. The stutter was the struggle. Southern University was the blessing made possible by caring teachers from Peabody High School. Before leaving for Southern, Ms. Baker gave me the names of three people to contact in Baton Rouge: Mr. Paul Duell, Dr. Jewel L. Prestage, and Dr. Frank J. Cook. I later learned that they were noteworthy Peabody alums. Mr. Duell had been one of the youngest principals in Rapides Parish and ultimately pursued a successful career in politics. Dr. Prestage grew up in Alexandria, and, at 22, became the first Black woman in the United States to receive a Ph.D. in Political Science. Dr. Cook, who shot pool on Lee Street, received an undergraduate degree from Grambling State University, a Ph.D. from Purdue University, and authored several books.

Until learning of them then, I had no idea Peabody had produced such giants in political science and education. It was at that time that I realized that they and the caring teachers at Peabody had created for me an open door to success. The struggle had been me trying to work my way out of the Sonia Quarters, and the blessing was more than I could ever ask for, a free ride to college!

## SOUTHERN UNIVERSITY

Peabody was great, but Southern was grand! The campus was imposing in its appearance with a beautiful view of the Mississippi River. Students came from all over the world, and so did the instructors. And some of those professors, Algebra for one, barely spoke English, which added an extra degree of difficulty to an already complex subject. Gone were the neighborhood teachers who would spend more time making sure you got what you needed to do your best in class. Between the yearning for my old friends and the academic challenge, I thought about going back home. But that was not an option; too many people had invested in me.

Leaving old friends is not easy, especially when they are all you have. Most of my Road Dogs did not attend college. I left them in the pool hall on Lee Street. At Southern, I made new friends with students I never hung out with at Peabody. Alfred Belvin, Ruben Coleman, Richard Clark, Michael Milton, Freddie Price, Johnny Freel, Marshal Winchester and Warren Zellars, to name a few. We were only acquaintances at Peabody until Southern where we became lifelong brothers and formed the group AMDs (Alexandria Main Dudes).

When I enrolled at Southern in 1968, ROTC (Reserved Officers' Training Corps) was mandatory. All land grant colleges during that era offered this program as a means of training future officers for the United States Army. Failure to enroll in ROTC exposed male students to the possibility of immediately being drafted into the regular Army. In addition to ROTC, I along with several homeboys joined AUSA (Association of the United States Army), an elite military fraternity which strengthened our character, common bond and exposed us to other potential leaders campus-wide. Most of us got out of ROTC after a two-year stint, but Freddie Price, a Peabody Class of 68 graduate, enrolled in advance ROTC, served in the United States Army and retired with the rank of Major. Below is a picture of AUSA in 1970. Many of its members are natives of Alexandria, LA.

During my senior year at Southern my stuttering started to disappear, and by the time I started student teaching it was barely recognizable. Thank God, I could finally read like a normal person. After undergraduate school (Fall 1972), I went straight into graduate school. I had become a professional student and loved every minute. My mind was crystal clear, and I had a memory like an elephant. By now I was researching selected political and educational topics for Dr. Prestage and Dr. Cook.

**Sitting**: *Lt. Col. W.B. Rhodes, P.M.S. D Robins, F. Price, 1st Sgt. B.H. Guillory, Capt. V.H. Brass, 1st Lt. A. Scott, MGS.M Maj. Leon D. Jackson, Sponsor.*

**Second Row:** *C. Montgomery, L. Smith, L. Gloston, R. Watley, F. Martin, J. Morris, A. Oliver, J. Colar, H. Harmon, C. Godfrey, R. Clark.*

**Third Row:** *S. Duper, J. Matthews, R. Frazier, M. Milton, M. Kennerson, W. Jones.*

I completed the coursework for graduate school in spring 1973, and while finishing my thesis, I ran into a major financial snag. I had grossly underestimated the publishing costs of the five bound copies of my work that needed to be submitted to the thesis committee. I didn't have the money, and neither did Mama. I couldn't borrow it, and I couldn't graduate. In summer 1973, I returned to Alexandria brokenhearted and defeated.

In an unforeseen totally unsolicited moment in the middle of the summer, my close-knit community again came to the rescue. I had told no one outside my family about my situation. One day that summer, Ms. Annie Wilson, a widowed retired teacher and our neighbor across the street, out of nowhere asked me over to change a few lightbulbs. As a teen, I had done odd jobs for her at no charge. After I finished the task, she handed me a check. As I had done before, I refused payment. She sternly refused my refusal, and in the stalemate I accepted. The check amount curiously was the exact cost for publishing my thesis. Ms. Ethel Bowie, who would eventually become my mother-in-law, contributed additional funds to also cover graduation fees. I received my master's degree in August 1973. It was close, but with the help of Ms. Wilson, Ms. Bowie and God's grace, I made it. What a struggle!

## ASSIMILATION INTO A DESEGREGATED WORK ENVIRONMENT

With two degrees in hand, I was off to the next chapter. Prior to that fall, I had interviewed with the East Baton Rouge School Board for a social studies and driver education teacher position at Zachary Senior High School. The interviewer said, "We need a teacher, and I will hire you, but you are not going to last 15 minutes at that school with long hair. The principal is a Navy ensign, and he runs a tight ship. Eventually, he will find a reason to fire you. I cannot tell you to cut your hair, but it would be in your best interest, if you want the job."

I told the interviewer I had no problem with cutting my hair. I was broke and needed a job. I got the job. Zachary is about 16 miles from Baton Rouge. I had no car, and I had nowhere to stay until two of my homeboys, Larry Roberts and Samuel (Sam) Culbert, let me stay with them. I had to borrow $3.50 from Dr. Cook to get a haircut. I also borrowed a car the first two days on the job and had to hitchhike to Zachary the third day. God showed me exceptional favor that morning, as I stood on the side of the road with my briefcase in the dark, and two other Zachary High teachers commuting offered me a ride. I did not know Ms. Slaughter and Ms. Bobby when they asked where I was going. Not only did they give me a ride that morning, they were also kind enough to let me join their carpool until I purchased a car. I will never forget them.

I taught school for a year-and-a-half, then decided to change career tracks. I moved to the Louisiana Department of Corrections where I worked at the Louisiana Training Institute (Project Instep) with mentally challenged youth for three years before transferring to the Louisiana State Penitentiary at Angola. Angola sits in a bend on the Mississippi River, an 18,000-acre farm with 5,000 offenders. In 1976, it was labeled the bloodiest prison in the nation. My first assignment was to manage the affairs of offenders on Death Row. I hated the job, but as a Classification Officer, I found solace in managing the concerns of those incarcerated. I advocated for them on prison matters when they could not speak for themselves. A good Classification Officer has to understand the nuts and bolts of the entire prison operation in order to be effective.

After a stint on Death Row, I moved to Main Prison, commonly called the Big Yard. It was a sprawling complex of single-story dormitories, where a significant portion of the prison population lived. As I entered the Big Yard in the morning, it was not uncommon to see offenders being brought out on stretchers from stabbings and beatdowns. Our job was to get the prison under control and reduce the violence, which at times seemed impossible. Many times, I thought about the home visit from my high school teachers when they told Mama, "If you can keep that boy out of the penitentiary and graveyard, we can get him an education." Ironically, I did go to the penitentiary, but not the way they thought.

The thought of quitting the job at Angola was constant, but I struggled there every morning because quitting represented failure, and failure was not an option. Like fixing the old rent houses in the Sonia, eventually, I developed a mastery knowledge of prison operations, and after three years, I was promoted to Director of the Classifications Department, a major administrative position with prison-wide impact. This was the first time in history that a Black man had been granted such authority within an adult prison in Louisiana. In a predominantly white environment, I made it plain that I didn't laugh when it wasn't funny, I didn't scratch where I didn't itch, and I didn't shuffle my feet when I had nowhere to go. Things were starting to look up.

My reputation as an efficient prison administrator started to exceed the boundaries of Angola.

In 1980, I began to see even more promise professionally. I got a call from the Department of Corrections Headquarters in Baton Rouge offering me the Director of Classification's job in the Central Office. It was a lateral transfer, but I would be placed in charge of the statewide Classification System, and I would no longer have to carpool. My new job site was on the State Capitol grounds and simply beautiful. For six years, I commuted 130 miles daily, the distance from Baton Rouge to Angola roundtrip, but my commuting days were almost over.

For every upside in life there is a downside. The upside of the new job was being in the city, having an office on the State Capitol grounds, and coming home at decent hours after work. The downside was my new boss, whom I shall refer to as Dr. Z. He was meaner than a rattlesnake; exceptionally clever, and a master politician. He threatened to fire somebody on staff every day, and if he told you to prepare a report, he could do it better.

Dr. Z was rude and did not mind embarrassing you publicly. He was the Assistant Secretary of Public Safety and Corrections, with authority over adult prisons, appointed by the governor. I did not know he had a few loose screws until after I had accepted the job. As a source of personal amusement, he gave all his section chiefs nicknames. His homeboy and best friend, the Director of Probation and Parole was called, "Dumb Ass." He called me "Draft Dodger" because I had no military experience. According to him, I was a long-haired hippie who passed the time "smoking dope, listening to Mick Jagger's music and badmouthing the country." Dr. Z was a hot mess with a foul mouth that would make a sailor blush. He managed the office with fear and intimidation, but he did not frighten me. I had dealt with bullies before in the Sonia Quarters. I knew what he really needed; a good old-fashioned butt whipping, but I would not accommodate him. I had come too far and worked too hard to throw it all away because of his foolish antics.

One day Dr. Z called a staff meeting. As usual, I was the only fly in the buttermilk. He said,

"Gentlemen, I have an announcement to make. I received permission from the Civil Service Department to create a Chief of Staff position and after careful consideration, I have decided to promote Draft Dodger. He's smart, tenacious and has what it takes to represent my office."

I was stunned and could not believe my ears because everybody else at the conference table were LSU graduates, and they usually got first preference; that was just the way it was. Against the odds, the boy with the stutter from Peabody had become as the teacher predicted, a full-blown eagle. I was 36, and by God's grace, I had been elevated from the bowels of Angola to the top of the mountain. Shortly afterwards, Mr. Z announced his retirement. I sighed with relief because I was close to the edge and couldn't take too much more of him.

Years later, I visited Mr. Z on his deathbed. He pleaded with me to not be angry with him. "I knew I was tough on you, but I was preparing for retirement long before I announced it, and I wanted to be sure that you could stand the pressure," he told me. "I knew my enemies would come after you because they hated me, but you were the right man for the job."

After Mr. Z retired, I eventually surpassed him in rank. For 12 years I was the chief troubleshooter for the department. During those days, if you were a warden, and I showed up at your doorstep, it was probably time for you to pack your bags. Three times I was appointed by three governors to serve as Deputy Secretary, the second in command of the entire system. I was fired by Governor Edwin Edwards for what he called "insubordination," or in simple terms, for being "a nigger who talked back." The same behavior exhibited by white men would have been called "just a little high strung."

I came roaring back to the same position after Governor Edwards left office, not because I was so charming, but I had a particular skill set that you can't buy from the grocery store. I was the only African American, then or now, to serve as warden of the Louisiana State Penitentiary (Angola). Having received a host of awards, I was one of the most decorated civil servants in my career field. In 2010, I was awarded the coveted, "Charles E. Dunbar Award," the highest honor bestowed upon civil servants.

I am deeply indebted to Assistant Secretary Whalen Gibbs, who recommended me for the award. After 37 years, I retired from state service in 2011.

## A HIGHER CALLING

My final career move involved the ultimate in service, and I would unknowingly be preparing for it long before my civil service career ended. In the 1990s, I was a Sunday School teacher and deacon at Shiloh Missionary Baptist Church in Baton Rouge, pastored by Dr. Charles T. Smith (no relationship). I was also a president of the Brotherhood, a Christian men's auxiliary dedicated to strengthening the men of the church and carrying out special assignments as directed by the pastor. It was during that time I started to hear God's voice calling me to the preaching ministry.

For years I had been ignoring the Lord, but it became unbearable. My wife, Pat, came to me one day and said, "Larry, you keep saying somebody is calling you. Well, I do not know who's calling you, but I wish you would go see what they want because you are about to drive us nuts. Plus, the neighbors are starting to wonder what is wrong with you because you are pacing up and down the sidewalk at night." After a few counseling sessions with Dr. Smith, I accepted God's call to preach the gospel in 1996. My peace was restored.

In 1999, at the invitation of Brother George White, I returned to Alexandria to preach on a rotational basis at Rose of Sharon Baptist Church, as the congregation began its search for a new pastor. While I was delighted to support God's work in my hometown and give back to a community that helped me, I had no intention of pastoring long distance, a 220 miles roundtrip, on a permanent basis.

As it was His will, God had a new plan for me in the new century. In 2000, I was elected the pastor of historic Rose of Sharon Baptist Church. Pat and I met new friends and were reacquainted with old ones. For 13 years I was bi-vocational, working for the state, and pastoring simultaneously. My day job afforded me the opportunity to come and go as needed, provided I put in my 40 hours. In addition, I enrolled in New Orleans Baptist Theological Seminary. By then, I was 50 and had been out of school a while. My memory was fading, and I really had to train it again to study. Seeing that my hands were full, Pat stepped up and accepted the job of being my full-time chauffeur. My daughter Brandi provided encouragement and financial support to our ministry. Members of Rose of Sharon accepted additional assignments, followed my lead and things started to come together. What seemed like an impossible task, now became doable and with all of us working together the church prospered.

Over the years I have had many daring, notable experiences, but nothing can compare to preaching God's word and leading His flock. Like many of my ancestors and contemporaries, my road has not been easy, and many times the struggles set before me seemed endless and unbearable. Yet, over the years I have come to realize that the totality of my life experiences were truly blessings in disguise. In June 2011, I retired from the Department of Public Safety and Corrections after 37 years. In September 2020, I retired from Rose of Sharon after 21 years. In May 2021, I was elevated to the lofty position of Pastor Emeritus. Wow, what a run!

As I look back over the road I have traveled, all I can say is summarized in words of the prophet Isaiah, *"But they that wait on the Lord shall renew their strength; they shall mount up with wings as eagles; they shall run, and not be weary; and they shall walk and not faint."* —Isa. 40:31, KJ

# STILL HERE

*"Always embrace the precious present, show, and give love to all, and maintain hope in the midst of uncertainty. This is our gift to GOD and others."*
—DR. LINDA GREEN

## Dr. Linda Smith Green—Ethel's daughter

*Music is an escape. A song can transport us to a time in our lives that we may want to forget or a time in our lives we happily embrace. As we grew up and sang and danced, my Mama never stopped us.*

EACH DAY OF our lives we make choices. We hope the choices we make will be the right ones. We learn from our parents, family, and friends during our childhood. We are blessed by God if we are in the right environment and have good role models. The person we have become at this moment is based on our life experiences. Who am I? I am a member of the Peabody Class of 1968. My name is Linda Smith Green, DNP, MSN, CNS, APRN. What does all that mean? Nothing, when it is all said and done. I have been a nurse for 47 years. I have cared for and comforted the sick, the dying. Served God's people by keeping hope alive in the midst of the shadow of death, and when death showed up, I have been there. Sometimes from the beginning to the end.

I cherish all mankind. I do not see color. It amazes me that people do not cherish each other. People do not follow the simple Golden Rule. Lest we forget, we are all given the perfect present, life. The secret is learning how to live it and learning from one's own, as well as others' mistakes. In early childhood, we have good and not so good memories from our homelife, the neighborhood and city we lived in, or ongoing wars in the world and racial injustices everywhere. In the turbulent 1960s, my mother never missed the 6 o'clock Chet Huntley-David Brinkley Report on NBC-TV nightly, and she never discussed the bad news with us. All my mother wanted to do was protect us from the harms of the times.

Our era was that of segregation. Many of us '60s children were protected, even overprotected by our parents from the hate of the period. Parents knew the pain and danger inflicted on children who experienced the loss of childhood innocence. They simply wanted us to stay safe. Our hope as members of the Peabody Class of 1968 is that we have and are making differences in people's lives. Please walk with me down memory lane, as I share some of my life with you.

## GRANDPARENTS

My mother, Ethel Smith, was born to Foster Smith and Adaline Gray Smith on August 10, 1918. My mother had one sister, Pearl, and two brothers, Robert and Oscar. We called her brother, Oscar, Uncle Buster. As adults they all lived on Bayou Rapides. In the early years, the family may have been required to pick cotton on Bayou Rapides. Mama was the only one that lived in Alexandria. My grandfather and Uncle Robert were veterans. Uncle Robert married Fannie Battles. They had 14 children. My grandmother died when my mother was 11 years old. My grandfather was away in the military, and my mother and her brother, Robert, were raised by aunts and uncles. Years later, my grandfather married our step grandmother, Louella Robinson. We called her Ma Ma. Uncle Buster and Aunt Pearl were older, and they grew up and married. The sister and brother married a sister and brother. When my grandfather returned from the military, I remember him visiting us. My last recollection of him was when I was 3. He brought a beautiful red leather rocking chair to our house for my birthday. My grandsons now use that rocking chair.

During my mother's adulthood, she cleaned houses for white families. She later trained to be a nursing assistant and worked at the Louisiana State Special Education Center on the nightshift for 22 years. Mama said she worked the nightshift so she could be home with us when we got out of school. When I was 3, she married Cleveland Hayes, and my sister Shirley Hayes was born in 1953.

## BAYOU RAPIDES

Mama would take my sister and me to the country on Sundays. Aunt Lucille (nicknamed Aunt Cile), Uncle Buster's wife, would have coffee for the grownups, and homemade ice cream and chocolate cake — five layers with pecans on top. It was delicious. They did not have any children. Aunt Pearl (nicknamed Aunt Sooky) always had a beautiful fire in the fireplace during winter, and she, too, had coffee and cake. They always had a beautiful garden. She was married to Alonzo Price, who was Aunt Cile's brother; they had 9 children. They would invite us to many cookouts after they slaughtered animals, which I did not like. I told Mama that I was not going to eat the meat because it was not USDA approved. She made me eat it anyway. I remember the juicy yellow plums. For a long time, the family did not have a bathroom. We had to go outside. I also remember we did not have a bathroom when we lived at 1620 Schnack Street in Alexandria. We took baths in a large tin tub. We often visited Uncle Robert and Aunt Fannie's house. I remember Uncle Robert and Uncle Buster were in a quartet, and we would listen to them practice at Uncle Robert's house. My cousin Joyce and I were visiting some years ago and talked about those days, when our parents would take us with them to visit our family, visit the old people. "Now *we* are the old people," she and I reflected playfully.

## PARENTS

My mother, Ethel Smith, had been divorced from her first husband for about a year when she met my dad, Leonard Simon LeMelle. He was from Opelousas, Louisiana, about an hour's drive south of Alexandria. Their relationship was brief. After it ended, she found out that she was pregnant. On Wednesday, September 13, 1950, at 10:30 a.m., I was born at Huey P. Long Hospital. I spent time with my father during my childhood and adulthood. He was a painter and a carpenter.

## SISTERS

My sister Shirley Hayes was born on August 16, 1953. She graduated from Peabody's Class of 1970. We had a fair childhood. Mama did the best she could in her situation. One of my happy memories is when Shirley was starting the first grade. Mama, who worked the nightshift, tried to get off early to get Shirley ready for the first day of school. When Mama got home, I had combed both of our hair and got us dressed for school. Mama bought us identical dresses in different colors. We were ready. Mama was so happy. We had fun during our childhood. I loved music, and we would listen to music on the TV, the radio, and our record player. We would dance and sing. Shirley had a beautiful voice. She sang in the choir at church. We would pantomime Diana Ross and the Supremes *Someday We'll Be Together*, along with songs by Jerry Butler, the Temptations, Jimmy Ruffin, Sam Cooke, and many others. Shirley worked at a local department store. Racism was frequently exhibited there, and the owner used the N-word. She also was a driver for UPS. I have two wonderful nephews.

After college, I lived in Lafayette for 18 years. I came home frequently, and Mama, my stepdad, and Shirley and her family visited Lafayette often. I moved back home in 1987. The family got together on Sundays, alternating cooking duties until we started going to Cousins Ernest and Geneva LeMelle's house on Cane River on Sundays. Sometimes Ernest and Geneva would travel to Alexandria, and then everybody would end up at my house. The girls and I were always on the go. Shirley, Mama, and I would say, "On the road again."

In 2000, cousin, Ernest LeMelle, told me that my father had another older child and that her name was Cecile Joffrion Jones. At that time, she lived in Atlanta, Georgia. He said that she wanted to meet me and asked if I wanted to meet her. I said, "Of course." We connected on the phone, and within a couple of weeks she came to visit me and Ernest and his wife, Geneva, on Cane River. Cane River became my adult version of country trips on Sundays. Geneva made delicious meat pies. Her mother and sisters are believed to have been some of the originators of the popular Natchitoches Meat Pies.

My sister, Cecile, never met our dad. Her mother died when she was 9 months old, and her aunt and uncle would not let my father see her. During our visit, I shared pictures, newspaper articles, and other items pertaining to him. We both sobbed as we got to know each other and shared moments together. After our meeting, we talked often on the phone, and she frequently drove to visit. Life is not about the length of time we spend with each other but the quality of the time we have together. I shared many stories with her. My dad made coffee in a little pot with gauze, and the coffee was so strong it made the hair on your head rise. In Lafayette, my dad had a contract with Holy Rosary Catholic School to do painting, and in my years after college in Lafayette, he and I got to spend a lot of quality time together.

In 1981, my mother and I had not heard from my dad for about a month. His neighbor called Mama and told her my dad was at Rapides General. Mama called me, and I went home to Alexandria. He was in a coma. He had been diagnosed with lung cancer the year before and did not tell me. The doctor told me that it was operable, but he had refused the surgery. This was devastating, and my sister Cecile and I cried when I told her. If only he had told me, maybe I could have convinced him to have the surgery. We made it through, but it haunted me for a long time that I was helping others but was not there to help my dad. Cousin Ernest was with him through most of it, and he would not let him tell me.

Many years of my career were devoted to working with cancer patients, trying to help them maintain hope, to receive treatment, and to be with them when all options had been exhausted. I remember taking a bereavement counseling course in New Orleans in 1992. There were approximately 40 students enrolled in the one-week course. The first two days we all were weary and in tears. The speaker told us that we were purging our own sorrows and that we had to begin to heal our own grief before we could help our patients. This is so true. I believe God had many of us in that class to help us heal.

## RELIGION

I believe religion is the thread that gives us as a race strength. The Bible, the songs, the closeness of families, and the culture as we know it. I was born and baptized a Baptist when I was about 6. My step grandmother was married to The Rev. P. M. Hall. They lived in her house on York Street. He was the minister of Starlight Baptist Church on Overton Street, where we were members. He had a giant Bible. It would hardly stay on my lap. The letters were huge. I loved reading it. We sat on the screened-in front porch on the swing. He would read it to me and my sister and explain everything about God and the Bible. He was the pastor of four churches: Starlight Baptist Church, Good Hope Baptist Church, Bright Morning Star Baptist Church, and Annadale Baptist Church. He was a God-serving man. His first wife died, and all of his children lived in California except one son, The Rev. Leon Hall. The younger

Reverend Hall lived in Alexandria with his wife, Pat, and their children. They were both schoolteachers.

As I write this, I'm remembering Ma Ma was the cook and maid for the Beasley Family that owned Guaranty Bank in Alexandria. She would make the best pancakes, and she would let my sister and me sneak and drink what I called coffee milk. She taught us all about etiquette, stirring the coffee with the spoon in the middle of the cup so no one would hear you stirring. I would spend the night on occasion with her. Ma Ma was a diabetic, and I would spend my high school weekends with her at Cabrini Hospital. Sometimes her blood sugar would drop too low, and she would pass out. That got me to thinking about being a nurse and helping people when they were weak and sick.

In junior high school, I played piano for a little Sunday school in Carver Village. Mrs. Howard (the mother of Peabody choir instructor, Mrs. Willie B. Morrison) and Mrs. White, who lived in Carver Village, started the Sunday school before regular church services would begin so that the children in the area would attend. Then they brought me to church where my mother and sister would meet us. They paid me $10 every time I played. Throughout junior high school, I played for them. In high school, I played the organ for Olive Branch Baptist Church on Third Street, and occasionally played for Pilgrim Baptist Church on Solomon Street. Reverend Jacob was the minister at Pilgrim. I promise you that was some good singing and some good preaching. Reverend G.C. Jacob would always sing after his sermon, and they would *tear the church up* with joy. These were such beautiful life experiences that I am thankful to write about.

When I went off to the University of Southwestern Louisiana (USL) in Lafayette, after leaving the library at night on my way back to the dormitory, I had to pass a Catholic church, and students were in the Catholic Student Union. On occasion I would sit in the church and pray. I remember the scent of the candles burning and the peacefulness of the church. This became a part of my serving God as well. Because my dad was Catholic and had had a strong connection to his church parish St. James, I felt a connection to the campus church. I loved to touch the Holy Water as I entered the sanctuary. I trusted and believed in God for getting all the nursing students through our schooling, especially the Black students.

After college, I married and settled in Lafayette. I played the organ at Trinity CME Church on Lee Street. I played for 11 years, from 1975 to 1986. We were on the radio on Sunday evenings. Our choir made a cassette, and it was sold to raise money to buy fancy choir robes. Of course, I was earning good money on a professional nurse's salary, compared to my first job playing the church piano in junior high for $10 a Sunday.

When I divorced, I moved home, and eventually joined St. James Catholic Church. The Catholic church was calling me, and my three daughters and I became Catholics. In 2009, my middle daughter Megan started going to Rose of Sharon Baptist Church. Those years, I went to St. James' Mass at 10 a.m. After Mass, I would attend 11 a.m. service at Rose of Sharon and eventually also would join the congregation. With dual memberships, I called myself a Catholic/Baptist. I promised God that if he helped me obtain a job in New Orleans, I would return permanently to the Catholic Church, and when I moved there December 2017, I did return. God is good and forever protecting us and answering our prayers. I am now a member of Our Lady of Guadalupe Church & International Shrines of St. Jude on North Rampart Street in New Orleans.

## Music

Music touches all cultures and is known as a universal language. Music has been in our lives as long as I can remember. Mama sang in the choir, and Shirley and I tagged along with her to choir rehearsal when we were little children. When Mama cooked or stood at the sink washing dishes, she always hummed a gospel song. Being a child, I did not even think to ask Mama why was she humming? Recently, I heard an interview with Sam Cooke, and he was asked to hum what "soul" meant to him. As he hummed, I was touched. It made me think about my Mama's humming. Music is an escape. A song can transport us to a time in our lives that we may want to forget or a time in our lives we happily embrace. As we grew up and sang and danced, my Mama never stopped us.

Of course, the lyrics to songs in the 1960s and 70s were not as they are today. As I share and think about these memories, I recall my Mama never hummed or sang a song that was not gospel. There is something called the "humming effect," which states that humming heals and transforms a person on a physical, emotional, mental, and spiritual level.

I am so thankful to God for giving us music. It has helped rescue me from many life events. Music has been my comforter, my healer. Music is in my life daily. When my children were coming up through the years, they would call out, "Mama turn the music down."

Here is my list of favorite gospel and secular songs.

## GOSPEL

- *Amazing Grace*, Bill and Gloria *Gaither*, featuring Wintley Phipps
- *I Remember Mama*, Shirley Ceasar
- *Angel's Keep Watching Over Me*, Cousin L. T. Blake (one of Mama's favorites)
- *Peace Be Still*, James Cleveland
- *Touch Me Lord Jesus* (one of Mama's favorites)
- *Touch the Hem of His Garment*, Sam Cooke
- *Soon I Will Be Done with the Troubles of the World*, Mahalia Jackson
- How Firm A Foundation
- I Don't Know about Tomorrow
- God Is
- Let the Church Say Amen
- Order My Steps
- Every Praise
- The Storm Is Passing Over
- What Is This?
- *I Can't Give Up*, Lee Williams and the Spiritual QC's
- *Goin' Up Yonder*, Walter Hawkins
- *Don't Call the Roll*, Debra Snipes
- *Change Is Coming*, Sounds of Blackness
- Walk Around Heaven All Day,
- Debra Snipes Version

## SECULAR MUSIC

- *Memories Don't Leave Like People Do,* Jerry Butler
- *Sailing,* Rod Stewart
- *Really Gonna Miss You,* Smokey Robinson
- *I Wanna Dance with Somebody,* Whitney Houston
- *To Dream the Impossible Dream,* Luther Vandross
- *Dancing In the Dark,* Bruce Springsteen
- *Love on Top,* Beyoncé
- *Love on the Brain,* Rihanna
- *The Whole Town's Laughing at Me,* Teddy Pendergrass
- *Wake Up Everybody,* Teddy Pendergras
- *What Becomes of the Brokenhearted,* Jimmy Ruffin
- *I Could Never Love Another,* The Temptations
- *Last Dance,* Donna Summer
- *My Girl,* The Temptations
- *Some Day We Will Be Together,* Diana Ross & the Supremes
- *A Change Is Gonna Come,* Sam Cooke
- *I Will Always Love You,* Whitney Houston
- *Dance with My Father,* Luther Vandross


## CHILDHOOD MEMORIES ROOTED IN MUSIC, CHURCH AND SEGREGATION

- Kress Store — colored water fountains
- Paramount Theatre — colored upstairs balcony
- White Dentist — colored entrance; did not fill bucktooth, instead pulled it.
- White Family M.D., Dr. Chicola, — colored entrance
- Piano lessons — Mrs. Ella D. Lawson
- Rev. P. M. Hall — Starlight Baptist Church

## School Days Life

- Elementary School—Lenora Johnson Kindergarten
  - South Alexandria Elementary

  - Silver City Elementary

- Junior High School—Jones Street Junior High
  - Cheerleader
  - Concert Band

- High School—Peabody Senior High
- Band Marching — Bell Lyre
- Band Concert — Bassoon
- Debate Club
- Junior Prom
- Senior Prom

## College Days—USL

I can say my college days were good. I sometimes felt out of place being a Baptist girl. Most of my high school friends went to Grambling State University and Southern University. At that time, nursing was not offered at those colleges. At University of South Louisiana in Lafayette, students liked to party on the weekends and drink wine. I did not drink. I pledged Alpha Kappa Alpha Sorority, Inc. and participated in other college activities, but majoring in nursing was time-consuming. I was too scared to party and not study.

In my freshman year, at the beginning of my nursing studies, there were about five Black students starting in fall 1968. I remember some protests on campus about equality, but, again, I was studying so I did not participate. There was a place on campus, the Collegian, where many of the Black students hung out. There was a juke box, and the place served food. We also went to the Union, but the Collegian was in the middle of campus, so we dropped in between classes.

We had a strong all-white faculty that appeared in general to treat all students fairly. After receiving a passing clinical evaluation, the clinical faculty member who was white told me she did not think I should stay in the nursing program. I became my own advocate, and I told her I was not a quitter and that I would not quit. I learned that many of the Black students on the campus were intimidated and had to stand their ground in similar circumstances. We all worked hard, up late many nights, taking NoDoz pills to stay awake for study. We all made it, thank God. The faculty member who tried to discourage me that year did not return the following year.

*My mother, Ethel Hayes, with my daughters: Lindsay, Heather, & Megan in 2002*

The football and basketball teams were mostly Black, and we enjoyed going to games and concerts at Blackham Coliseum. The fraternity on campus was Alpha Phi Alpha, and the sorority was Alpha Kappa Alpha. In 1970, I was nominated for A Phi A Sweetheart and happened to meet their graduate advisor, Patrick Green, who was seven years my senior. I was pursued by him, and we married in July of 1971. Patrick was the son of Jeanné Broussard Green and Gerard Green, Sr. He was the youngest son of seven children. The Broussard and Green families were so close that one of Mrs. Green's brothers married one of Mr. Green's sisters. The family lived in an area of Lafayette that was originally called Long Plantation.

Mr. Green's father was one of the first black men in the community with a car. He started a tradition of helping his neighbors who lacked transportation by collecting their bills and money and making their payments. I witnessed Mr. and Mrs. Green continue this tradition through the years.

Mr. Green was a farmer and a school bus driver. He planted sweet potatoes and grew corn and okra every year. Mrs. Green taught me how to make maque choux, a stewed corn dish. The Greens were great cooks, and I learned their way of seasoning beef and poultry. So many memories of good times. We were eventually blessed with three beautiful daughters. We divorced in September 1988, and he died in 1991. Today, our children have numerous degrees, are married, have purchased homes. I have four grandchildren. We are all grateful. In 1998, I married Freddie Price, Sr. We divorced in 2001.

## Nursing Career

My nursing career has been very rewarding. I believe that as a nurse, I and others who have worked with me, have made a difference in many lives. I recall a white patient not wanting me to take care of him. He later apologized for his behavior and brought crawfish to me while I was on duty at the hospital. I believe that many racist stereotypes are held because of what someone has been told by their family and friends. Nursing is about treating all people the same—the Golden Rule.

## Epilogue—The Year 2021

I'm writing this on January 17, 2021. Friday, January 15, was Dr. Martin Luther King's birthday. This weekend is celebrated throughout the United States in observance of his legacy. Last week, on January 6, there were violent riots at the U.S. Capitol. This upcoming week is the Inauguration of the country's 46th president, Joe Biden, and the first Black and Asian American and female vice president, Kamala Harris. These happenings are taking place in a country divided. Racial injustices began to return to the forefront during the presidency of Barack Obama. We must do the right thing in all situations. I refuse to let the injustices around me dictate my attitude toward gratitude and the blessings that God has surrounded my family and me with. We lived through 2020 and are thankful to still be here. Langston Hughes wrote:

"Still Here"
I've been scarred and battered.
My hopes the wind done scattered.
Snow has friz me, sun has baked me.
Looks like between 'em
They done tried to make me
Stop laughin', stop lovin', stop livin'
But I don't care!
I'm still here!

—*Selected Poems of Langston Hughes, 1987*

Yes, I have had gains and losses, but I have cherished each moment of the experience. I have embraced everyone throughout my life. It did not take me becoming a nurse to value life. I thank God for my memories. Like Jerry Butler sings, "Memories don't leave like people do." I have cried my tears and strived to move on. After the sudden death of my children's father, I always maintained a happy appearance. I cried many nights in the shower. I did not want them to worry, be concerned, or fretful.

We must maintain hope and keep it alive, as Dr. Martin Luther King, Jr. said. We must strive to be the change that we want to see. We should never make excuses for who we are or who we have become. Know that God never leaves us alone. He is always watching over us. We must hold our dreams, hopes, and values close. We must be a role model for all people. Lastly, know this: There is a reason why we are *still here*. Be thankful for the perfect present.

# LIFE LESSONS

*"...Fear God and keep his commandments,*
*for this is the whole duty of man."*

ECCLESIASTES **12:13**

## Aubrey Woodley

MY RECOLLECTIONS OF growing up in Alexandria, or simply becoming aware of my existence, started when I was around 5 years of age. That time was filled with innocence, to be sure, but it included periods of social awareness through friendships forged and visits made to relatives, not to mention parental and sibling influences. Being the youngest of the first five siblings and living in a diverse working-class neighborhood helped to shape us all and brought a set of lessons that stayed with me.

I was raised in the Lower Third area of Alexandria on a street that was close to the city limit. The major landmark in the area was a cotton gin, but the neighborhood also included various retail businesses owned by Blacks and whites. Many storefronts sold foods, cookies and candies, and sundry items. The store functioned not only as a place of business but as the family residence as well. A tractor company to support the farming community outside the city limits, service stations, fish market, and mechanic shops also were nearby.

Whenever we had a taste for fresh pastries, we ventured outside the neighborhood to the Black owned bakery located in the Sonia Quarters. My street and all the streets in the neighborhood were dirt roads until they were paved in the late 1950s and early 1960s. Many changes occurred during this period, including the addition of Silver City Elementary and Jones Street Junior High School. The neighborhood was bound on the east by the Red River with a levee less than a half mile from my home. The levee was a source of joy for my brothers and me because it allowed us to thrill-ride on a makeshift go-kart we had constructed or our bicycle or to slide down on a big piece of cardboard. The trick was to avoid any traffic that might have been passing by when we got to the bottom. Every now and then the Red River would overflow its banks, and the levee would provide security from flooding. The other side of the levee contained many Blackberry patches, which we and many in the surrounding area took advantage of. I still remember the Blackberry cobblers

*"Be careful about stereotyping…All Black people do not talk the same, and it should not be assumed that as a white person, you would have to learn slang to communicate with your new employees."*

and jelly my mother used to make. My brothers and I also picked berries in season to earn a little spending money.

The majority of the homes in the neighborhood were owned by the residents. In fact, my father and uncle built our house and my uncle's house as well. My uncle was a carpenter, and my father learned homebuilding through him and trade school. His official employment was at the Veteran's Administration (VA) Hospital, but being the resourceful man that he was, he saw the value in learning homebuilding and auto mechanics and electronics, which all came in handy as you can see. I often wonder what the outcome would have been for my five brothers and me if my father had pursued this craft as his livelihood. In retrospect though, I know that he was being prudent as he and my mother had many mouths to feed, mine, as well as those of my three sisters and five brothers over the years. Being a cook at the VA provided the stability needed to raise a family.

> **Life Lesson #1: Do not put all your eggs in one basket. Prepare yourself for life alternatives.**

My father was raised in Ruby, Louisiana, and was educated in Alexandria at Kelso Elementary and Peabody High School when it was located on Third and Bogan Streets. A tour of duty in the U. S. Army followed high school and trade school followed that. After serving in Europe during World War II, he returned home and started work at the VA Hospital. My mother was raised in Big Bend and Magda, Louisiana, where she was educated through the seventh grade. Both towns were in the Alexandria metropolitan area with Alexandria being the "big city" that provided more job opportunities. She moved to Pineville as a young woman, lived with an aunt, and started work laundering and ironing clothes to earn her keep before marrying my father and moving across the river to Alexandria.

My parents had nine children, which I look at as two groups. Since I am the middle child, you can better understand why I might look at it that way. I grew up with the first group that consisted of two sisters and two brothers with the girls being the elders. The second group consisted of a sister and three bothers born after me. My older brothers, a first cousin, and I grew up together and as youngsters spent our time doing what boys do: playing marbles, building popguns and slingshots, repairing and assembling bicycles, arguing and trying to stay out of the way of our sisters who had control of the house when our parents were away at work.

*The Woodley Family: Seated from left are Dr. Annie Brown, Nell Kelley, my mother Rebecca Woodley, and Sherlene Humphrey. Standing from left are Greg Woodley, Capt. Sherman Woodley, James Woodley, Aubrey Woodley, Glynn Woodley, and Dr. Charles Woodley.*

Summers were filled with fun and often included many other children in the neighborhood. One of the good things about a big family is that you always had somebody to play with. When we had disagreements with our other playmates, we always had each other to stay engaged and occupied. Fortunately, our disagreements with playmates would not last more than a day or two, and we would be right back playing as if nothing had happened. Trying to keep up with my brothers not only made me fleet of foot but increased my curiosity and toughened me.

An elderly man in the neighborhood lived in a boarding house that was used to accommodate Black seasonal workers who were employed at the cotton gin. He was trusted by my parents, and my brothers and I would occasionally visit him, as he was one of the first to own a television and would allow us to watch it and just fool around. Everyone in the neighborhood was known by each other and felt it was their duty to make sure any mischief you were involved in did not go unreported and that helped keep us in line.

▶ **Life Lesson #2: It does "take a village to raise a child".**

My mother saw to it that we be of help to others. Any elderly neighbor needing someone to run to the store for them knew that all they had to do was call, as she let them know that my brothers and I were available. For my mother, doing good deeds for others was not only about volunteering us but also about our family leading by example. Even though she had many mouths to feed, she would always provide a plate of food for anyone needing a good hot Sunday meal. She tried to help any family having a hard time in any way she could whether it was food or clothing. She really got joy from helping others and taught us all that it is more blessed to give than receive.

To this day, I can remember how a fish dinner smelled when it was wrapped on a paper plate with wax paper and placed in a brown paper bag. Fish fries were a popular way to earn money for the church and were always well attended by family and friends. I delivered many of these dinners in the neighborhood. My mother also baked single-serve lemon and sweet potato pies for fundraisers, whether it was for her community event or one of her sisters' or brothers'. I spent whatever change I had accumulated on those pies because they were so good!

My mother always made time to support whatever activities we were involved in whether school or church related and found a way to provide whatever we needed to participate. In general, children get uneasy when their parents show up at school with them or at a PTA meeting when they are required to speak. It did not take long for me to find out that my mother was really smart and could talk with anyone. She always had a well thought-out opinion and could communicate it well. I found out that whatever the occasion, she knew exactly what to say.

► **Life Lesson #3: A selfless person is to be esteemed above a selfish person. It doesn't matter what you have or do not have in life, there is always someone who isn't faring as well as you. You should seize upon opportunities to be of service and help to others.**

I truly believe that the firstborn child in a family, whether male or female, has a big influence on all the other siblings. My oldest sister definitely had an impact on the rest of us. She was very smart, valedictorian of her class, open to new things, and a regular trailblazer. Summers were not all play, as those months had afforded her an opportunity to exercise her authority as the firstborn and to feed her nurturing spirit. I recall lining the kitchen chairs out on the front porch for school lessons during the summer, not only for me but for all of us at the time. I am sure I learned my alphabet and how to count from these lessons and a desire for knowledge. When she got to high school and started bringing home a band instrument, we were all ears and were hooked. All of us ended up playing in the school band. Both of my sisters also participated in a community choir formed by a lady in the neighborhood.

We were raised during a time when people had caring attitudes and realized we were in a common struggle. We had excellent educators who did their best to make sure we had a broad education and the tools to succeed in life. For example, if the school band had not provided instruments for members, we would not have been able to participate to the extent we did given the restricted expense of owning our own. Sure, there were students who did buy their instruments, but the majority of participants could not afford to, me included. The opportunity has given me a lifelong appreciation and enjoyment of music.

> ► **Life Lesson #4: Exposing one to something new could open the door to a great contribution to mankind. Depriving people of the opportunity to explore their limits or learn new things ultimately deprives us all.**

To earn money for school clothes, supplies and other interests, my brothers and I always looked for summer work and did odd jobs mostly on the weekends — mowing lawns, cleaning house, painting houses, picking berries and pecans for sale, and even babysitting. We learned early that one way to improve our chances of landing a job in the summer was to start looking a minimum of two weeks before school ended, going to the employment office and making a nuisance of ourselves by calling and/or visiting the office at least twice a week to inquire about the status of our application. That generally led to success for at least one of us, but when the Neighborhood Youth Corps was initiated by the government, we had even greater success landing a job. I cut grass on the former England Air Force Base and worked as a Nursing Assistant at the VA Hospital. To this day, I still make a bed and put pillow slips on the military way. We learned early the value of work and were willing to do whatever job was available. The thought of staying home following high school graduation never crossed our minds. We knew we were not only expected to go out and make a living for ourselves once we completed high school, but we looked forward to making it on our own. We also understood that as long as we were in college, we had a place at home.

> ► **Life Lesson #5: Whatever job you do, do it to the best of your ability, and learn all you can from it.**

My mother was from a big family, so several of her younger siblings ended up staying at our house for periods to attend school. Anything approximately five miles outside the city limit we considered the "country," and my aunts would come to the city to pursue higher education. Many went on to college and encouraged my oldest sister to do the same, which in turn set in motion the rest of us following suit. All eight of my siblings and I attended college with seven of the nine graduating from college and two going on to earn doctorate degrees. Undergraduate degrees were obtained from Dillard University, Grambling State University, Southern University, and Louisiana Tech University, in the fields of Sociology, Education, Electronics, Business Administration, Chemical Engineering, and Psychology. Postgraduate degrees were obtained at Washington University in Missouri, Texas A&M University, and Howard University. All my siblings went on to successful careers in their chosen fields.

When I was in the sixth or seventh grade, I made up my mind that I wanted to be a chemical engineer. At the time, I really did not fully understand what that entailed, as I did not know anyone in that field or anyone who worked at a chemical facility. The paper mill was probably the only employer in the Alexandria metropolitan area that utilized that discipline, and I did not know anyone working there. I got the idea for this profession from perusing a set of encyclopedias my parents had bought for us. A section on occupations with salaries and skill requirements caught my attention one day, and after evaluating those against my interests, chemical engineering sounded good to me. After all, I enjoyed the experiments my brothers and I used to conduct when they received a chemistry set for a Christmas or birthday present. Stink bombs, chemical snakes, disappearing ink, various chemicals mixing, and solving litmus test results really got my attention, and math came easy to me.

However, when it came to choosing a college or university, money was a big consideration, as it always is. I had learned something about this through my older siblings and listened attentively to the conversations my brothers used to have concerning life on the campus of Southern University. Since they had experienced the good and the bad, I felt I could make it there, and Southern was my first choice. In addition, I spent two summers on the Southern University campus attending Bayou Boys State as a citizen and later as a counselor and liked the campus. And, I was familiar with the layout. It was really my only choice even after I learned one summer that they did not offer a degree in chemical engineering. I decided that a major in accounting would be the avenue I would take. But as fate would have it, representatives from Louisiana Tech University (LA Tech) visited the Peabody campus my senior year, and I learned that not only did Tech provide a degree in chemical engineering, but the university could provide grants and loans to finance my education.

With the financial assistance offered and the scholarships I would receive, Tech was doable. Even though I had only vaguely heard of LA Tech, the thought of financial assistance resonated with me. My only reservation was that LA Tech was a predominately white school, and I was not sure how welcoming it would be since I had always attended segregated schools. After reflecting on the fact that I was not going to college to socialize but to pursue a career and that my success was in my hands only, I put that behind me. When I learned that a close friend from junior high school would be attending LA Tech, I was resolved to go. Little did I know that four of my classmates from Peabody had made plans to attend as well. I was surprised and pleased when I saw them on campus.

When I informed my parents of my selection, I remember my father voicing concern in asking if that was where I really wanted to go. I knew then that he had some reservations, not about whether I could make it there, but rather about how well I would be treated there. I learned sometime later that my father had been refused service at a donut shop in Ruston where LA Tech is located. He and my two older brothers were confronted with this racism when they stopped in Ruston after dropping my second oldest sister off at Grambling, about five miles from Ruston. I am sure that incident entered his mind. My father never really talked about his experiences with white people, but my siblings and I knew about racial inequality and injustice. Nevertheless, we were never told nor did we get any hint from our parents that we should lower our goals or expectations due to racism, or that we could not aspire to be anything we wanted to be. Even though they had limited opportunities, my parents did not restrict us in any way and only offered encouragement. Parents are always concerned about their children's welfare and happiness, though, and my decision would be a new experience for us all.

As children, we knew that whenever we chose to ride the city bus downtown, we were to sit in the back of the bus. This did not really matter when riding from the Lower Third area to downtown because very few whites lived in that area of town or needed the bus service. We knew whenever we went to the Paramount Theater downtown that there was a certain entrance we were expected to use. During this period, Black patrons were seated in the upper (balcony) section of the theater and whites in the lower. Separate concession areas were also provided so that contact between Blacks and whites was minimized. About the only time I would see the white patrons would be if I looked over the balcony and saw them down below. The Ritz Theater on Lee Street catered strictly to the Black population. Whenever we went to see a movie there, we would go early in the day to avoid being on Lee Street at night. Lee Street had many nightclubs and a reputation for shootings and stabbings, and our parents did not want us spending anytime in that area for safety reasons. With the exception of going to the theater or to a funeral home or two, we had no reason to go there.

We did not have to ride the bus often because my brothers and I would generally walk downtown or ride our bikes for short trips. I really did not think much of it because we used to walk everywhere before my father bought a car in 1956. I remember my father carrying me when I was the youngest child after visiting his sister about a mile or more away from our home. There was a little plank bridge we had to walk over to cross a canal or drainage ditch on Sixth Street, as this was the shortest route on foot. This was a little scary to me especially when we had to cross in the dark. Once we got a car, we would just take the Ninth Street route to my aunt's and grandmother's house on the other side of Broadway.

When I entered college fall 1968, the Civil Rights Movement was in full swing, and the Vietnam War was raging. Most of what I learned about the Civil Rights Movement was through discussions my older brothers had concerning the activism on the Southern University campus. I started hearing about H. Rap Brown, Stokely Carmichael, Angela Davis, and the Black Panthers, also about freedom rides and demonstrations and the dangers involved. It sounded so exciting. Most of the activity around the Movement appears to have occurred in isolated pockets around the state of Louisiana. I do not recall any specific organized actions being taken in Alexandria in support of the Movement. The bigger issue in 1968 in my recollection was the Vietnam War. When it was time for me to register with the Selective Service, I was already committed to college and registered with an education deferment. All this meant was that as long as I was pursuing a college education, I would not be drafted. Men were being drafted left and right to feed the manpower requirement to conduct a war, including our high school classmates.

During my freshman year at LA Tech, I joined the U.S. Air Force ROTC in lieu of taking physical education or some other courses in case things did not work out as I had planned. This would allow me to enter the armed forces as a second lieutenant in the event my education was interrupted for any reason — failure to make the grade in engineering or an unforeseen escalation in the war. By my sophomore year at Tech, a lottery system through random drawings was implemented by the Selective Services agency, dictating the order in which men would be drafted. The various deferments, including my education deferment, were still applicable. My March 24 birthday was the 258th day chosen, which meant that with my number at 195, I probably would not be inducted. I had picked up a few things from the ROTC program and had enjoyed the classes. After, however, the result from a plane simulation test to qualify as a jet pilot (my goal) showed that the best I could be was a navigator, I felt safe from the draft my sophomore year and left the program.

Things went smoothly at Tech from a race standpoint. There was one incident during my freshman year where a prankster(s) jammed a coin between the door and doorjamb to my roommates' and my room one night. When we arose the next morning and got ready to go to class, we found that we could not get the door open. We calmly assessed the issue and after finding what the root cause was, we were able to dislodge the coin and make it to class on time. Another issue that was definitely racially motivated involved one of my English professors. At the start of a quarter, we had several Black students in this particular class, and we all naturally sat together. I was generally the only Black student in my classes and was glad to have some company. Well, the professor came in, and after calling the roll, loudly proclaimed that the Black students could not sit together and would have to separate. You can imagine what we Black students were thinking: "What about all of these White students sitting together?" I've always had a sort of laidback attitude and am not easily riled. I believe the Lord blessed me with patience because he knew what I was capable of, and things could have gotten ugly. Generally, I take an "I'll show you" attitude after I ponder an issue and then decide a course of action. English was not a course I had trouble in, so it really did not matter where I sat, so I just kept my cool. As (again) fate would have it, though, someone came looking for me one day to let me know I was wanted by the head of the English department. I was not aware of anything I had done wrong but did not have a clue as to why I was being summoned. As it turned out, I was informed that I had scored the highest among the entire freshman class in what I believe was some sort of placement test that we all had taken. I had not given a second thought to that test since taking it, but the department head was really impressed and wanted to know if I were pursuing a career in the arts or humanities. Following that revelation, I had no more problems with my English professor.

► **Life Lesson #6: The Lord works in mysterious ways.**

I took enough math at LA Tech that, when I graduated, I had a minor in math. Since I had taken math at Peabody through Calculus, some of these courses, I feel, I should not have had to take, but I did to ensure I was not missing something I would need in my engineering courses. Anyway, I enrolled in what I believe was my third math class in the progression I had mapped out. There was nothing special about this course, but I did not do well on the first test. In retrospect, I believe I had put too much thinking into the processes, or maybe I thought it should have been more difficult than it was. On the second test, I regained my form and made a 100. As my professor was returning each student his test, when he got to me, he said, "this test could not have been that hard because Woodley made a 100 on it." I cannot say for sure that his comment was racially motivated or not, due to my initial test score, but it gave me the incentive (not that I needed it) to show him. After I'd shown him that my score was not a fluke by acing all subsequent tests, he would turn his head whenever I would meet him walking across campus. Despite that slow start, my test results in the class exempted me from the final exam.

► **Life Lesson #7: Success is not always revealed in how you start, but in how you finish. Persevere through life's ups and downs.**

During my junior year, my roommate and I were approached about establishing a chapter of Alpha Phi Alpha, Inc. Fraternity on campus with other likeminded Black male students. I had not thought about it and certainly had not considered joining one of the white fraternities. I had heard the stories about fraternity life on Southern University's campus from my older brothers and thought that this might be fun and allow me to form some other bonds of friendship. In April 1971, after much planning and work, seven Black men from central and north Louisiana were initiated into the Alpha Phi Alpha Fraternity as charter members of the Eta Kappa Chapter, the first Black fraternity on campus. This was accomplished with the support of the University with no resistance that I am aware of. We gained a seat on the Panhellenic Council along with the numerous white fraternities and with the same rights and privileges. Although I was voted the first president of the chapter, we all shared the responsibility out of necessity because of our small number and the fact that the pursuit of our education was the members' top priority.

Although we were the first Black fraternity on campus, we were not the first Black organization. That distinction goes to Soul Tech, and organization that was not only a social group but a vehicle for change and awareness of Black students on campus. The university's annual event, "Old South Day", raised the ire of both the fraternity and Soul Tech. The use of local Black kids in the parade through campus was a particular area of concern. We felt that our presence on the Panhellenic Council, the governing board for the fraternities, provided us a voice in eliminating this injustice, and ultimately it did. The fraternity provided a true avenue for brotherhood and lifelong friendships, as well as opportunities for civic involvement and campus activities support. LA Tech's Eta Kappa Chapter introduced the student body to the Black Greek organizations pledge stomp tradition, which began at midcentury and still is celebrated at Historical Black Colleges and Universities throughout the country. Fraternity brothers choreographed stomp performance (a mix of creative stepping moves with original chant verses) at LA Tech's Greek shows was no competition, and the shows were enjoyed by all students on campus. We were invited to lead the homecoming parade to the stadium on one occasion.

During the summer of my sophomore year, one of my engineering professors encouraged me to apply for a summer job at a manufacturing plant in Pineville, Louisiana. I did not realize it at the time, but it became obvious to me later that he had talked with someone at the plant about providing summer employment for a LA Tech student. When I went to the plant for an interview and physical, I left thinking I had a job for the summer as a Safety Engineer. However, when I showed up for work, I was informed that the company's doctor had found a heart murmur during my physical exam. Because the job involved some climbing, which could be stressful on my heart due to the exertion, I was advised to get an opinion from my doctor before I could work. My doctor examined me and did not find any such thing, so I rushed back to inform my plant contact only to be told that the job had been given to someone else. I still wanted to work. There was an opening in the labor pool. Since this occurred over the span of maybe a day and a half, I smelled a rat. It turns out that the safety job was given to a white student and a good opportunity was taken from me, not by the student, but by the manufacturing company. I thought that was pretty lowdown to scare me by claiming I had a health issue just to keep from giving me an essentially white-collar position. Nevertheless, based on my experience in what it took to land a summer job, I knew I would be very lucky if anything was still available at that late point; therefore, I accepted the labor position. I spent my summer cleaning out storage bins between batches of the different detergents that were produced at the plant or sweeping floors in response to spills and the cricket invasion. Occasionally, I would be given an opportunity to work on a production line. The pay was much better than what I would typically receive from my summer jobs through the Neighborhood Youth Corp, but not enough for me to abandon my career pursuit in engineering. Nevertheless, as with any job I worked, I tried to learn all that I could and would put in an honest day's work.

John Donne wrote that "No man is an island, entire of itself". No sentiment was truer when it came down to how I was to get back and forth to work since my family had one car, and my work schedule did not coincide with my father's by a long shot. Fortunately, there are some good people in the world, and I was able to arrange for a ride with a young lady who worked at the manufacturing facility and lived not too far from me. I caught a ride with her all summer, and she would not let me pay her when she learned I was in school. She was a Godsend. Acts of generosity continued throughout my college years. The summer I worked at the VA Hospital, I learned how to type, thanks to a generous white supervisor. He arranged for interested students wanting to learn typing during lunchbreaks to have access to a room with several typewriters and training manuals. I had not taken typing in high school because it had not aligned with my career choice, as other curriculum choices at the time had. The decision benefitted me enormously during college and throughout my career. The kindness also taught me that good people come in all races, including the white race. I returned to school in the fall and resumed my studies and fraternity activities.

► **Life Lesson #8, paraphrased from Dr. Martin Luther King Jr's "I Have A Dream" speech: Judge people not by the color of their skin, but by the content of their character.**

In the summer of my junior year, one of my professors arranged a summer job for me at the Kaiser Aluminum Company in Baton Rouge, Louisiana. This afforded me the opportunity to work in my chosen field of chemical engineering and was a totally different experience than what I had the previous summer. Being away from home, though, necessitated the need for me to have a car, so my father found me a car, and I was able to pay it off with my summer earnings. After I had been at Kaiser a week or so, my mother called to tell me that the manufacturing company I had worked at previously had been calling the house wanting to know if I wanted a job for the summer. Well, you can just imagine the satisfaction I felt when I called to inform them that I was already employed for the summer and would not be returning to their facility. This was another of those occasions where I thanked God for giving me an even greater opportunity. That summer, as well as the time I had spent in Baton Rouge with Bayou Boys State, convinced me that Baton Rouge was the place for me after graduation.

After that summer, I returned to LA Tech as a senior, and at the end of the fall quarter, I realized I was close enough to graduation that if I attended summer school, I could graduate in November 1972, the following year. Up to that point I had never attended summer school and had always looked at summer as a time to rest and rejuvenate my mind and earn money for school and expenses. The lure of finishing school just in time for the holidays was too great. Fortunately, a few fraternity brothers also were heading to summer school, so with the opportunity to split living and food expenses, I saw it as doable with the money saved from my Kaiser Aluminum job, even after purchasing a car. Four of us rented an apartment off the Grambling campus, and since two of us had cars, we were able to commute to the Tech.

During this final year at LA Tech, I experienced my very first plane ride when I started interviewing for a job upon graduation. Not just a job, but the job that would launch my career and establish my independence and the responsibility that came with it. I flew out of Shreveport on a sunny, 65-degree winter day headed to Indianapolis, Indiana for an interview with Dupont and arrived at the Chicago O'Hare Airport at dusk. After landing and boarding a small plane in Chicago, we took off for Indianapolis about 45 minutes away, if I remember correctly, and were greeted with a light snow and a 35-degree temperature when we landed. The next day was dreary and cold, as I drove out to the Dupont facility and pretty much made up in my mind then, that a warm sunny climate was more to my liking. I hoped, at that point, that I would get additional interviews in warmer states.

An interview at a Stauffer Chemical plant in Alabama followed that, and after graduation I received an offer from Kaiser Aluminum where I had worked a couple of summers before. Since I liked Baton Rouge and had had a pleasant work experience at the Kaiser plant, I had pretty much made up my mind to accept their offer. I later interviewed with Gulf Oil Chemicals in Orange, Texas, after the Christmas. After my interview at the Orange plant, I interviewed at the Gulf Oil Refinery in Port Arthur, not too far from Orange. Port Arthur, Orange, and Beaumont were all a part of what was known as the Golden Triangle for the region's concentration of industrial facilities. As I set off for Port Arthur, I came upon the tallest bridge I had ever seen, the Rainbow Bridge, a two-lane monstrosity (or engineering marvel depending on how you looked at it) that rose from the road and reached to the sky it seemed. I manned up and drove across. It was not as bad as I thought, and. I've since driven across it many times. I received offers from both Gulf Oil facilities and decided on the Orange site, a polyethylene manufacturing facility, with January 3, 1973, the official employment date.

I worked at the Orange plant as a Product Development Engineer for three years before being transferred with the rest of my department to the Gulf Oil Chemicals facility in Baytown, Texas. Orange turned out to be a friendly town of about 25,000 people with a significant Black population. I rented apartment space from a former Gulf Oil Black employee, an independent businessman who owned and operated a mortuary and sold insurance. He and his family, friends, and kinsmen welcomed me and made me feel right at home. The people I worked with at the plant were warm and cooperative and made my tenure at the plant pleasant. I do not recall any instances of racism and that made my job easier. I patterned my work habits after an elderly gentleman who worked in our group but was not an engineer. I found him to be thorough and meticulous in his work, and if his manner resulted in job security for him, it could very well work for me.

In the 1970s, the federal government began its focus on diversity in the workforce, and companies started trying to address the issue. I have no doubt that this played a part in my being hired, but I had had no illusion that if I did not perform to expectations, I would not continue to be employed. An incident at the plant occurred during probably my second year, one that I viewed as a learning experience for my coworkers. A training session for new employees entitled "Understanding the New Workforce" was conducted at the facility for the engineers in my group and those in our Technical

Service department entitled. The new hires were the result of an anticipated increase in the employment of Black professionals in all areas of the plant. This process had already begun, as there were quite a few Black workers at the Orange plant when I was hired, but I was the first and only Black engineer.

There was a point in the training session when the engineer, a white person in my department conducting the training, put a question to the group that was along the line of "If your Black employee called to let you know that he was going to be late for work because his hog had died, how would you interpret that?" Keep in mind that being late for work is a major infraction at a chemical manufacturing facility that is not taken lightly without a legitimate excuse. The response he was looking for was that the employee would be communicating the fact that he was having car trouble. After no one responded to his question, he asked me to respond, assuming I would know what was being communicated. Well, my face was as blank as anyone else's because that is not how Blacks talk in a professional setting. Of course, I had heard that reference by Black people to a Cadillac, but in this setting, it was all wrong.

► **Life Lesson #9: Be careful about stereotyping people.**

► **Life Lesson #10: All Black people do not talk the same, and it should not be assumed that as a white person, you would have to learn slang to communicate with your new employees.**

Engineering is a challenging and demanding but gratifying profession. It is a magnet for the brightest technical minds, and competition can be stiff for the higher-level jobs. Advancement is predicated not only on your experience and knowledge but how well you cultivate relationships with those above you. It requires a proper introduction and guidance for young engineers, which was not necessarily the case when I started working. I noticed over time that conversations between management and me were not as expansive as conversations between management and other engineers. So much of what I have learned was through personal attentiveness and tenacity. I ended my career having worked for Gulf Oil, briefly with Chevron when they acquired Gulf Oil, Amoco Chemical Company, and British Petroleum after they acquired Amoco Corporation. In my career, I held positions of Product Development Engineer, Process Engineer, Quality Administrator, Plant Hazard and Operability Study Coordinator, and Plant ISO 9000 Coordinator.

Following my retirement from British Petroleum in March 2000, I worked as an independent contractor for 14 years, facilitating hazard and operability studies for British Petroleum and numerous engineering firms, including Bechtel, Kellog Brown & Root, Worley Parsons, and Fluor to name a few. Working as an independent contractor, allowed me to travel all over the United States and to some faraway places as well, such as Kuala Lumpur in Malaysia and Queensland in Australia. I found this contract work to be rewarding, fulfilling, and challenging. I took great pride and gained much satisfaction from interfacing with the brightest minds in the chemical business and contributing to the safe and efficient operation of chemical facilities handling highly flammable and hazardous chemicals as dictated by the Occupational Health & Safety Administration of the federal government.

All my employers encouraged community involvement, and I was more than happy to take up the mantle of service. I was involved in Junior Achievement with two other Orange plant employees when I was employed at that facility. And while living in Orange, I was invited by my landlord's cousin, to assist in coaching little league football and had a grand time. Since moving to Baytown, I've been actively involved in voter registration drives through my church, as well as voter registration as a Deputy Voter Registrar, and I plan to continue service in these areas. I've been the Sunday School superintendent at my church for many years and find that to be most rewarding. I've been married 46 years and am the proud father of four children, two sons and two daughters.

I hope this narrative is found to be informative and a little entertaining. I leave you with this thought: Black history is such a rich history, filled with strength and humor. And it is so profound.

# ...THE STRUGGLE CONTINUES

*"It's disheartening that we are still fighting."*
— LINDA BROWN THOMPSON, TOPEKA, KS, 1984

## Jean Nash Johnson, Coeditor

A S THIS BOOK'S 24 essayists were finishing their first year at all-Black Peabody High as sophomores, I was completing eighth grade, preparing for freshman year at Marion High, one of the two all-white high schools in Lake Charles Louisiana, 96 miles southwest of the city of Alexandria. My hometown school integration experience in 1966-67 was a message of caution for the country's new era in education.

I was a year old when the U.S. Supreme Court ruled in *Brown v. Board of Education* that racial segregation in public schools was against the equal protection clause in the Fourteenth Amendment. The court's declaration, which rendered separate but equal useless, impacted schools in 21 states, including my home state of Louisiana. There, starting high school at age 13, 12 years after Brown and two years past the Civil Rights Act of 1964, I began my lifechanging journey in Louisiana's early attempt at school desegregation.

Before my 1966 freshman year, I had spent my early education years up to Grade 8 at my neighborhood Black Catholic school on the corner of the street I lived on. The school was founded and funded by hardworking church parishioners such as my parents. It ultimately would become the foundation for a solid education for me. There were two all Black public high schools and one Black Catholic school in the city. My oldest brother who graduated from Washington High, our neighborhood all-Black high school, a block beyond my Catholic school, the same year would be starting college, and my other older brother, also at the school, would be following him a year later.

As states and cities were beginning to mount tactics to desegregation, Louisiana chose freedom of choice, a structure that fundamentally meant if you were a Black student, you or your parent could choose to opt out of attending the neighborhood black school and enroll in the all-white school of your choosing. While the system in theory was supposed to work both ways, it did not. It would be many years before white students enrolled at predominantly Black campuses.

High school for me loomed, and my parents decided that it was impractical for me to attend the only Black Catholic high school across town in another separate all Black area. In their minds, with a freedom of choice, the timing was right to consider public education at the closest all white school. It had always been the whisper in our community that white public schools were preferentially equipped with more up-to-date textbooks and curriculums.

I wanted to attend my Black neighborhood high school and follow my two older brothers' paths. By the time the Catholic school was built they already were at higher grade levels and happily settled at the neighborhood public school from first to 12th grades. There, under the leadership of the exceptionally bright and caring teachers, they were able to thrive and prepare for college. They were my blueprint. My parents were my heroes. They supposed that in some way that busing me 15 minutes to the bordering white school I would get a better education.

The apprehension weeks leading up to the big day gave me nightmares and stomachaches. The 13-year- old me was afraid, given my very limited TV news exposure of the civil rights struggle. My parents had no idea how deeply anxious I was about this lifechanging day. They were proud of me, and I took comfort in their pep talk leading up to the moment. "Hold your head up high," Mama especially said. Daddy discussed the Nash Family dignity and respect for others. I kept a brave front for them, got on the bus that stopped in front of our house, and off I went in search of my "superior" education.

Today when I look back on the historic first day, I muse about its uneventfulness. I remember that the bus was practically empty with two other girls, one I recognized from my old school, the other unfamiliar. I think we were too afraid to talk during the ride. I remember rationalizing how I was part of some experiment. There were no demonstrations that first day. No angry throng, no U.S. Marshal escort, nothing thrown at us. A humdrum experience that was met with sighs after uncountable minutes of nervous breathing. From early months on, I soared academically with the anticipated A's and rare B. There were only two incidents where I was the indirect target of a sneer that I wasn't supposed to hear. The words came in murmurs I chose not to acknowledge, thinking my dignified daddy would be proud.

The worst part of my new experience was the loneliness and disregard. In my youngest and earliest reasoning stage, I always prided myself as happiest and at my best when I was around people who loved me and appreciated me. During my freshman year routinely, I felt isolated and often invisible not only by students but also teachers. I was always the girl who was the first to raise her hands. The Spanish teacher would not call on me. At my Catholic school, Black lay educators and white nuns who taught there were always encouraging, supportive and nurturing.

Lunchtime was the worst, sitting alone with no one to talk to. In grade school, I went home for lunch to Mama's homecooked meals and would eat with my younger siblings. I had looked forward to eating in the school cafeteria and socializing with friends and classmates. There, we were segregated, and even worse the handful of Black students enrolled rarely had same time lunch periods. After school I would return home to stories from my big brother, cousins and friends about their day, the joys of high school life – the extracurriculars, the socials, the antics, favorite teachers, mean teachers, the friendships. During my school day, I felt like a robot going through the motion. Nobody said I couldn't join in, but I felt shut out of campus events, never participating because I knew I was not wanted. There was no hands-on counseling, no teacher to talk to, no remedy in sight, and I was too scared and naïve to demand the emotional help I needed.

As brave as I tried to be, the sadness and the stomachaches didn't go away and by midway the schoolyear I was dreading returning to campus. I finally got up the courage to approach Mama and Daddy. Both were born and raised in Louisiana in the height of Jim Crow. Daddy was a World War II veteran and worked at one of the local oil refineries, and Mama was a homemaker who was raised on a farm that had been in her family two generations. Both smart and kind and like all of their fellow Black contemporaries had endured in spite of Jim Crow rule. They wanted more for their children. They wanted us to get the college degrees. I wanted desperately to please them, but I also knew they would want me to be happy. My parents were blessed with commonsense and immediately recognized that underneath my pretense of contentment was distress. My Dad grasped the situation, and in his most serious tone, words I'll never forget, he said. "There is a time and place for everything. This is not the time or the place." As we talked, he recognized that sheltering me (and my younger siblings) from racism only had put me at a disadvantage.

I grew up bigtime that year. I aced ninth grade academically and completed the year at the white school. I could not wait to start sophomore year at my neighborhood Black high school. I joined the drill team and was part of its percussion section, served as a French Club officer twice, became president of the National Honor Society senior year and received the local Daughters of the American Revolution Citizenship Award at graduation. The best teachers I had were the Black teachers there that taught me history, math and science. As a student I was at my happiest, and I flourished the three years. Senior year, I met my first journalism mentor. William Alley, my 12th grade English teacher, was one of the first white faculty members at the school. As a word nerd, our linking was unavoidable, and he was in person proof that change was coming. He called me aside after grading my first essay and told me I had the goods for becoming a writing pro. He gave me extra, more challenging assignments and took a sincere interest in my career goals and college searches.

I was salutatorian of my class of 172 and received a scholarship to the school of my choice. Predominantly white universities wanted me, but it would be years before I would take another dip in the integration waters. I said no to my second choice, St. Mary's Dominican, the then-sister school to Loyola University in New Orleans. Instead, I chose the safe harbor of Grambling State University, the historically Black university that had become a Nash family tradition. Grambling's biggest attraction was its brand-new Journalism program. Attending GSU also meant that I would be following in the footsteps of my older brothers and a host of Nash first cousins going back to the late 1940s. It was a best decision all around. The summer before college graduation, during a newspaper editing internship in Dubuque, Iowa, Black population less than a tenth of a percent, I befriended a white person, my housemate, for the first time, and the experience enriched me in ways that serve me greatly today. I also remained friends with one of the young white staff reporters at the paper.

As for the once all white school I attended, other Black students after me succeeded. It became more integrated each year, and student campus life for Blacks improved. But by my senior year, there still were no whites at my Black school. It would be a decade or more before a white student integrated a predominantly

Black high school. Interesting sidenote, the two high schools from my integration experience merged as the school district's magnet school in the '80s, as was the fashion. Economics and politics forged odd bedfellows. My older brother is an assistant principal at the school. And, of course, the majority of the population is black, the effects of white flight and failed gentrification efforts.

Looking back on the nation's racial tumult of the '60s and '70s, I am grateful for the path I took. I had caring teachers, a stellar education and a school home. While the early integration history at 13 left a few fading scars, it prepared me for adult life. Most close to me — Black and white — don't even know the story, but the deep feeling of relief from not having to ride that bus never left me. It's there for whenever life's tough markers come into play. Still, there are times I wish I had been bolder and had stayed at the all-white school, the way Elizabeth Eckford and the other Little Rock Nine did in 1957, or New Orleans first-grader Ruby Bridges in 1960, or my superhero journalist Charlayne Hunter-Gault, who in 1961 became the first black woman to attend the University of Georgia.

On the 50th anniversary of the Brown ruling, in 2004, I wrote an essay about my journey. As I pointed out, by the time my integration saga played out in 1966, the racist hubbub had quieted appreciably. There were laws then to protect students. I wonder how my story would have ended had someone acknowledged me directly – even through confrontation. If I might have dared to stay? Would I, could I have made any difference?

Linda Brown Thompson, the student whose father, Oliver Brown, was a plaintiff in the Brown case, passed away in 2018. Ms. Brown still lived in Topeka, Kan., in 1984, and spoke about the Supreme Court decision with a sense of dismay when she said, "It's disheartening that we are still fighting."

In 2021, copy that.

# WORKS CITED AND CONSULTED

Advertisement for Colored teachers. *Weekly Town Talk,* May 20, 1916, p. 11.

Advertisement for Negroes for sale. *Louisiana Democrat.* October 19, 1859, p. 3.

Advertisement for $50.00 reward *Louisiana Democrat.* October 19, 1859, p. 4.

Advertisement for Valuable Servant Woman to Dispose of. *Louisiana Democrat.* July 23, 1859.

Bannister, Steven. "Known for Local Work in Civil Rights." *Alexandria Daily Town Talk,* 14 June 1992, pp. 11-12.

———. "Quiet power." *Alexandria Daily Town Talk,* 14 June 1992, pp. 11-12.

Blokker, Laura Ewen. *Education in Louisiana.* State of Louisiana Department of Culture, Recreation and Tourism Office of Cultural Development Division of Historic Preservation, May 15, 2012, https://www.crt.state.la.us/Assets/OCD/hp/nationalregister/historic_contexts/Education_in_Louisiana.pdf.

"Board of Trustees," *Red River Republican,* 6 January 1849, p. 2.

"Central Louisiana Academy." *Alexandria Daily Town Talk,* 15 September 1908.

"Commencement Exercises." *Alexandria Daily Town Talk,* 15 May 1908, p. 7.

"Council Rejects Negro Center Plea, Approves Drive for Building Funds." *Alexandria Daily Town Talk,* 8 April 1947, p.1+.

Curtin, Phillip D. *The Atlantic Slave Trade: A Census.* University of Wisconsin Press, 1972.

Dillingham, George A. *The Foundation of the Peabody Tradition.* United Press of America, 1988.

"History of Rapides Parish Desegregation." *The Town Talk,* 4 September 2003, p.5.

"Home of Dunbar Aunt Site of Cross Burning." *Alexandria Town Talk*, 18 May 1963.

"Saturday Session in Dunbar Trial; Ten Jurors Selected. *Alexandria Town Talk*, 18 May 1963.

Kramer, Ethel. *Slavery Legislation in Ante-Bellum Louisiana, 1803-1860.* 1944. Louisiana State University, M.A, Thesis.

Laurent, N.B. Carl. *From This Valley, A History of Alexandria, Pineville, and Rapides Parish, Louisiana.* Red River Express, 2002.

"Lawyer Louis Berry Devoted to 'Cause'." *Alexandria Daily Town Talk*, 8 April 1983, pp. 91-95.

"Louis Berry Dead at 82." *Alexandria Daily Town Talk*, 4 May 1998.

*The Louisiana Baptist.* 2 May 1901.

Matthews, Ralph. "Louisiana Riots Planned by Whites." *The Afro American*, 24 January 1942

Matthews, Ralph. "M.P.s Used Gas and Guns on Unarmed Soldiers." *The Afro American*, 24 January 1942.

Partrain, Chad. *Images of Alexandria.* Arcadia Publishing Library Editions, 2013.

"Remain Awake, King Tells Delegates to LEA Meeting." *Alexandria Daily Town Talk*, 23 November 1966, pp. A1+.

Rollins, Judith. *All Is Never Said: The Narrative of Odette Hines.* Temple University Press, 1995.

Sanborn Fire Insurance Map from Alexandria, Rapides Parish, Louisiana. Sanborn Map Company, Mar 1951. Map. Retrieved from the Library of Congress, www.loc.gov/item/sanborn03267_010/.

"Sanders to Discuss Bolton Mixing Only with Parents." *Alexandria Daily Town Talk*, 21 January 1965, p.9.

"Suit Filed to Desegregate All Rapides Parish Schools." *Alexandria Daily Town Talk*, 22 March 1965, p.1.

Seip, Terry L. "Slaves and Free Negroes in Alexandria, 1850-1860." *Louisiana History: The Journal of the Louisiana Historical Association*, vol. 10, no. 2, Louisiana Historical Association, 1969, pp. 147—65, http://www.jstor.org/stable/4231060.

Simpson, William M. "A Tale Untold? The Alexandria, Louisiana, Lee Street Riot (January 10, 1942)." Louisiana History: The Journal of the Louisiana Historical Association, vol. 35, no. 2, Louisiana Historical Association, 1994, pp. 133—49, http://www.jstor.org/stable/4233092.

Spletstoser, F. *Talk of the Town: The Rise of Alexandria, Louisiana, and the "Daily Town Talk"*. Louisiana State University Press, 2005.

"Twenty-eight Negro Soldiers Shot in Riot," *Alexandria Daily Town Talk,* 12 January 1942, p.1.

U.S. Census Bureau (1870). The Statistics of the Population of the United Stated, Embracing the Tables of Race, Nationality, Sex, Selected Ages, and Occupations, From https://www2.census.gov/prod2/decennial/documents/1870a-01.pdf.

Usner, Daniel H. "From African Captivity to American Slavery: The Introduction of Black Laborers to Colonial Louisiana." Louisiana History: The Journal of the Louisiana Historical Association, vol. 20, no. 1, Louisiana Historical Association, 1979, pp. 25—48, http://www.jstor.org/stable/4231866.

West, Earle H. "The Peabody Education Fund and Negro Education, 1867-1880." *History of Education Quarterly*, vol. 6, no. 2, [History of Education Society, Wiley], 1966, pp. 3—21, https://doi.org/10.2307/367416.

# PHOTOGRAPH CREDITS

- "African Americans Lined up to Vote in 1953." The Newcomb Collection at the Alexandria Historical and Genealogical Library & Museum.

- "Alexandria Black Aces." The Newcomb Collection at the Alexandria Historical and Genealogical Library & Museum.

- "Attorney Louis Berry." *The Town Talk*, 8 April 1983.

- "Cotton Picking at Inglewood Plantation near Alexandria, Louisiana." State Library of Louisiana Historic Photograph Collection.

- "Librarian Hazel Harris with young library patrons at the Carver Branch of the Rapides Parish library in Alexandria, Louisiana in the 1950s." State Library of Louisiana Historic Photograph Collection.

- "Rose of Sharon Baptist Church Vacation Bible School," Rose of Sharon Baptist Church archives.

- "Soldiers Reading Books at the Rapides Parish Library at the USO Building in Alexandria, Louisiana in the 1940s." State Library of Louisiana Historic Photograph Collection.

- "St. Lawrence Baptist Church Vacation Bible School." St. Lawrence Baptist Church archives.

*Helen and Jean (African American Museum of*
*Dallas, Photo by Irwin Thompson)*

YEARS AGO, *Helen Benjamin* was described by one of her college professors as being "concerned about the world and those who people it." Throughout her life, she has focused on the underserved, having been in that category herself. She looks back with pride and appreciation for the life-altering education and support she received from Peabody High School. Upon her graduation in 1968, she moved to Dallas, TX and 22 years later to California seeking opportunities to apply the educational abilities and leadership skills she acquired and honed in the South. She worked in the Contra Costa Community College District in the San Francisco Bay Area for 26 years in several positions, including serving as president of two of the colleges, retiring in 2016 as chancellor of the District.

Dr. Benjamin holds a bachelor's degree in English from Bishop College, and master's (education) and doctoral degrees (English with a concentration in rhetoric) from Texas Woman's University, which recognized her as Distinguished Alumna in 2017. In 2019, the American Association of Community Colleges honored her with its Leadership Award in recognition of her contributions to the community college field. Her publications include *Harvest from the Vineyard: Lessons Learned from the Vineyard Symposiums (co-author)* and *The Chocolate Truth: An Anthology of Perspectives from Community College CEOs (Coeditor and contributor)*.

Since retiring, Dr. Benjamin established HSV Consulting, Inc., and she has worked with dozens of colleges, boards, and CEOs to advance student-centered organizational and leadership improvement. She chairs the Board of Trustees of Excelsior College and is a member of the Texas Woman's University Foundation Board of Directors. She now resides in Dallas. Over the years, Dr. Benjamin has remained connected to her Peabody High School 1968 classmates and her hometown. She is the mother of two (Michael and Traci) and grandmother of three (Marquis, Ezekiel, and Emerson).

*Jean Nash Johnson's* award-winning journalism career as a daily newspaper features writer, news and features editor and columnist spans almost three decades. With her Southern Black upbringing firmly rooted and an eye for culture, trends and lifestyles issues, Jean sought after unforeseen storylines and untold angles with a keen understanding of communities of color. She began first in Houston out of college as a cub reporter for *The Houston Chronicle*, and ultimately as a veteran staffer for *The Dallas Morning News*. In between her two newspaper periods, Jean served as staff assistant to Sen. Russell B. Long in Washington D.C. On behalf of the senator, she worked as a liaison between U.S. education and housing agencies and Louisiana government counterparts to champion federal funding needs in her home state.

In 1999, as millennials came of age and Zoomers came into the world, Jean's work at *The News* expanded, focusing on the youth voice. She established a Lifestyles teen advisory board for input on local and national stories and also created a prize-winning in-person children's book club series and wrote stories on each event. After retiring from daily news life, Jean turned to life in her North Texas community. As volunteer, she helped form and sponsor an afterschool campus writing club and annual writing contest at her neighborhood Title I middle school, inspiring a new generation of wordsmiths.

Among her honors are the 1987 *Dallas Morning News* Award of Excellence for Best General Interest Column, the 2001 Texas State Teachers Association School Bell Outstanding Feature Story Award, Southern Newspaper Publishers Association Foundation 2003 Literacy & Newspapers in Education Writing Award for Best Feature, and American Association of Sunday and Feature Editors 2006 Excellence in Feature Writing Contest for Short Feature.